BOUNDARY AND SPACE

An Introduction to the Work of
D.W. WINNICOTT

BOUNDARY AND SPACE

An Introduction to the Work of
D.W. WINNICOTT

MADELEINE DAVIS and
DAVID WALLBRIDGE

Brunner-Routledge
New York & London

Library of Congress Cataloging-in-Publication Data
Davis, Madeleine.
  Boundary and space : an introduction to the work of D. W. Winnicott
  by Madeleine Davis and David Wallbridge.
    p. cm.
  Includes bibliographical references and index.
  ISBN 0-87630-641-5
  1. Child psychology.   2. Child psychopathology.   3. Winnicott, D.
W. (Donald Woods), 1896–1971.   I. Wallbridge, David   II. Title.
BF721.D325 1990
155.4—dc20   90-48118
                                                                    CIP

British Library in publication data available
upon request from British Library

Appendix material is reprinted with permission from the *International Review of Psycho-Analysis.* Copyright © 1987 by the *International Journal of Psycho-Analysis.*

Published by
Brunner-Routledge
29 West 35th Street
New York, NY 10001

Published in England by
H. KARNAC BOOKS LTD.
58 Gloucester Road
London, SW7 4QY
British ISBN 1-85575-001-5

10 9 8 7

To Clare Winnicott

Felix, qui potuit rerum cognoscere causas,
atque metus omnis et inexorabile fatum
subiecit pedibus
—VIRGIL, *Georgics II*

Contents

Foreword by Robert J. N. Tod   ix
Preface   xi
Acknowledgments   xv

I.   **The Background   1**
    1. Personal Qualities   3
    2. The Evolution of the Theory   8
    3. The Spatula Game   17

II. **The Theory of Emotional Development   25**
    A.   BASIC ASSUMPTIONS   27
        1. Self and Ego   27
        2. The Fact of Dependence   30
    B.   EARLY PSYCHIC FUNCTIONING   32
        1. Integration and Unintegration   32
        2. Personalization   37
        3. Primitive Object Relating and the Experience of
           Omnipotence   39
        4. Impingement and Trauma   43
        5. Self Defense   46
        6. The False Self   48
        7. Intellect and the False Self   49
        8. The Expectation of Persecution   52

    C.   ADAPTING TO SHARED REALITY   53
        1. Growth of the Inner World   54
        2. The Area of Illusion   55
        3. Transitional Objects and Transitional Phenomena   57
        4. Playing   61
        5. The Potential Space   63

6. The Use of an Object and the Roots of Aggression 67
7. Innate Morality and the Capacity for Concern 73
8. The Antisocial Tendency 78
9. Adolescence 81

D.   THE ENVIRONMENTAL PROVISION 86
1. Mothering and Biology 87
2. The Accumulation of Experience in the Mother and in the Parents 90
3. Primary Maternal Preoccupation 93
4. Holding 97
5. Handling 100
6. Object Presenting 103
7. De-adaptation and Failure 110
8. Ego-relatedness and Communication 113
9. The Ordinary Devoted Mother 121
10. Dependence and Domination 126
11. The Father 128
12. The Family 131

III. **Boundary and Space** 137
1. Form and Content 139
2. Security and Risk 141
3. The Individual and Democracy 144
4. The Broken Boundary 147
5. The Oppressive Boundary 151
6. Space Without Boundary 159
7. Time and Continuity 169

Endpiece 172
Appendix: The Writing of D. W. Winnicott 173
Bibliography 195
Index 201

Foreword

The Winnicott Publications Committee was formed in 1975 in order to make better known to students the work of Donald W. Winnicott. Many of his ideas are already known through his books and through papers that have appeared in professional journals. There is, however, nowhere any general introduction and appraisal of his work and the Committee considered it important that a short book should be written to introduce students to his main concepts. Madeleine Davis and David Wallbridge undertook to make this attempt and they had access to all his unpublished writings that were available. The result is this book written by Madeleine Davis with the advice and assistance of David Wallbridge.

Donald Winnicott died just ten years ago and I write this short note in the capacity of a friend who always felt enriched from any meeting with him. I hope that this book will introduce many new readers to Winnicott's way of thinking and help them to understand his concepts and so lead them to further study of his work.

—ROBERT J. N. TOD
Chairman, Winnicott
Publications Committee 1981

ix

Preface

Donald Winnicott has a reputation here and there of being difficult to understand. There is no doubt that his theory of development is complex, and there is also no doubt that some of the things he says are blindingly simple. In a recent textbook of child psychiatry we find the opinion that Winnicott's exposition of developmental theory is characterized by a "poetic evocation of child development and maternal experience in an individual language difficult to link with other approaches" (135). This perhaps touches the heart of the matter, and there are two reasons why it may be so. The first is that Winnicott took the theory of emotional development back into earliest infancy, even before birth, and much of this work was therefore devoted to the verbal exploration of what is preverbal in the history of the individual. The invention of a purely technical vocabulary would have been useless here because it would have had no *meaning*, so he needed to borrow the "poetic" to help him with work that he himself certainly considered scientific.

The second, and allied, reason is that he felt in any case that "a writer on human nature needs to be constantly drawn to simple English and away from the jargon of the psychologist" (87). Believing it impossible to talk about human nature without the intrusion of his own life experience and that of his reader (or audience or student or patient), he actively sought through his style of writing and talking to enlist these experiences in bringing about an understanding of what he had to say. So the reader is invited to respond not with the intellect alone but with the whole self, including all that is remembered and all that is forgotten. Wherever this response can be made it is likely that something of what Winnicott is saying will already be familiar, and the rest, on the basis of this familiarity, will begin to fall into place.

Because his method of communicating owed so much to the overlap of experience it is not surprising that Winnicott found it difficult to address himself to an indeterminate readership. Nearly all that he wrote consists in lectures prepared for specific groups of people whose problems and interests he made for the time being his own, so that he was able to relate specifically to them. It is especially through this relatedness that he emerges as a unique person, preserving for the reader something of the charm and the vitality that were his in life. But perhaps it should be mentioned that the resulting diversity in his approach can lead to confusion where an overall surface consistency is expected. For example, when talking to psychoanalysts he was always emphasizing and re-emphasizing the crucial importance of the environment for the infant and the small child. This was because psychoanalysis had its beginnings in the study of conflicts *within* the individual, and the concepts derived from this study had been extended to cover infancy in such a way that he found a tendency to "explain all that can be known about babies in terms of the baby alone" (109)—something completely alien to his own views. On the other hand, when addressing teachers, social workers or other groups concerned with the care of children he often pleaded that a child's illness should be recognized as belonging to the child (88), because in such groups he found a tendency to stress the social and familial aspects of a child's problems at the expense of personal factors.

Occasionally, also, Winnicott used terms to express his ideas that belonged more to the group he was addressing than to his own usual vocabulary. This was particularly true when he was talking to members of the British Psychoanalytical Society, among whom the influence of Melanie Klein and her followers was very strong at the time that he was making his major contributions. Thus words like "projection," "introjection" or "good breast," which have a very specific meaning in Klein's language, were sometimes used by him out of context, as it were, in order to make his ideas "click" with his listeners.

So it is a good idea when reading Winnicott to keep in mind, as he always did, the audience he was addressing. It is also worth remembering that his writing spans a period of apprenticeship and a period of mastery, roughly divided by the Second World War; and that during the last years of his life (1965 to 1970), while still pursuing new lines of thought, many of his papers present a condensation or distillation of his ideas that has made readers independently compare them to the late Beethoven Quartets that he himself loved to listen to.

Then, too, there is often the feeling that Winnicott was using his writing to clarify—even to discover—his own ideas. In this he was spiritually akin to Freud himself, and no doubt future annotators of his work will encounter the same perplexities and apparent contradictions that have been found in Freud. To this it can only be said how enormous would have been the loss if only what was cut and dried had been entrusted to us: if he had not had the courage as well as the ability to reveal the ripening of his thought—the courage, in fact, to contradict himself in the interest of new discovery.

We do not, however, believe that the individuality of Winnicott's style diminishes the susceptibility of his hypotheses to rational appraisal. For his theory of emotional development is, beneath the surface, both consistent and coherent. Even what may seem to be simple expressions of intuitive or poetic truth—"truth arrived at in a flash" (89)—turn out on further acquaintance to be integral parts of this theory that reveals itself in different lights and from different angles throughout his work. It was part of himself: it was, so to speak, in his bones, growing and changing as he himself grew and changed through observation and experience.

It is this that gives his writing an intellectual unity even where the theory is not explicit, and provides an underlying form that adds depth and significance to the meeting of experience. The result is that the reader can go back to his books year after year and discover in them each time some new understanding, and some new stimulus to reflection.

The purpose of the essay that follows is therefore truly introductory. It has not been written for psychoanalysts or for others whose researches have already included Winnicott's work, but for all with an interest in the study of human nature who are not familiar with him. This especially includes those who are professionally involved with infants, with children and with young people: those, in fact, for whom many of his papers were written, such as doctors, nurses, health visitors, teachers, social and probation workers, and students in these fields.

What we have tried to do is to gather together the main strands of Winnicott's theory of personal development and to show how he contributed to an understanding of the significance of infancy in the total life of human beings. We have also tried to furnish a glimpse of the way he worked. Our aim has been accuracy rather than analysis or critical comparison: these must be left to others better qualified. By quoting extensively from Winnicott's writing and listing our sources in an index of references at the end of the text, we hope to help the reader find his way among the many books and papers: for where we do not persuade the reader to become familiar with Winnicott through his own writing we shall have failed.

Although our essay is set out under ordered headings, as is customary in such an undertaking, it must be confessed that the result is not altogether tidy. Bits belonging to one section will invade another, and repetitions occur. For this we ask the reader's indulgence: our only excuse is that with Winnicott it is particularly difficult to separate idea from idea, and impossible, as we have mentioned, to separate the ideas from the man. He will not be fitted into pigeonholes: he was all of a piece.

Acknowledgments

For permission to quote from material already published we wish to thank: Basic Books, Inc.; Faber and Faber Ltd; Fontana Paperbacks and Fontana/Open Books, Glasgow (Wm. Collins Sons & Co. Ltd); Harper & Row, Inc.; Harvard University Press; International Universities Press; Little, Brown and Company; Tavistock Publications Ltd; The Hogarth Press Ltd; and the International Journal of Psycho-Analysis.

We also wish to thank the members of the Winnicott Publications Committee, and particularly Clare Winnicott, for help and advice and for access to Donald Winnicott's unpublished work; and the Winnicott Trust for permission to use a Winnicott "squiggle" on the cover.

To Professor Rudolf Schaffer our thanks are due for generously agreeing to his conclusions being used in debate.

Finally, we most gratefully acknowledge the continual and generous help of John Davis, whose resources of learning and intellect we have unashamedly used.

BOUNDARY AND SPACE

An Introduction to the Work of
D.W. WINNICOTT

I. The Background

1. Personal Qualities

Perhaps the most important temperamental influence on Donald Winnicott's work was simply his belief that life is worth living. There was nothing romantic or sentimental in this: he was fully aware that "life is difficult, inherently difficult for every human being, for every one of us from the very beginning" (13), and he could identify with the people who came to consult him because he knew about anxiety and doubt. But his immense sense of pleasure and profit in his own life must at least in part have been responsible for his conviction that, for each individual, life can be creative and valuable. Bound up with this was the belief that every human being, given a facilitating environment, intrinsically contains the momentum for growth towards emotional as well as physical maturity, and towards a positive contribution to society.

It seems likely that the ambience of his childhood had something to do with this. He was born and brought up before the watershed of the First World War, at a time when people still profoundly believed that things would go on getting better as human beings became more and more enlightened. By all accounts his early years were passed in a secure and affectionate household where he was allowed the freedom to deal with the difficulties inherent in growing up and to develop that confidence in himself which enabled him to be confident in others.

His faith in human nature embraced the whole person, including the "old Adam" in us. He could not believe that human beings are *born* with the seeds of their own destruction in themselves. He was unable, for instance, to accept Freud's explanation of aggressiveness in terms of a death instinct. Instincts and the impulses to which they gave rise were for him the natural source of spontaneity and creativity through which alone life can be worth living for the individual and productive for society. "The adult who is mature," he wrote, "is able to identify with the environment, and to take part in the establishment, maintenance, and alteration of the environment, and to make this identification without serious sacrifice of personal impulse" (43). To this we can add, as a corollary, the following:

> In some way or other our theory includes a belief that living creatively is a healthy state, and that compliance is a sick basis for life. There is little doubt that the general attitude of our society and the philosophic atmosphere of the age in which we happen to live contribute to this view, the view that we hold here and that we hold at the present time. We might not have held this view elsewhere and in another age (67).

Here too the attitude of his own family probably influenced him. His parents were nonconformist in religion in the tradition that is associated with the west of England. Their approach was not doctrinaire. Winnicott wrote this description of an incident in his childhood:

> My father had a simple (religious) faith and once when I asked him a question that could have involved us in a long argument he just said: Read the Bible and what you find there will be the true answer for you. So I was left, thank God, to get on with it myself (151).

"Applied morality bores us," he wrote elsewhere; and indeed he could be ruthless in the face of imitation, of cant, and of what was false, wherever these seemed to him to appear, even though he was at pains to explain the aetiology of the false and compliant in early environmental failure. In compliance he felt that integrity was lost, and this possibly accounts for that trace of defiance in his own nature which led his colleagues to think of him at times as an *enfant terrible*. He once introduced a paper of almost revolutionary ideas at the time (1945), given to the British Psycho-Analytical Society, with the words:

> I shall not first give an historical survey and show the development of my ideas from the theories of others, because my mind does not work that way. What happens is that I gather this and that, here and there, settle down to clinical experience, form my own theories, and then, last of all, interest myself to see where I stole what. Perhaps this is as good a method as any (21).

Provocative though this statement may be (and no doubt was), there is something refreshing in its honesty.

It may be that this *enfant terrible* in Winnicott found an ally in children themselves, and that he could fully indulge his delight in the unexpected and the spontaneous in the company of those from whom society does not exact too great a compromise. At any rate, he was drawn towards children and to the practice of children's medicine and later child psychiatry, and the children in turn were drawn to this man who took such a pleasure in being himself with them. Here is what a paediatric colleague, speaking at his funeral, had to say about his capacity for relating to children:

> I first got to know Donald Winnicott twenty-two years ago when I became a physician at the Paddington Green Children's Hospital. I went there with a poor opinion of the general usefulness of child psychiatry but I soon found that, however difficult and damaging a child's past and present circumstances, the situation always changed for the better once Dr Winnicott became involved. At first I attributed this to his obvious high intelligence, his intuitive powers and the fact that he was "good with children'; but while all these attributes were correct, I later realized—and I am sure he would have liked me to say so—that his success also owed much to his professional discipline and his training as a psychoanalyst. Donald Winnicott had the most astonishing powers with children. To say that he understood children would to me sound false and vaguely patronizing; it was rather that children understood him and that he was at one with them. He used to allow some of his younger colleagues at Paddington Green to be present while he interviewed a child. The presence of others would be regarded by most doctors as prohibitively disturbing, but the fact was that within a few minutes of a child entering his consulting room both the child and Dr Winnicott were oblivious of the presence of anyone else. A good example of his acceptance by and communication with children is what happened when he was about to visit a Danish family for the second time after an interval of a few years. The children remembered his playing with them very well and were delighted at the prospect of again meeting an Englishman who could speak Danish. When their father said that Dr Winnicott could not speak a word of their difficult language his children simply did not believe him (150).

This extraordinary capacity for being "at one with" extended to people

of all ages and conditions, contributing to a success as psychoanalyst and
therapist that had made him famous by the end of his life. Colleagues
might differ quite strongly with some of his ideas but they agreed that
his patients were lucky.

It has sometimes been said that Winnicott idealized infancy and
childhood and the business of baby and child care. It is true that there
are to be found in his writing Wordsworthian overtones, as when he
refers to "the native honesty which so curiously starts in full bloom in
the infant and then unripens to a bud" (15). It is also true that in his lectures and talks he felt a need to emphasize the positive side of what happens naturally between babies and children and their parents, and the
positive side too of the distresses and difficulties that arise, for these he
saw primarily as manifestations of the innate tendency in all human
beings to grow and to mature. This emphasis does, indeed, set him
apart from many other writers on child development. But it needs to be
remembered that he spent many of his working hours in contact with
life's casualties—casualties that sometimes spilled over into his private
life as well. He described one such occasion when, during the war, he
and his wife took into their home for three months a boy of nine who
had run away from a hostel for difficult evacuated children.

> Three months of hell [wrote Winnicott]. He was the most lovable and
> most maddening of children, often stark, staring mad . . . It was really a
> whole time job for the two of us, and when I was out the worst episodes
> took place . . . The important thing for me is the way in which the evolu-
> tion of the boy's personality engendered hate in me, and what I did about
> it.
>
> Did I hit him? The answer is no, I never hit. But I should have had to
> have done so if I had not known all about my hate and if I had not let him
> know about it too. At crisis I would take him by bodily strength, without
> anger or blame, and put him outside the front door, whatever the
> weather or the time of day or night. There was a special bell he could
> ring, and he knew that if he rang it he would be admitted and no word
> said about the past. He used this bell as soon as he had recovered from
> his maniacal attack.
>
> The important thing is that each time, just as I put him outside the
> door, I told him something. I said that what had happened had made me
> hate him. This was easy because it was so true.
>
> I think these words were important from the point of view of his pro-

gress, but they were mainly important in enabling me to tolerate the situation without letting out, without losing my temper and without every now and again murdering him (24).

So we may take it that, though Winnicott had no children of his own, he had no illusions about what is involved in caring for them. "Children *are* a burden," he said in a talk to parents, "and if they bring joy it is because two people have decided to take that kind of burden; in fact, have agreed to call it not a burden but a baby" (14).

It was also written of Winnicott when he died that "the world . . . has lost a practical man of extraordinarily felicitous and fertile ideas" (140). This is particularly apt because the word "practical" comes first: somehow or another the phrase "an intellectual" never applied to him. He was far too down-to-earth. The development of his ideas had always the aim of helping in therapeutic work, of understanding the aetiology of mental illness, and above all of defining the conditions in which the individual can grow, without hindrance, to maturity. These practical aims are reflected in the fact that this theory embraces development in the environment alongside the development in the individual from earliest infancy. The environment is considered in terms of the actual lives and attitudes of those caring for infants and small children, and even the paraphernalia of infant care customary in our society—the bath, the feeding bottle, the cot and the blanket, the spoon and the teething ring—are part of it. It was Winnicott's ability to share the common sense of those engaged in the actual business of child rearing that made him truly remarkable as a builder of theory. It would have seemed as futile to him to describe the growth of a human being in isolation from his specific environment as it would be for a farmer to think about growing a field of corn without taking into account its position, the climate, the nature of the soil and, indeed, the feel of the place.

Winnicott was, in fact, a marvellous natural observer. A sensuous rather than a sensual man, he had the ability to be vitally present and engaged in any situation even when quiet and still, so that he was continually experiencing what went on around him in all sorts of ways. He also had a huge capacity to contain and to use experience, and this was enhanced by his medical training and was crucial to his work. A colleague said about him "he was reared in the tradition of his people, the English. For him facts were the reality, theories were the human stam-

mer towards grasping the facts" (141). Indeed, the strict logical or
formal consistency of his theory of development was never of paramount importance to him, although at a deeper level consistency is
clearly discernible in his thought. For him understanding was not the
same thing as intellectual acceptance, for understanding necessarily
contained an element of experience. And because he himself understood what it was like actually to care for and manage children, he fully
realized the limitations of his theory. He once said, talking about residential social workers, "The nearer a worker is to the child the more difficult it will be for him or her to discuss theory without being
overwhelmed by a sense of the unreal. Theory seems futile to someone
who wants to know now what to do with a problem of management"
(126).

Nevertheless it is also true of Winnicott that he had a deep sense of a
need in himself, and in all of us to a greater or lesser extent, to discover
structure in what we know and to try to make an objective approach to
truth. He saw this as an element in the drive towards personal independence and maturity.

2. The Evolution of the Theory

The belief that the ordering of knowledge into science—the objective
study of groups of phenomena—helps us in the achievement of autonomy was expressed by Winnicott in a lecture given to the sixth form of
Saint Paul's School in 1945. Describing the feeling he himself had as a
schoolboy when he came across Darwin's *Origin of Species*, he said:

> I could not leave off reading it. At the time I did not know why it was
> so important to me, but I see now that the main thing was that it showed
> that living things could be examined scientifically with the corollary that
> gaps in knowledge and understanding need not scare me For me this idea
> meant a great lessening of tension and consequently a release of energy
> for work and play.

Certainly Winnicott cannot have been unique in finding the study of biology a help amid the mysteries of adolescence. As he went on to explain, "If, in a subject that is being approached through the scientific method, there is a gap in our knowledge, we just record it as a gap in knowledge, a stimulus to research, but the intuitive person's gaps are unknown quantities with somewhat terrifying potential" (120).

This principle can easily be given a historical perspective. There is no doubt that the growth of modern physics has brought us relief from the fear of the environment just as physiology and biology have removed doubts and superstitions about certain aspects of ourselves. It could also be said that the more scientific discovery and technology enable us to be masters of the environment, the more consuming does our anxiety about our own human nature become, and that it is not surprising that psychology—to give the term its historical meaning as the objective study of human nature—has, since its beginnings in the last century, fallen upon fertile ground.

In the personal history of Donald Winnicott, too, the discovery of a method for the study of human nature—namely psychoanalysis— seems to have come at a time when it was particularly needed. As a schoolboy he had decided that he would study medicine, and here again the need for independence appeared as a motive. Clare Winnicott has written this about his decision:

> It was when Donald (aged 16) was in the sick room at school, having broken his collar bone on the sports field, that he consolidated in his own mind the idea of becoming a doctor. Referring to that time he often said "I could see that for the rest of my life I should have to depend on doctors if I damaged myself or became ill, and the only way out of this position was to become a doctor myself, and from then on the idea as a real proposition was always in my mind . . ."(151).

His preliminary study towards this end was biology, which he read at Jesus College, Cambridge. His chosen course was interrupted by the First World War, bringing with it the loss of many friends. He himself served for a time as Surgeon Probationer on a destroyer, where he had spare time to reflect and to read. From what he later wrote, it can be gathered that when he came to the study of physiology he found it disappointing.

The physiology I learned was cold, that is to say, it could be checked up by careful examination of a pithed frog or a heart lung preparation. Every effort was made to eliminate variables such as emotions, and the animals as well as human beings seemed to me to be treated as if they were always in a neutral condition in regard to instinctual life. One can see the civilizing process which brings a dog into a constant state of frustration Consider the strain that we impose on a dog that *does not even secrete urine into the bladder* until some indication is given that there will be opportunity for bladder discharge How much more important it must be that we shall allow physiology to become complicated by emotion and emotional conflict when we study the way the human body works (100).

It must, therefore, have been a relief to Winnicott when he began the clinical part of his training, where there was contact with patients as whole people. Particularly in paediatrics, which became his speciality and which in some ways he helped to shape in Great Britain and to influence in the United States, he found an opportunity to "deal with the whole individual, and to think of the child in the family and social setting" (126). That he increasingly had such opportunity he acknowledged as owing much to medical discovery, particularly the discovery of penicillin, which put an end to many epidemics and acute illnesses, and "transformed physical paediatrics into something which could afford to look at the disturbances which belong to the lives of children who are physically healthy" (130).

Nevertheless, in the necessarily empirical nature of the practice of medicine there was always something unsatisfactory to him. There were so many questions unanswered—or, to be more precise, unasked. In 1931 he wrote in *Clinical Notes on Disorders of Childhood:*

> If enuresis is explained as a disturbance of the pituitary or thyroid gland, the question remains, how is it that these glands are so very commonly affected in this way? If cyclical vomiting is explained along biochemical lines the question must be asked: Why is the biochemical balance so easily upset, when everything points to the stability of the animal tissues? The same applies to the toxaemic theory of tiredness, the glycopoenic theory of nervousness and the theory that stuttering is due to lack of breath control. All these theories lead to blind alleys (19).

Consequently, it is not surprising that when Winnicott, as a newly qualified doctor, came across the work of Freud in a bookshop, the encounter changed his life. Here was a distinguished neurologist—and it is not always well known outside medicine that Freud was a pioneer in neuropharmacology and wrote what is still one of the standard works on the pathology of cerebral palsy—who, in Winnicott's words, "became dissatisfied by his own results and those of his colleagues, and moreover, found that if he removed a symptom by hypnotism he was no further in his understanding of the patient" (81). Out of Freud's dissatisfaction, as is better known, came his adaptation of the setting for hypnotism that resulted in the method of psychoanalysis, by means of which he was able to build his theory.

For Winnicott, psychoanalysis formed a bridge that linked what he observed in medical practice back to biology, making sense of what he had felt to be irrational. It was a way of preserving that one article of faith that he believed the scientist could legitimately bring to his work—that there are "laws that govern phenomena." "Psychoanalysis," he wrote, "goes on where physiology leaves off. It extends the scientific territory to cover the phenomena of human personality, human feeling and human conflict. It claims therefore that human nature can be examined, and where ignorance is exposed psychoanalysis can afford to wait, and need not indulge in a flight to superstitious formulations" (81).

There are, of course, problems about the extension of the scientific territory into the realm of psychology, no matter what branch of the subject we consider. One of the most intractable of these is the problem of subjectivity in the observer. Winnicott was fully aware of the dilemma; as he pointed out, the study of psychology includes "not only the phenomena of other people's human nature but also our own. In this respect psychology is distinct from other sciences and must always remain so. With our minds we are examining the very minds we are using, and with our feelings we are examining our feelings. It is like trying to examine a microscope under its own high power" (120). There is not only the question of the effect of the observer on the observed—a question pertinent in physics—nor even of what the observer brings to his observations in the way of conceptual theory; there is also the question of the observer's personal nature getting in the way of his search for objective truth.

In some branches of psychology, knowledge is sought in ways that attempt to avoid this dilemma by restricting the study to such phenomena as are capable of measurement by standardized procedures. This can be seen, for instance, in the compiling of normative data, such as the distribution of I.Q. within a given population, or in epidemiological studies, such as the relative incidence of delinquency in the different social classes. Standardized questionnaires are often used in diagnosis.

Psychoanalysis, on the other hand, approaches the problem of the irrationality of surface phenomena in human nature by assuming that behaviour and emotional (and therefore sometimes physical) well-being are influenced by "the unconscious"—that is, by motives and psychological conflicts of which we are unaware. It also assumes that within the context of a relationship between therapist and patient, given a simple and constant setting, these motives and conflicts can be communicated and understood, allowing the patient to discover what he has hitherto been unaware of in himself. Diagnosis and therapy are therefore simultaneous and, because psychoanalysis patently depends on a relationship, the analyst has to make use of many emotional complexities that standardized procedures attempt to eliminate. He keeps in sight the whole individual human being who is lost (or compartmentalized) in the broad survey. Talking of psychoanalysis as an instrument of research, Winnicott wrote, "Within the psychoanalytic framework there is room for an infinite variety of experiences, and if from various analyses certain common factors emerge, then we can make definite claims" (26).

Psychoanalysis thus provides rich material for the generation of hypotheses, but is always prone to the criticism that, from the almost limitless variety of experience available, the observer (who is also the therapist) will choose observations to support rather than to test attractive hypotheses and that objectivity will be lost. There is, therefore, a particular need for integrity on the part of those engaged in research. Ideally this need is recognized by psychoanalysts: one of the aims of their training, the *sine qua non* of which is a personal analysis lasting for a number of years, is to promote insight and an understanding of the effect that they as individuals may have on a given situation. And, indeed, it is surely impossible to fully exclude the subjective in the observer from research. As Winnicott put it, "To do research one must have ideas. There is a subjective line of enquiry. Objectivity comes later through planned work, and through comparison of the observations made from various angles" (22). Because he always recognized the personal element, as when he wrote "This work . . . is in the direct line of development that is peculiarly mine," and "my own stage of development at the present time gives my work a certain colouring," it is the easier to accept the statements he also made about ideas being "forced upon him" by his work or arising "out of clinical experiences" (65). Then, too, he was capable of criticizing himself, and indeed of laughing at himself. Among his unpublished papers there is a particularly lucid criticism of Melanie Klein's position regarding envy and aggression in early infancy. It ends with a peroration of two finely turned sentences expressing the essence of his own view. When he had finished he added the words (112):

$$I = D.W.W. = GOD$$
$$\text{Late night}$$
$$\text{FINAL}$$

In any event it is important that Winnicott believed that psychology, including psychoanalysis, was a science related to other sciences, and that in the construction and testing of his theory of emotional development he always tried to impose on himself the discipline appropriate to this conviction. In this he followed Freud, who believed that, by using as a starting point the method that he invented and refined, man would be able to study his own nature in the way he can study his own physiology. It is worth quoting a passage from Winnicott's book *The Family and Individual Development* in which, while stating his own position, he sums up Freud's contribution to the study of human nature:

> The reader should know that I am a product of the Freudian or psychoanalytic school. This does not mean that I take for granted everything Freud said or wrote, and in any case that would be absurd since Freud was developing, that is to say changing his views (in an orderly manner, like any other scientific worker) all along the line right up to his death in 1939.
>
> As a matter of fact, there are some things that Freud came to believe which seem to me and to many other analysts to be actually wrong, but it simply does not matter The point is that Freud started off a scientific approach to the problem of human development; he broke through the

reluctance to speak of sex and especially of infant and child sexuality, and he accepted the instincts as basic and worthy of study; he gave us a method for use and for development which we could learn, and whereby we could check the observations of others and contribute our own; he demonstrated the repressed unconscious and the operation of unconscious conflict; he insisted on the full recognition of psychic reality (what is real to the individual apart from what is actual); he boldly attempted to formulate theories of the mental processes, some of which have become generally accepted (35).

Winnicott began his training for psychoanalysis in 1923, the same year that he obtained two consultant appointments in children's medicine, one at Paddington Green Children's Hospital and one at Queen Elizabeth's Hospital in the East End of London. Of this early period in his life he wrote,

> . . . you can imagine how exciting it was to be taking innumerable case histories and to be getting from uninstructed parents all the confirmation that anyone could need for the psychoanalytic theories that were beginning to have meaning for me through my own analysis. At that time no other analyst was also a paediatrician, and so for two or three decades I was an isolated phenomenon (59).

It soon became apparent to him, however, that for his purposes classical Freudian theory had its limitations. These lay in the fact that at that time (at least in England) analysis was thought feasible as a treatment only for the sophisticated—for the type of patient, in fact, that Freud himself had treated. Furthermore, generally speaking, only the psychoneuroses (that is, those difficulties which arise in conjunction with the triangular relationship between a child and his two parents) were thought amenable to analysis. Observational studies of infants and small children in a clinical setting had not been seen to be important for psychoanalytic theory, nearly all of which was founded on experience seen backwards through the analysis of adults. In Winnicott's words,

> At that time, in the 1920s, everything had the Oedipus complex at its core. The analysis of the psychoneuroses led the analyst over and over again to the anxieties belonging to the instinctual life at the four to five

year period in the child's relationship to the two parents . . . Now innumerable case histories showed me that the children who became disturbed, whether psychoneurotic, psychotic, or antisocial, showed difficulties in their emotional development in infancy, even as babies . . .
Something was wrong somewhere (59).

It happened that, in the meantime, Anna Freud in Vienna and
Melanie Klein in Berlin had begun to open up the study of the infant
as a new area for psychoanalytic research. Psychoanalytic treatment of
children, even at a preverbal stage, was undertaken using new techniques, particularly play, for communication. Klein went, in Winnicott's
words, "deeper and deeper into the mechanisms of her patients and
then . . . applied her concepts to the growing baby" (59). This made
it possible to increase the scope of psychoanalysis for people of all ages
and to study the emotional growth that belongs to infancy. When
Melanie Klein came to England, Winnicott became for a time her pupil,
and was able to take advantage of her work to resolve his own difficulties
and, eventually, through his unique position as a paediatrician with psychoanalytic training, to make his own contribution to developmental
theory. This involved tracing the foundations of emotional maturity to
the beginning of the self in the earliest days of life.

Of course, it took time for his theory to grow and develop into its
definitive form, for practical experience was an essential ingredient of
it. There is no doubt, for instance, that his specific statement of the antisocial tendency derived to some extent from his experience with evacuated children during the Second World War. As he described it:

> Children evacuated from big cities were sent to ordinary people's
> homes. It soon became evident that a portion of these boys and girls were
> difficult to billet, quite apart from the complementary fact that some
> homes were unsuitable as foster homes.
> The billeting breakdowns arising in these ways quickly degenerated
> into cases of antisocial behaviour. A child who did not do well in a billet
> either went home and to danger, or else changed billet; several changes
> of billet indicated a degenerating situation, and tended to be the prelude
> to some antisocial act.

Eventually, hostels became organized for residential care of difficult
evacuated children, and Winnicott, as a consultant psychiatrist, worked

in close conjunction with the staffs of a group of these hostels. It was found that "evacuation breakdowns occurred for the most part in children who had originally come from unsettled homes, or in children who had never had in their own homes an example of a good environment" (75).

These wartime experiences with difficult children linked up with a certain type of disturbance he had encountered in infants in his clinic; he also found a correspondence between his observations and Bowlby's work with deprived children (130). Taken in conjunction with psychoanalysis (particularly the work of Klein) these observations crystallized into a theory of the antisocial tendency and its aetiology that he found serviceable in diagnosis and therapy, including the idea of "delinquency as a sign of hope" (85).

It was, in fact, after the war that Winnicott's prolific period of lecturing and writing began—a period that lasted until his death. Education, training and experience had become assimilated and what emerged was truly his own. His theory became second nature to him. It made sense of the relationship between paediatrics and psychiatry, informing his practice and providing a framework within which he could allow for the subjective without being arbitrary. Even so, it did not remain static, but, like Freud's theory, it continued to grow and change in certain ways, just as he himself grew and changed throughout his life, according to experience and to the discovery of new facts.

When considering the actual substance of the theory, it is necessary to keep in mind the two distinct sources of these facts: direct observation of infants and children and those who cared for them; and "indirect" observation made during the course of psychoanalysis of patients of all ages. In using these two kinds of observation in conjunction, Winnicott was a pioneer, along with a very few other analysts—notably (in Great Britain) Susan Isaacs and Anna Freud. Having found that (given our present lack of knowledge) "direct observation is not able of itself to construct a psychology of infancy" (57), he used psychoanalysis to throw light on what was implicit in the observed behaviour of infants and their parents. But it was in direct observation that his theory was rooted. At the end of his life he wrote, ". . . direct clinical observations of babies . . . have indeed been the main basis for everything that I have built into theory" (64). When we consider that during his lifetime Winnicott completed the full psychoanalysis of some seventy individuals, and also that he held his post of consultant physician and then psychiatrist at Paddington Green Children's Hospital for forty years and was able to state that during the first twenty-five of these years he had personally taken 20,000 case histories (47), we can see that neither of the bases of his theory was negligible.

3. The Spatula Game

To get an idea of the development of Winnicott's methods for therapy (and hence for observation) along with the evolution of his thought, it is helpful to look at some very early work afterwards described by him under the heading *The Observation of Infants in a Set Situation* (20). This paper explains his use of what he called the "Spatula Game," at first for diagnostic purposes. A shiny metal tongue depressor was placed on a table within reach of an infant seated upon his mother's knee. The typical behaviour of the infant was divided by Winnicott into three stages (57):

First Stage   Initial reflex grasp;
                      withdrawal;
                      tension covering renewed voluntary grasp and
                            slow passage of object to mouth.
  Here the mouth becomes suffused, saliva flows.
Second Stage   Mouthing of the object;
                      carefree use of the object in experimental exploration,
                        in play and as something with which to feed others.
  Here the object drops by mistake. Let us assume that it is picked up
    and returned to the infant.
Third Stage   Riddance

It is easy to imagine how this game arose in the first place simply from the nature of the paediatric consultation. The doctor was talking to the mother; the baby in the meantime was busy; the bowl of spatulas was on the desk. Probably at first Winnicott saw in the baby's play the possibility of a simple test of motor development. But being interested not only in what a baby *could* do in the circumstances, but also in all the things that each baby *did* do, he noticed that there was a common pattern of behaviour that over a period of time could be accurately observed and noted. Given enough cases, a "norm" could be established and deviations could be used in diagnosis. Useful diagnosis, however, could only be made when he had found an answer to the question: "Why do babies *normally* behave as they do when confronted with the spatula?" It was only when in possession of this knowledge that he could begin to understand what the baby whose behaviour was abnormal needed. To answer the question he used psychoanalysis.

Thus, when a baby was referred to his clinic with symptoms for which no organic cause could be discovered, he became able to use one or other of the stages in the Spatula Game to get at the root of the trouble. Early on he used the first stage, the "stage of hesitation," in relation to such disorders as a colic, disturbed sleep and asthmatic attacks. Here is a description of a seven-month-old baby referred for asthma whose case is particularly apposite because her symptom appeared during the playing of the Spatula Game itself:

> I stood up a right-angled spatula on the table and the child was immediately interested, looked at it, looked at me and gave me a long regard with big eyes and sighs. For five minutes this continued, the child being unable to make up her mind to take the spatula. When at length she took it, she was at first unable to make up her mind to put it to her mouth, although she quite clearly wanted to do so. After a time she found she was able to take it, as if gradually getting reassured from our staying as we were. On her taking it to herself I noted the usual flow of saliva, and then followed several minutes of enjoyment of the mouth experience.

This same pattern was repeated at a second consultation, only this time there was a prolonged period of playing with the spatula and then with the bowl and spatula and her toes, and of looking "very pleased with life."

Winnicott went onto explain about the symptom,

> The baby sat on her mother's lap with the table between them and me.

The mother held the child round the chest with her two hands, supporting her body. It was therefore very easy to see when at a certain point the child developed bronchial spasm. The mother's hands indicated the exaggerated movement of the chest, both the deep inspiration and the prolonged obstructed expiration were shown up, and the noisy expiration could be heard. The mother could see as well as I did when the baby had asthma. *The asthma occurred on both occasions over the period in which the child hesitated about taking the spatula.* She put her hand to the spatula and then, as she controlled her body, her hand and her environment, she developed asthma, which involves an involuntary control of expiration. At the moment when she came to feel confident about the spatula which was at her mouth, when saliva flowed, when stillness changed to the enjoyment of activity and when watching changed into self-confidence, at this moment the asthma ceased.

Recently (that is, twenty-one months after the episode I have described), the child had had no asthma, although of course she is liable to it.

Discussing the case, Winnicott continued, "Because of the method of observation it is possible for me to make certain deductions from this case about the asthma attacks and their relation to the infant's feelings. My main deduction is that in this case there was a close enough association between the bronchial spasm and anxiety to warrant the postulation of a relationship between the two" (20).

Obviously, psychoanalytic theory is not needed for an observer to equate hesitation in taking the spatula, which is then so patently enjoyed in play, with anxiety. But the question remains, anxiety about what? Winnicott knew that the attitude of a particular mother could have a bearing on what happened, that some mothers would not allow their babies to put things in their mouths. But the stage of hesitation was normal: "In the ordinary case the child hesitates in spite of the fact that the mother is quite tolerant of such behaviour and even expects it" (20). For an explanation Winnicott drew on the work of Melanie Klein: he came to see the danger that makes the child anxious, and the whole sequence in the Spatula Game, as emanating from "infant fantasies," that is, from the (largely unconscious) imaginative elaboration of the actual experiences of the infant, including experiences of the outside world and especially of the child's own bodily functions and feelings. "It is in analysis," he wrote, "that the full significance of the infant's play becomes recognized, play which indicates the whole of the fantasy of incorporation and elimination, and of the growth of the personality through imaginative eating" (57). More specifically, the hesitation in the first stage of the Spatula Game was seen to come about through fantasies of harm, destruction and loss connected with mouthing and biting. It represented the beginnings of a social sense. This is discussed in greater detail later, in the sections about *The Use of an Object and the Roots of Aggression* and *Innate Morality and the Capacity for Concern*.

While continuing to see significance in deviations from the norm in the Spatula Game, Winnicott increasingly used it also as a positive indication of a child's personal achievement in terms of the richness and variety of the imagination in playing and of the capacity for total involvement in the experience. A symptom for which a baby was referred could thus be either a part of an illness or incidental in healthy development. In the latter case, it would be likely to disappear with "time and ordinary good management." Normality had come to be equated with health. It meant the capability, "given reasonably good and stable surroundings, of developing a personal way of life, and eventually of becoming a whole human being, wanted as such, and welcomed by the world at large" (13), in spite of troublesome symptoms.

At the same time, the theory that was emerging from Winnicott's involvement with psychoanalysis was being refined in the light of his observations. For practical purposes, for instance, it was necessary to know the age range within which common patterns of behaviour normally occur. Of the Spatula Game he wrote:

Typical is eleven months. At thirteen and fourteen months infants have developed so many other interests that the main issue is likely to be obscured. At ten months or nine months most infants will pass through the phases normally, though the younger they are the more they need some measure of that subtle cooperation which mothers can give which supports yet does not dominate. It is not common in my experience for a six-month-old baby to show clearly the whole physical performance. Immaturity at that age is such that it is an achievement that the object has been grasped and held, and perhaps mouthed. Direct observation shows that the baby must have a physical and psychological maturity of a certain degree before being able to enjoy the full emotional experience (57).

Psychoanalysis proper, looking backwards as it does into the past, cannot accurately date early infantile phenomena nor gauge the time lapse between them. Winnicott's clinical experiences enabled him to give a chronology to very early events which in turn made his theory more serviceable in practice and in understanding the needs of infants at a given age.

Looking at the Spatula Game, it is also possible to see how for Winnicott the diagnostic and therapeutic roles of the interview became inseparable. He found that there was satisfaction for the infant, and often a dramatic lessening of troublesome symptoms, where the "full course of the experience was allowed." Sometimes it needed to be allowed more than once for a particular infant, but the principle was always to "give the baby the right to complete an experience which is of particular value to him as an object lesson." He saw that this reinforced and gave an added importance to the intuitive behaviour of mothers with their infants: ". . . a mother naturally allows the full course of various experiences keeping this up until the infant is old enough to understand her point of view" (20).

This detail of maternal care, along with others, such as the "subtle cooperation which mothers can give, which supports yet does not dominate," came to be incorporated in Winnicott's concept of "holding," which is how he described the environmental provision indispensable to emotional development in earliest infancy. The concept was applied by him to psychoanalysis proper, where it was the provision of a holding environment by the analyst that allowed analysis to extend backwards beyond the psychoneuroses to more fundamental elements in the personality. He believed that it was only when the infant or patient was being held—in the Spatula Game the infant was physically held by the mother and the situation was held by himself as the doctor—that the truly spontaneous gesture, the revelation of the self, could arise and be felt by the infant or patient to be safe.

All of these elements contributed to the emergence of the beautifully economical method of interview described by Winnicott in the posthumously published *Therapeutic Consultations in Child Psychiatry.* Here communication came about through the technique that he developed with older children called "The Squiggle Game." He would draw a line on a piece of paper for the child to turn into something, and then in turn he would complete an initial line, or squiggle, made by the child. Where each contributed something to the situation, the child was soon at ease and, because Winnicott did not dominate the interview, spontaneous gestures and approaches could be made. Moreover, his method presented no bar to such spontaneity: the only limit to what could be expressed was imposed by the nature of the blank sheet of paper and the pencil, for the squiggles themselves could be used to represent "impulse, incontinence, madness, etc. according to the emotional state of the particular child" (111). Eventually, even the accepted procedures of adult analysis were modified by him in the interest of the spontaneous gesture. At the end of his life he wrote about his analytic work with adults:

> It appalls me to think how much deep change I have prevented or delayed in patients in a certain classification category by my personal need to interpret. If only we can wait, the patient arrives at understanding creatively and with immense joy, and now I enjoy this joy more than I used to enjoy the sense of having been clever. I think I interpret mainly to let the patient know the limits of my understanding. The principle is that it is the patient and only the patient who has the answers. We may or may not enable him or her to encompass what is known or become aware of it with acceptance (68).

It can be truly said that for Winnicott psychoanalysis was the only basis for therapy in keeping with his intrinsic respect for other people. There is little doubt that psychoanalytic theory can be, and indeed has been, used by unscrupulous people for gaining power over others. This fact could even be said to constitute a kind of support for the validity of the theory. But to Winnicott the professional ethic was of paramount importance and it was of the essence of psychoanalysis and psychotherapy that they involved a relationship in which "the patient is on equal terms with the doctor" (47). "We find that when we are face to face with a man, woman or child in our speciality," he wrote, "we are reduced to two human beings of equal status. Hierarchies drop away" (86). He believed that "in time it will be accepted that the findings of psychoanalysis have been in line with other existing trends towards a concept of society that *does not violate the dignity of the individual*" (89). This was one reason why the physical treatment of mental illness was alien to his nature, and his repudiation of such treatment opened up a gulf between him and many "adult" psychiatrists. It was not that he did not recognize the immense strain put on the psychiatrist by the mentally ill: "Every psychiatrist," he wrote, "has an immense load of serious cases. He is always threatened by the possibility of suicide among the patients in his immediate care and there are heavy burdens associated with taking responsibility for certification and de-certification and with the prevention of such things as murder and the abuse of children. Moreover, the psychiatrist must deal with social pressures since all those who need protection from themselves or who need to be isolated from society inevitably come under his care and in the end he cannot refuse them. He may refuse a case but this only means that someone else must take it" (103).

Nevertheless, his native antipathy to physical treatments remained. He saw danger in them, partly a direct danger to society because "there must, in fact, always be a borderline in which there is no clear distinction between the corrective treatment of the political of ideational opponent and the therapy of the insane person. (Here lies the social danger of physical methods of therapy of the mental patient, as compared with true psychotherapy, or even the acceptance of a state of insanity)" (47). Further, as he put it, physical methods of therapy can be "an escape from the acceptance of the psychology of the unconscious," and he could see no basis for this type of treatment in objective knowledge. "Scientists hate empiricism and regard it as a stimulus to research" (113). A description of E.C.T. (electroconvulsive therapy) by the neurobiologist Steven Rose makes the point clear: "The treatment is analogous to attempting to mend a faulty radio by kicking it, or a broken computer by cutting out a few of its circuits" (147). But Winnicott's most fundamental and simple objection to the physical treatment of mental illness was that it interfered with the person. Leucotomy to him was an extreme example of such interference, for "the psyche, and for those who use the term, the soul, depends on the intact brain" (28). "Leucotomy has *really shocked me.* In Leucotomy, which has now mercifully gone out, I can only see the patient's insane delusion being met by a delusion on the part of the doctor" (61).

Throughout his career Winnicott never ceased to regard his medical

training and practice as the natural preparation for his role as psychiatrist. He used to say that during his training at St Bartholomew's Hospital it was "Lord Horder who taught him the importance of taking a
careful case history, and to listen to what the patient said, rather than
simply to ask questions" (151). In 1963 he wrote: "Paediatrics gives the
student and the doctor the very best opportunity for getting to know
the child patient and the parents . . . it was as a practising paediatrician
that I found the therapeutic value of history taking . . . Psychoanalysis
for me is a vast extension of history taking, with therapeutics as a
by-product" (61).

To sum up, it seems appropriate to use some words that Winnicott
wrote about himself in the introduction to *Therapeutic Consultations
in Child Psychiatry*, published soon after he died:

> If the reader should *enjoy* reading the details of a series of these cases
> it is likely that there will emerge in the reader a feeling that I as the psy-
> chiatrist am the constant factor and that nothing else can be predicted.
> I myself come out of these case descriptions as a human being, so that
> in no case would the same results have been obtained if any other psy-
> chiatrist had been in my place. The only companion that I have in explor-
> ing the unknown territory of the new case is the theory that I carry round
> with me and that has become part of me and that I do not even have to
> think about in a deliberate way. This is the theory of the emotional devel-
> opment of the individual which includes for me the total history of the
> individual child's specific environment. It cannot be avoided that changes
> in this theoretical basis for my work do occur in the course of time and
> on account of experience. One could compare my position with that of
> a cellist who first slogs away at *technique* and then actually becomes able
> to play *music*, taking technique for granted. I am aware of doing this work
> more easily and with more success than I was able to do it 30 years ago
> and my wish is to communicate with those who are still slogging away
> at technique, at the same time giving them the hope that will one day
> come from playing music. There is but little satisfaction to be gained from
> giving a virtuoso performance from a written score (73).

II. The Theory of Emotional Development

The baby new to earth and sky,
What time his tender palm is prest
Against the circle of the breast
Has never thought that this is I;

But as he grows he gathers much
And learns the use of 'I' and 'me',
And finds 'I am not what I see,
And other than the things I touch.'

So rounds he to a separate mind
From whence pure memory may begin
As through the frame that binds him in
His isolation grows defined.*

Tennyson, *In Memoriam XLIV*,
first published 1850

*Our attention was first drawn to these stanzas in a paper written by Dr. St John Vertue of Guy's Hospital.

It will be seen by people who have studied emotional growth in infancy and childhood that Winnicott's theory owes much to others—not only to Freud and Klein and to the ego psychologists who were prominent at the time of its evolution, but also to the philosophers and poets of our civilization. As Winnicott himself said, "It is not possible to be original except on a basis of tradition" (69). Of the originality of his work there can be no doubt for those conversant with it; and even though a word or a phrase, an analogy or an idea may be found to have been borrowed, it always reappears enlarged and transmuted by his particular use and associations. In one of his lectures given to an American audience he said, "It might happen in practising my scales and arpeggios I may provide material for discussion. I am not concerned either with being original or with quoting from other writers and thinkers (even Freud)" (106). Just here we should like to follow his example and try to present a coherent outline of his theory, referring to other writers only when similarity or contrast seem to illuminate his own concepts.

A. BASIC ASSUMPTIONS

1. Self and Ego

Winnicott's theory of emotional development was principally stated in terms of the developing self. For him the concept of self, while inseparable at one end of the scale from anatomy, physiology and biology, was, at the other end, essential in a full evaluation of what is meant by mental health in the human being. In spite of being central to his theory, the self is not easy to define: in his writing there are variations in its meaning according to the context in which it is found. It does, however, carry the connotation of personal identity that is embedded in everyday language.

At first the personal identity is only potential. At the very beginning there is a primary "central self" later to become the "core of the self," also spoken of as a "potential true self." Of the central self Winnicott wrote,

> The central self could be said to be the inherited potential which is experiencing a continuity of being, and acquiring in its own way and at its own speed a personal psychic reality and a personal body scheme (51).

Here the initial self is defined in terms of the *growth* that is already taking place in order for a personal identity to be realized. The idea of growth as a moving and motivating force in the individual from the very beginning is essential in Winnicott's theory, and the absolutely primary inherited potential spoken of here was seen mainly by him as the poten-

27

tial for growth, manifested in a tendency towards psychological development "which corresponds to the growth of the body and the gradual
development of functions" (53), and which takes place according to a
personal (inherited) pattern. In other words it is the "maturational processes" that are there from the beginning—the capacity to become who
one is. This becoming of who one is was described by Winnicott as a
"progress" which in the course of time involves the "evolution of the
individual, psyche-soma, personality and mind with (eventually) character formation and socialization" (30). To this we can add, on his authority, the capacity to "take part in the establishment, maintenance and
alteration of the environment" (43) or, as he put it elsewhere, to make a
"contribution to the world's [cultural] fertility which is the privilege of
even the least of us" (22). Of this progress he wrote that it "starts from a
date certainly prior to birth," and he added, "There is a biological drive
behind progress" (30).

Like Freud's "id," Winnicott's central self is the source of energy or
spontaneity. But Winnicott does not give quite the same primacy as
Freud to the id-drives (libidinal and aggressive): these are seen more by
Winnicott as *serving* the maturational processes. The difference here is
one of emphasis, and it can be seen in the theory of infantile development; for while Freud's theory, where it touches on earliest infancy, is
concerned mainly with the pleasurable and unpleasurable effects of
orgiastic (id-driven) experience (tension, satisfaction, frustration), Winnicott's is not. Although always recognizing the id instincts as fundamental in the infant's difficult task of adapting to external reality,
Winnicott believed that before any use can be made of these instincts
there must be present an *experiencing person*, however rudimentary. It
is here that the "ego" comes in, because it is through the ego that the
psychic organization takes place in the infant that makes an id-event
into a personal experience. The following passage concerning earliest
infancy makes this clear:

> It must be emphasized that in referring to the meeting of infant needs
> I am not referring to the satisfaction of instincts. In the area that I am
> examining the instincts are not yet clearly defined as internal to the
> infant. The instincts can be as much external as can a clap of thunder or a
> hit. The infant's ego is building up strength and in consequence is getting
> towards a state in which id-demands will be felt as part of the self, and not

as environmental. When this development occurs, the id-satisfaction becomes a very important strengthener of the ego (58).

It was thus with the genesis of the experiencing person that Winnicott was most particularly concerned, and hence with the extension and development not of Freud's id-psychology but of Freud's ego-psychology.

It is helpful to think of the ego (or "I") as the organization of the infant that in time results in the self of everyday language: that is, in the sense of identity that comes with self-awareness. In Winnicott's words this self of common usage arrives "after the child has begun to look at what others see or feel or hear and what they conceive of when they meet this infant body" (52). Looked at from this point of view "the ego offers itself for study long before the word self has relevance."

Through the ego the components of the inherited constitution are gathered bit by bit to the nascent self: examples of this would be the baby's fingers or toes, or the sound of his own crying, which according to Winnicott are not necessarily felt as part of himself at the beginning. As this gathering together occurs, so sensory and motor events become personal and usable experience. The ego is intimately bound up with neuro-physiological development, and with perception and the development of intellect, memory and cognition, which become its allies in bringing about each individual's orientation to a world outside the self.

A vitally important function of the ego is the organization of the mental elaboration of sensory and motor events into what becomes the "personal psychic reality." Winnicott called this "Freud's concept . . . that was clearly derived from philosophy," and he added that our understanding of it had been enriched by the work of Melanie Klein (49). The inner reality is seen as an extension of the "fantasy" of the infant, which, at the beginning of life, consists in a very simple "imaginative elaboration of somatic parts, feelings and functions" (28). This simple elaboration, though an integral part of each individual that is never lost, is at first so primitive that it is totally lost to consciousness. Eventually, on the basis of broadening experience together with concurrent neurological development, the inner world emerges: "Of every individual who has reached to the state of being a unit with a limiting membrane and an outside and an inside, it can be said that there is an inner reality to that individual, an inner world that can be rich or poor and can be at peace or in a state of war" (27).

It seems that the primary central self or core of the self becomes isolated: it is something that "never communicates with the world of perceived objects"; moreover "the individual knows that it must never be communicated with or be influenced by external reality" (60). It is therefore through the inner reality, which the infant acquires like the flesh around the core of an apple, that the infant becomes recognizable as an individual; and it is under the influence of the inner reality that the world takes shape for the infant and child. When it becomes possible to attribute an inner reality to the infant the phrase "true self" comes to include this reality (60).

Finally, some sentences from a description of the self written by Winnicott towards the end of his life make the best summary:

> For me the self, which is not the ego, is the person who is me, who is only me, who has a totality based on the operation of the maturational process. At the same time the self has parts, and in fact is constituted of these parts. These parts agglutinate from a direction interior-exterior in the course of the operation of the maturational process, aided as it must be (maximally at the beginning) by the human environment which holds and handles and in a live way facilitates . . . It is the self and the life of the self that alone makes sense of action or of living from the point of view of the individual who has grown so far and who is continuing to grow from dependence and immaturity towards independence . . . (109).

2. The Fact of Dependence

"Ego-psychology," wrote Winnicott, "only makes sense if based firmly on the fact of dependence" (48). The same statement was made in another way when he said, "There is no such thing as a baby—meaning that if you set out to describe a baby, you will find you are describing *a baby and someone.* A baby cannot exist alone, but is essentially part of a relationship" (10).

The actual physical helplessness of the human infant means that the *sine qua non* of the infant's growth, both physical and emotional, is dependent upon a "facilitating environment" or "the maternal care which together with the infant forms a unit." The inherited potential which is at the core of the person cannot be realized without an adequate environment. "If the inherited potential is to have a chance to become actual in the sense of manifesting itself in the individual's person, then the environmental provision must be adequate. It is convenient to use a phrase like 'good-enough mothering' to convey an unidealized view of the maternal function" (98). The study of the maternal function is therefore inseparable from Winnicott's study of psychic processes in infancy. For our purposes here, it is convenient to make a separation of the two themes, but this is clearly artificial. We return to the subject of the maternal provision in Section D.

Dependence was seen by Winnicott to have three stages:

> (i) *Absolute Dependence.* In this state the infant has no means of knowing about the maternal care, which is largely a matter of prophylaxis. He cannot gain control over what is well and what is badly done, but is only in a position to gain profit or to suffer disturbance.
>
> (ii) *Relative Dependence.* Here the infant can become aware of the need for the details of maternal care, and can to a growing extent relate them to personal impulse.
>
> (iii) *Towards Independence.* The infant develops means for doing without actual care. This is accomplished through the accumulation of memories of care, the projection of personal needs and the introjection of care details, with the development of confidence in the environment. Here must be added the element of intellectual understanding with its tremendous implications (51).

To this may be added a further statement:

> Independence is never absolute. The healthy individual does not become isolated, but becomes related to the environment in such a way that the individual and the environment can be said to be interdependent (55).

B. EARLY PSYCHIC FUNCTIONING

In the infant's journey from absolute dependence to relative dependence, Winnicott mapped out three major achievements: integration,
personalization and the beginnings of object relating. These achievements are not necessarily consecutive; they are interdependent and
overlapping. Nor are they consolidated all at once, but are reached only
momentarily at first and then lost and reached again. Winnicott
believed that by the end of the first half year of life (in health) they are
consolidated to a degree significant to the observer. He pointed out,
however, that "most of the processes that start up in early infancy are
never fully established, and continue to be strengthened by the growth
that continues in later childhood, and indeed in adult life, even in old
age" (54).

1. Integration and Unintegration

Winnicott wrote this description of a baby at the beginning of life:

> What is there is an armful of anatomy and physiology, and added to this
> a potential for development into a human personality. There is a general
> tendency towards physical growth, and a tendency towards development
> in the psychic part of the psycho-somatic partnership; there are in both

the physical and the psychological areas the inherited tendencies, and these inherited tendencies on the psyche-side include those that lead towards integration or the attainment of wholeness.

To this he added:

> The basis for all theories about human personality development is continuity of the line of life, which presumably starts before the baby's actual birth; continuity which carries with it the idea that nothing that has been part of an individual's experience is or can ever be lost to that individual, even if in various complex ways it should and does become unavailable to consciousness (98).

Ego-integration, then, has as its basis the continuity of the line of life. The infant self cannot be said to have started until the ego has started (52), and the beginning and foundation of the self and of identity is this first organization of the ego that results in going-on-being. Of the crude beginnings of ego-integration, Winnicott also wrote:

> It is useful to think of the material out of which integration emerges in terms of motor and sensory elements, the stuff of primary narcissism. This would acquire a tendency towards a sense of existing. Other language can be used to describe this obscure part of the maturational process, but the rudiments of an imaginative elaboration of pure body-functioning must be postulated if it is to be assumed that this new human being has started to be, and has started to gather together experience that can be called personal (52).

In the natural course of events (given, that is, a good-enough environment) continuity of the line of life gives rise to wholeness, starting with moments when unit status—I AM—is achieved. In order to understand this achievement it is helpful to look at the baby in the state of unintegration from which integration emerges—the state that Winnicott describes here as "primary narcissism," when absolute dependence is a fact.

To begin with the baby does not feel himself to be separate from the environment: insofar as it is possible to talk about a self at all there is no difference between what is "me" and what is "not-me." "No object external to the self is known" (34) (cf. Freud, Piaget). The mother especially is merged in with the baby, her actions, heartbeat, breath and warmth felt as no different from his own. There is to some extent a continuation of the state of affairs that obtained before birth.

The unintegrated state involves temporal as well as spatial dissociations (or, to be more accurate, non-associations: "dissociation" is more usually used to describe a state where integration is faulty, or has been achieved and lost). Not only are aspects of the baby felt as environmental, and aspects of the environment felt as self, but even where there is continuity in the line of life and moments of I AM, the nascent self is not felt to be the same at all times. For instance, experimental psychology has shown that there are patterns of behavior established before birth that correspond to rhythms in alternation between the states of waking and sleeping, activity and non-activity, observed in the newborn baby (144, 149). Doubtless the feelings of the baby in some of these states (especially active ones) could provide material for primitive mental elaboration—the beginnings of fantasy. In time such states could also contribute, like the more rapid rhythms of breathing and heartbeat probably do at first, to a sense of continuity of process that is an integrating factor. But at the beginning Winnicott believed there is not enough ego-strength to carry the baby through these states as a single self. He wrote, "I think an infant cannot be aware at the start that while feeling this and that in his cot or enjoying the skin sensations of bathing, he is the same as himself screaming for immediate satisfaction, possessed by an urge to get at and destroy something unless satisfied by milk . . . and I think there is not necessarily an integration between a child asleep and a child awake. This integration comes in the course of time" (21).

So the attainment of wholeness means the coming together of the various somatic and psychic components into a unit self. I AM moments are at first especially "linked to the more definite emotional or affective experiences, such as rage, or the excitement of a feeding situation" (33). Integration comes to include orientation in three-dimensional space with a sense of process and of finite time gradually added. The organization of a personal psychic reality leads to an individual relationship with the environment; and the environment comes to be felt as external and eventually as permanent, the human environment—the mother— being at first all important. For integration, and indeed even continuity of the line of life, absolutely depend on the care given by the good-enough mother.

The mother's function at this time of absolute dependence was encompassed by Winnicott in the word "holding." Holding involves principally

> 1. Keeping the baby safe from unpredictable and therefore traumatic events that interrupt going-on-being.
> 2. Caring for the baby: meeting all physiological needs through an understanding of what the baby is feeling like: i.e. through empathy.

Reliable holding means that the immature and weak ego of the infant is made strong by the "ego-support" that the mother is able to give, having "the child in her mind as a whole person" (121). Through the holding of the mother there arises in the infant in the course of time a sense of trust in the mother and in the environment; and there also comes about a special kind of relationship between infant and mother that Winnicott called "ego-relatedness" to contrast it with the relationship built on id-instincts that is at the root of the classical psychoanalytic theory.

One other aspect of unintegration needs to be mentioned here. Winnicott wrote: "It is almost certain that rest for the infant means a return to an unintegrated state" (33). Insofar as the mother's ego-support is reliable the infant is able to return to this state without threat to personal continuity. In the fragmentary transcript of one of Winnicott's lectures there is a description of this restful unintegrated state:

> . . . in the quiet moments let us say that there is no line but just lots of things they separate out, sky seen through trees, something to do with mother's eyes all going in and out, wandering round. Some lack of need for any integration. That is an extremely valuable thing to be able to retain. Miss something without it. Something to do with being calm, restful, relaxed and feeling one with people and things when no excitement is around (121).

The experience of a return to unintegration in the infant is thus the precursor of the adult ability to relax, to be inconsequential and to enjoy solitude. Winnicott later called this "the capacity to be alone," and considered it "one of the most important signs of maturity in emotional development" (50).

It can be seen that the capacity to be alone is not the same as actually being alone. "A person may be in solitary confinement, and yet not be able to be alone. How greatly he must suffer is beyond imagination. However, many people do become able to enjoy solitude before they are out of childhood, and they may even value solitude as a most precious possession." This sophisticated capacity to be alone can only come about when the mother's actual alive presence at the beginning makes a return to the state of unintegration possible. Hence the paradox that the capacity to be alone is "the experience of being alone while someone else is present. This is the essence of ego-relatedness." "In the course of time," Winnicott added, "the individual becomes able to forgo the *actual* presence of the mother or mother-figure. This has been referred to in such terms as the establishment of an 'internal environment'" (50).

That the capacity to be unintegrated without loss of personal going-on-being is vital for emotional development is indicated in this passage:

It is only when alone (that is to say, in the presence of someone) that the infant can discover his own personal life. The pathological alternative is a false life built on reactions to external stimuli. When alone in the sense that I am using the term, and only when alone, the infant is able to do the equivalent of what in an adult would be called relaxing. The infant is able to become unintegrated, to flounder, to be in a state in which there is no orientation, to be able to exist for a time without being either a reactor to an external impingement or an active person with a direction of interest or movement. The stage is set for an id experience. In the course of time there arrives a sensation or an impulse. In this setting the sensation or impulse will feel real and be a truly personal experience

It will now be seen why it is important that there is something available, someone present, although present without making demands; the impulse having arrived, the id experience can be fruitful, and the object (recipient of the impulse) can be a part or whole of the attendant person, namely the mother. It is only under these conditions that the infant can have an experience which feels real. A large number of such experiences forms the basis for a life that has reality instead of futility. The individual who has developed the capacity to be alone is constantly able to rediscover the personal impulse, and the personal impulse is not wasted because the state of being alone is something which (though paradoxically) always implies that someone else is there (50).

These ideas connect up with Winnicott's insistence in his later writing that the only true basis for "doing" is "being." "Creativity," he wrote, "is the doing that arises out of being" (82), and, "After being, doing and being done to. But first, being" (67).

2. Personalization

A particularly important aspect of integration was referred to by Winnicott as "personalization," by which he meant the acquisition of a personal body scheme with the "psyche indwelling in the soma." In *The Ego and the Id* Freud wrote, "The ego is first and foremost a bodily ego; it is not merely a surface entity [i.e., dealing with outside world] but is itself the projection of a surface" (139). Winnicott expanded this in his concept of personalization:

> The basis for this indwelling is a linkage of motor and sensory and functional experience with the infant's new state of being a person. As a further development there comes into existence what might be called a limiting membrane, which to some extent (in health) is equated with the surface of the skin, and has a position between the infant's "me" and his "not-me." So the infant comes to have an inside and an outside, and a body scheme. In this way meaning comes to the function of intake and output; moreover it gradually becomes meaningful to postulate a personal, or inner psychic reality for the infant (51).

Psychosomatic collusion is a development from "the initial stages in which the immature psyche (although based on body functioning) is not closely bound to the body and the life of the body." Even after the establishment of psychosomatic collusion there may be periods when the psyche loses touch with the body:

> There may be phases in which it is not easy for the infant to come back into the body, for instance, when waking from deep sleep. Mothers know

this, and they gradually wake an infant before lifting him or her, so as not
to cause the tremendous screaming of panic which can be brought about
by a change of position of the body at a time when the psyche is absent
from it. Associated clinically with this absence of the psyche there may be
pallor, times when the infant is sweating and perhaps very cold, and
there may be vomiting. At this stage the mother can think her infant is
dying, but by the time the doctor has arrived there has been so complete
a return to normal health that the doctor is unable to understand why the
mother was alarmed (33).

Personalization means not only that the psyche is placed in the body,
but also that eventually, as cortical control extends, the whole of the
body becomes the dwelling place of the self. It is possible to see in small
babies, before this state of affairs comes about, that, while at times they
seem purposeful in the way they use their hands, for instance, at other
times they will regard the movement of their fingers and toes with fasci-
nation and even astonishment. Dr. Tom Bower, in a psychological experiment concerned with skill in reaching for objects, has observed that
babies under five months "have particular difficulties in monitoring
hand transport, which shows up as an interruption of reaching whenever the hand enters the visual field. The baby will simply stop the act
of reaching and stare fixedly at his hand" (131).

We could relate this to the plight of an adult psychotic patient of Winnicott's in whom personalization was undeveloped. She ". . . discovered in analysis that most of the time she lived in her head, behind her
eyes. She could only see out of her eyes as out of windows and so was
not aware of what her feet were doing, and in consequence she tended
to fall into pits and to trip over things. She had no "eyes in her feet."
Her personality was not felt to be localized in her body, which was like a
complex engine that she had to drive with conscious care and skill" (21).

Like the achievement of "I am," that of indwelling in the body relies
upon good enough environmental provision. Winnicott specifically
linked the *handling* of the infant with personalization.

Handling describes the environmental provision that corresponds
loosely with the establishment of a psycho-somatic partnership. Without
good-enough active and adaptive handling the task from within may well
prove heavy; indeed it may actually prove impossible for this develop-

ment of a psycho-somatic interrelationship to become properly established (52).

Adaptive handling carries with it the implication that "the person who is looking after the child is able to manage the baby and the baby's body as if the two form a unit" (114).

The achievement of personalization has its manifestations in good coordination and satisfactory muscle tone. But even apart from this it is of vital importance in Winnicott's scheme of emotional development. Without it he believed that a relationship to shared reality is difficult because instinct experiences, which are an essential basis for this relationship, cannot be felt with the full intensity of total involvement.

Total involvement includes, as the psyche comes to inhabit the body, a joining up of the initially uncoordinated movements (motility) of the infant to the experiencing of significant events. In time movement becomes harnessed in the service of specific goals and purposes.

3. Primitive Object Relating and the Experience of Omnipotence

The use of the term "object" in psychoanalytic literature is confusing. It needs to be taken in its particular meaning as the opposite of "subject." In fact, it more often applies to a person or part of a person than to a thing. So "object relationship" really conveys the idea of a personal relationship. A further complication arises here out of the fact that at the stage of development with which we are concerned, that is, where absolute dependence is reaching towards relative dependence, the "me" of the infant is only at times separated out from the "not-me." The object in the most primitive relationships is, to the infant, indistinguishable from his own self. Winnicott referred to such an object as a "subjective object" to contrast it with an "object objectively perceived."

It is possible to see from what has been said about integration why

Winnicott held that "the ego *initiates* object relating," taking object relating in the sense (derived from Freud) of the infant's relationship to the mother on the basis of instinctual (id) satisfaction, gratification, frustration, etc. "With good-enough mothering at the beginning the baby is not subjected to instinctual gratifications except in so far as there is ego-participation. In this respect it is not so much a question of giving the baby satisfaction as of letting the baby find and come to terms with the object" (52).

Here as always in Winnicott's work there is emphasis on the initiation of action in the infant (or child or patient) and not in the environment, though the environmental framework and the technique supplied by a particular infant's particular mother are vital. Too much doing and not enough responding on the part of the mother or mother-substitute can result in impingement to which the infant has to *react*, and the reaction may threaten his continuity of being. On the other hand, doing or being done to on the part of the infant because of a need or sensation or impulse arising spontaneously out of an integrated state will be felt by the infant to come from himself. He can initiate fulfillment of his needs by himself affecting his environment, though in a way at first unknown to him. Where his needs are met as they are felt by the good-enough mother's adaptive behaviour, a "this is just what I needed" experience turns, on the basis of repetition, into an "I have created this" experience. Here fantasy and reality are one, and the infant becomes the creator of the world. This created world, which consists of subjective objects, is felt by him to be under his control. Thus the mother allows him "a brief period in which omnipotence is a matter of experience" (52).

Here is a description of the process in terms of infant feeding:

> Imagine a baby who has never had a feed. Hunger turns up, and the baby is ready to conceive of something; out of need the baby is ready to create a source of satisfaction, but there is no previous experience to show the baby what to expect. If at this moment the mother places her breast where the baby is ready to expect something, and if plenty of time is allowed for the infant to feel round, with mouth and hands, and perhaps with a sense of smell the baby "creates" just what is there to be found. The baby eventually gets the illusion that this real breast is exactly the thing that was created out of need, greed, and the first impulse of

primitive loving. Sight, smell and taste register somewhere, and after a while the baby may be creating something like the very breast that the mother has to offer. A thousand times before weaning the baby may be given just this particular introduction to external reality by one woman, the mother. A thousand times the feeling has existed that what was wanted was created, and found to be there. From this develops a belief that the world can contain what is wanted and needed, with the result that the baby has hope that there is a live relationship between inner reality and external reality, between innate primary creativity and the world at large which is shared by all (10).

Writing about object relating in a paper for psychoanalysts in 1960 (51) Winnicott quoted a footnote concerning earliest infancy from Freud's *Formulations Regarding the Two Principles of Mental Functioning* (138):

> Probably it [the baby] hallucinates the fulfillment of its inner needs; it betrays its pain due to increase of stimulation and delay of satisfaction by the motor discharge of crying and struggling, and then experiences the hallucinated satisfaction.

The similarity between the two accounts is obvious. Characteristically, Winnicott points out that "the theory indicated in this part of the statement [Freud's] depends on his taking for granted the requirements of the earlier phase": that is, the holding phase when the meeting of ego-needs has allowed valuable experiences to be made of id-events. In other words, Freud's statement cannot be applied to the very beginning, but belongs to the time when the baby is already "creating something like the very breast the mother has to offer." But another important difference here is Winnicott's use of the word "create" instead of "hallucinate," which indicates the particular way that Freud's brief statement is expanded in Winnicott's scheme of emotional development. It is the joining up of the "innate primary creativity" of the infant, first manifested in fantasy, with the actual details of the world at large that comes to be a crucial aspect of the life of each individual leading to a "whole colouring of the attitude to external reality" which continues to make life worth living as long as life lasts. We return to this subject below (II C2).

Bound up with his idea of the baby's creation of the world is Winnicott's use of the concept of omnipotence as something that is an *actual experience* for the baby when fantasy and reality correspond. It is more usual in psychoanalytic theory to find omnipotence conceived of as a quality of feeling accompanying a denial of impotence or helplessness in the face of reality (external or internal). An interesting exception to this last rule is to be found in the work of Ferenczi, the friend and colleague of Freud, who, like Winnicott after him, seems to have had a particular understanding, both through observation and empathy, of what went on in early infancy. In his paper called *Stages in the Development of the Sense of Reality* (137) he wrote:

> If . . . the human being possesses a mental life when in the womb, although only an unconscious one—and it would be foolish to believe that the mind begins to function only at birth—he must get from his existence the impression that he is in fact omnipotent.

Ferenczi called the period before birth the "period of unconditional omnipotence" and the period immediately after birth, when there is maximal adaptation to the baby's needs, the "period of magical-hallucinatory omnipotence." While it is doubtful that Winnicott would have attributed such a sophisticated capacity for experience to the infant before birth (the full-blown experience or impression of omnipotence relying to some extent on the memory of what are in fact environmental details), the two are alike in assuming that omnipotence is an actual experience and also in assuming that this experience depends first upon the maximal adaptation to the baby's needs naturally supplied in the womb and then supplied by sensitive mothering, or, as Ferenczi put it, by the ability of the nurse to "feel herself into the soul of the new-born babe."

"Object-presenting" was Winnicott's way of describing that part of the maternal provision that facilitates the first object relationships and the experience of omnipotence. Something of his ideas of the nature of this function can be seen from these words:

> The process is immensely simplified if the infant is cared for by one person and one technique. It seems as if the infant is designed to be cared for from birth by his own mother, or failing that by an adopted mother, and not by several nurses.

It is especially at the start that mothers are vitally important, and indeed it is a mother's job to protect her infant from complications that cannot yet be understood by the infant, and to go on steadily providing the simplified bit of the world which the infant, through her, comes to know . . . Only on a basis of monotony can a mother profitably add richness (21).

4. Impingement and Trauma

The concept of psychic trauma has been familiar in psychoanalytic literature since it was first used by Freud. Winnicott linked it particularly with the idea of impingement, and in order to get an idea of what he meant by trauma it is useful to look at the ways in which the infant and the environment first come into contact in terms of impingement.

1. Within the context of ego-support, the baby acts upon the environment by a need or an impulse, perhaps expressed in a gesture or movement. The mother responds in a sensitive way (for example, feed when hungry, comfort, reassurance, etc.). Contact is made with the world creatively.

2. Again within the context of ego-support, the environment acts upon the baby in a way that is within the baby's competence because it is predictable and because the mother has the baby in her mind as a person (for example, moving from place to place, bathing, playing, etc.). Here is impingement, but again the result is increment to the baby.

3. Because of lack of ego-support or lack of protection, the environment impinges upon the baby in such a way that the baby must react (for example, repeated change in technique, loud noise, head not supported, baby abandoned, etc.). The continuity of being is interrupted, and where the baby cannot rest and recover within an environment that has once more become maximally adaptive, the thread of continuity cannot easily be restored. An accumulation of traumatic impingements at the stage of absolute dependence can put at risk the mental stability (sanity) of the individual.

In this place which is characterized by the essential existence of the holding environment, the "inherited potential" is becoming itself a "continuity of being." The alternative to being is reacting, and reacting interrupts being and annihilates Being and annihilation are the two alternatives. The holding environment therefore has as its main function the reduction to a minimum of impingements to which the infant must react with resultant annihilation of personal being. Under favorable conditions the infant establishes a continuity of existence and then begins to develop the sophistications which make it possible for impingements to be gathered into the area of omnipotence (51).

It is in this context that Winnicott defined trauma: "Trauma is an impingement from the environment and from the individual's reaction to the environment that occurs prior to the individual's development of the mechanisms that make the unpredictable predictable" (106).

Trauma at the beginning of life, then, "relates to the threat of annihilation." The concept of annihilation is expanded in Winnicott's list of what he called the "primitive agonies" or "unthinkable anxieties":

1. Going to pieces
2. Falling forever
3. Having no relation to the body
4. Having no orientation (52)
5. Complete isolation because of there being no means of communication (98).

It will be understood that the relation of these unthinkable anxieties to *actual* environmental impingement is complex. From what Winnicott wrote the following sequence can be postulated:

1. An impingement occurs—either obviously external to the observer or in the nature of some overwhelming impulse or body need in the infant which, if ego-support is missing, does not come within the infant's competence.
2. There is a body reaction (reflex, chemical, etc.). Primitive agony "intense beyond description" is suffered for a split-second before defences in the ego can be organized against it (103) (see Section II B5).
3. The imaginative elaboration (fantasy) of the reaction to the impingement appears in one of the forms listed by Winnicott, *"according to*

the degree of integration that survives the trauma" (106). These fantasies can sooner or later turn up as "the stuff of psychotic anxieties" (52).

It can be seen that primitive agony results in *dis*integration—a reversal of the maturational process. The sequence would be: primary unintegration, partial integration, trauma, disintegration, with defences in the ego that do not allow of re-integration along the same straight pathways as before.

"If reacting that is disruptive of going-on-being recurs persistently," Winnicott wrote, "it sets going a pattern of fragmentation of being. The infant whose pattern is one of fragmentation of the line of continuity of being has a developmental task that is, almost from the beginning, loaded in the direction of psychopathology" (52).

Here, however, Winnicott is talking about extremes. His ideas of impingement and trauma can be put into perspective by considering what he wrote about common experience at the time of birth. He did not believe such experience to be harmful if the birth is normal; he explained that in psychological terms a normal birth means

> 1. "that the birth is felt by the infant to be the result of his own effort. Neither precipitation nor delay interfered with this" and
> 2. that "in the natural process the birth experience is an exaggerated example of something already known to the infant. For the time being, during birth, the infant is a reactor and the important thing is the environment; and then after birth there is a return to a state of affairs in which the important thing is the infant, whatever that means. In health the infant is prepared before birth for some environmental impingement, and already has had the experience of a natural return from reacting to a state of not having to react, which is the only state in which the self can begin to be.
>
> "This is the simplest possible statement that I can make about the normal birth process. It is a temporary phase of reaction and therefore of loss of identity, a major example, for which the infant has already been prepared, of interference with the personal 'going along,' not so powerful or so prolonged as to snap the thread of the infant's personal process" (23).

5. Self Defense

It will by now be seen that for Winnicott the aetiology of psychotic illness is to be found in failure of environmental adaptation at the stage of
absolute dependence. This is not to say that he did not believe in the
importance of constitutional and hereditary factors in emotional development, but he did believe that, given an infant with "brain intact," the
growth of the infant's personality depends upon a sensitivity to his or
her individual needs that naturally takes innate predispositions into
account. The psychoses were therefore essentially thought of by him as
"environmental deficiency diseases" organized as defences against the
trauma of unthinkable anxiety and hence as a way of relating to reality
that does not betray the self (26). They were found to include:

1. "distortions of the ego-organization that lay down the basis for schizoid
   characteristics"; that is, dissociations, or "splitting" which is the "extreme of dissociation" and
2. "the development of a caretaker self and the organization of a self that
   is false."

In the first of these categories he included

(a) *Infantile Schizophrenia or Autism.* "It is a common experience in
child psychiatry for the clinician to be unable to decide between a diagnosis of primary defect, mild Little's disease, pure psychological failure of
early maturation in a child with brain intact, or a mixture of two or all of
these. In some cases there is good evidence of a reaction to failure of
ego-support."

(b) *Latent Schizophrenia,* which can be hidden in an apparently normal child and appear later, in adolescence or adult life, under stress or
strain.

(c) *Schizoid Personality,* which is a less extreme form of dissociation.
"Commonly there develops personality disorder which depends on the fact

that a schizoid element is hidden in a personality that is otherwise sane. Serious schizoid elements become socialized insofar as they can hide in a pattern of schizoid disorder that is accepted in a person's local culture" (52).

The theme of self defense is elaborated in the following passage:

> What we observe in children and in infants who become ill in a way that forces us to use the word schizophrenia, although the word originally applied to adolescents and adults, what we see very clearly is an *organization towards invulnerability*. Differences must be expected according to the stage of the emotional development of the adult or child or baby who becomes ill. What is common in all cases is this, that the baby, child, adolescent or adult *must never again experience* the unthinkable anxiety that is the root of schizoid illness. This unthinkable anxiety was experienced initially in a moment of failure of the environmental provision when the immature personality was at the stage of absolute dependence.
>
> The autistic child who has traveled almost all the way to mental defect is not suffering any longer; invulnerability has almost been reached. Suffering belongs to the parents. The organization towards invulnerability has been successful. It is this that shows clinically along with regressive features that are not in fact essential to the picture (106).

To this we may add what Winnicott called his "axiom": "Clinical fear of breakdown is the *fear of a breakdown that has already been experienced*. It is a fear of the original agony which caused the defence organization which the patient displays as an illness syndrome" (101).

So Winnicott believed that sanity is the result of a good-enough environment at the beginning of life. He did, however, make it very clear that there is "clinically no sharp line between health and the schizoid state or even between health and full blown schizophrenia" (65). Writing about autism, he said, "this is a clinical term that describes the less common extreme of a universal phenomenon" (124). Moreover, he found that his patients with schizoid characteristics could see things with a special clarity that is lost in those more firmly rooted in external reality, and he admired their honesty. "For schizoid persons (I feel humble in their presence) wicked means anything false, like being alive because of compliance" (77). He believed that healthy people can "play about with psychosis . . . Psychosis is . . . down to earth and concerned with the elements of human personality and existence . . . and (to quote myself!) we are poor indeed if we are only sane" (39).

6. The False Self

The second category of illness arising from early environmental failure was described by Winnicott as the "false self." The aetiology of the false self is to be found particularly in failure in object-presenting at the stage of absolute dependence.

> The good-enough mother meets the omnipotence of the infant and to some extent makes sense of it. She does this repeatedly. A True Self begins to have life, through the strength given to the weak ego by the mother's implementation of the infant's omnipotent expressions.
>
> The mother who is not good enough is not able to implement the infant's omnipotence, and so she repeatedly fails to meet the infant gesture; instead she substitutes her own gesture which is to be given sense by the compliance of the infant. This compliance on the part of the infant is the earliest stage of the False Self and belongs to the mother's inability to sense her infant's needs.
>
> Through this False Self the infant builds up a false set of relationships, and by means of introjection even attains a show of being real, so that the child may grow to be just like mother, nurse, aunt, brother, or whoever dominates the scene. The False Self has one positive and very important function: to hide the True Self, which it does by compliance with environmental demands (58).

There are degrees of false self. At the pathological extreme there is "the truly split-off compliant False Self which is taken for the whole child." Because the true self, being totally hidden, can have no relationship to reality, life itself becomes futile.

> Instead of cultural pursuits one observes in such people extreme restlessness, an inability to concentrate, and a need to collect impingements

from external reality so that the living time of the individual can be filled by reactions to these impingements.

At the other end of the scale (that is, in health):

> . . . there is a compliant aspect to the True Self . . . an ability of the infant to comply and not to be exposed. The ability to compromise is an achievement. The equivalent of the False Self in normal development is that which can develop in the child into a social manner, something which is adaptable. In health this social manner represents a compromise. At the same time, in health, this compromise ceases to become allowable when the issues become crucial. When this happens the True Self is able to override the compliant self (58).

Here again it can be seen that Winnicott is dealing with something familiar and accepted in our society, as he himself pointed out when referring to the arts:

> I think you will agree that there is nothing new about the central idea. Poets, philosophers, and seers have always concerned themselves with the idea of a true self, and the betrayal of the self has been a typical example of the unacceptable . . . You could quote to me from almost any poet of standing, and show that this is a pet theme of people who feel intensely. Also you could point out to me that present day drama is searching for the true core within what is square, sentimental, successful or slick (84).

7. Intellect and the False Self

Very often in Winnicott's writing we are reminded in some form or another that "the opposite partner of the soma in life's waltz is not the mind" (129). On the other hand, the development of the true partner, the psyche, depends upon the intact brain and intellectual functioning.

In the body of an anencephalic infant functional events, including instinctual localizations, may be taking place, events that would be called experiences of id-function if there were a brain. It could be said that if there had been a normal brain there would have been an organization of these functions, and to this organization could have been given the label ego. But with no electronic apparatus there can be no experience, and therefore no ego (52).

The intellect, then, from the very beginning is essential in organizing experience, and out of this organizing function thinking comes into being. Describing the process Winnicott wrote, in lecture notes,

> A list can be made of the properties of the human baby
>   Body functioning, sensori-motor
>   Imaginative elaboration of body functioning (fantasy)
>   add The cataloguing, categorizing and collating faculty
>   Memories: not conscious ever
>   conscious.

Winnicott saw the rudiments of these properties as present at least at birth, except for conscious memory. He continued with this explanation:

> The collation function develops its own life, enables prediction to be made. This comes into the service of the need to preserve omnipotence. Parallel with this, the elaboration of function [fantasy] enriched by memories passes over into creative imagination, dream and play (also serves omnipotence).
> In this way thinking comes into being as an aspect of the creative imagination. It serves the survival of "experience of omnipotence." It is an ingredient of integration (104).

Thinking itself, that is, "deliberate directing of the mind in a specific task" (104), probably has little relevance at the stage of absolute dependence. When the next stage is reached, however, where the "infant can become aware of the details of maternal care" (51), the mother can begin to use the developing intellect of the infant to help her.

It could be said that at the beginning the mother must adapt almost exactly to the infant's needs in order that the infant personality shall develop without distortion. She is able to fail in her adaptation, however, and to fail increasingly, and this is because the infant's mind and the infant's intellectual processes are able to account for and so to allow for failures in adaptation. In this way the mind is allied to the mother and takes over part of her function (33).

As a "crude example of the use of the mind," Winnicott wrote, "think of a baby expecting a feed. The time comes when the infant can wait a few minutes because noises in the kitchen indicate that food is about to appear. Instead of being simply excited by the noises, the infant uses the news item in order to be able to wait" (55). Put in other words, it is thinking that converts "good-enough environment into perfect (adapted) environment" (28). Here is where thinking comes into the service of omnipotence.

Sometimes, however, there is too rapid and too early a failure in maternal adaptation, or there is erratic mothering. In these cases,

> . . . the baby survives by means of the mind. The mother exploits the baby's power to think things out and to collate and to understand. If the baby has a good mental apparatus this thinking becomes a substitute for maternal care and adaptation. The baby "mothers" himself by means of understanding, understanding too much. It is a case of "Cogito, ergo in mea potestate sum."
>
> In the extreme the mind and the baby's thinking has enabled the baby, now growing up and acquiring a developmental pattern, to do without the most important aspect of the maternal care that is needed by all human babies, namely reliability and adaptation to basic need (104).

The result of this state of affairs, particularly if there is "an element of difficulty in the psychosomatic field," is that "the baby begins to develop a false self in terms of a life in the split-off mind, the true self being psychosomatic, hidden, and perhaps lost" (83). In the extreme case there thus comes into being "a mind-psyche, which is pathological" (28).

In clinical terms the picture of the intellectual false self

> . . . is peculiar in that it very easily deceives. The world may observe academic success of a high degree, and may find it hard to believe in the

very real distress of the individual concerned, who feels "phoney" the
more he or she is successful. When such individuals destroy themselves
in one way or another, instead of fulfilling promise, this invariably produces a sense of shock in those who have developed high hopes of the
individual (58).

8. The Expectation of Persecution

Winnicott referred to the first "I am" moments that contain the idea that
everything else is "not-me" as "raw moments." Assertion of the self
brings with it an expectation of persecution from the new thing, the
"other-than-me" which is momentarily felt as separate and rejected, and
the infant feels "infinitely exposed." At such moments, the infant relies
for safety upon the holding environment. "Only if someone has her
arms round the infant at this time can the I AM moment be endured, or
rather, perhaps, risked" (46).

A breakdown in support of adaptation at such moments means a
breakdown in integration. Clinically there can appear, together with the
dissociations mentioned above, a continuing expectation of persecution.
Here again such paranoid states were seen by Winnicott as the extreme
of something normal: separateness from the mother in any case
demands an awareness of the environment; being merged with her
ensures a sort of safety. "The most aggressive and therefore the most
dangerous words in the languages of the world are to be found in the
assertion 'I am'. It has to be admitted, however, that only those who
have reached a stage at which they can make this assertion are really
qualified as adult members of society" (88).

C. ADAPTING TO SHARED REALITY

Where the needs of the absolutely dependent infant have been met by the good-enough environment, there comes a transition to the state of relative dependence. Here the developing intellect of the infant makes possible a growing awareness of maternal care and of his need for it. The "not-me" becomes separate from the "me" and objectivity is achieved, leading eventually to living in a world where objects can be felt as permanent in time and space and can be used because they are separate and indestructible. The infant acquires the capacity to deal with the disillusionment involved in forgoing the continued experience of omnipotence and begins to feel responsible for his own actions. At this point, a graduated failure of adaptation to the needs of the infant becomes an important aspect of maternal care:

> As soon as the mother and infant are separate, from the infant's point of view, then it will be noted that the mother tends to change in her attitude. It is as if she now realizes that the infant no longer expects the condition in which there is an almost magical understanding of need. The mother seems to know that the infant has a new capacity, that of giving a signal so that she can be guided towards meeting the infant's needs. It could be said that if now she knows too well what the infant needs, this is magic and forms no basis for an object relationship (51).

1. Growth of the Inner World

We have referred to the concept of a "personal psychic reality" which in Winnicott's scheme of emotional development comes into being as a part of the self as soon as the infant has "reached the state of being a unit with a limiting membrane and an inside and an outside." The establishment of this state of affairs roughly corresponds to, or is soon followed by, the beginnings of self-consciousness, so that it becomes possible to talk about an individual self with the connotation of personal identity that belongs to everyday language.

    Winnicott's description of the inner psychic reality owes much to Melanie Klein, though the original concept and the phrase are Freud's. It is seen as the personal organization of the fantasy of the infant; an organization in which the "imaginative elaboration of somatic parts, feelings and functions," and especially of instinctual experiences (erotic and aggressive), becomes interwoven with increasingly complex mental representations of the essential human environment. In Klein's writing this is felt by the infant to happen on a body function model, so to speak: that is, it comes about through imaginative eating, and material is said to be introjected. What is felt to be good (ego-supportive) is preserved, and what is felt to be bad (persecutory) is eliminated (projected outwards). Winnicott made use of these ideas both in his clinical work and in his theoretical formulations, especially the earlier ones. There is, however, a difference in emphasis: in Klein's psychology personal heredity is seen as the greater determinant of what within the infant shall be felt as good or persecutory, while with Winnicott the actual behaviour of the (human) environment is more important in this respect.

    The inner psychic reality is largely unconscious (though, of course, the feelings to which it gives rise are not); it is the place from where the dream emanates. It is that part of the total self that can be called the "psyche"—that part, in fact, that is available to psychoanalysis.

    The inner psychic reality is seen as the basis for what becomes the personality of the individual, and it is also related to what in Winnicott's writing is called "character." In the course of time responsibility comes to be taken for "the total fantasy of what belongs to the instinctual moment" (33), and there develops in the infant the beginning of a social sense, or a capacity to feel guilt (see below II C7). This capacity, modified by the expectations of the parents and other significant people in the life of the child, also becomes an integral part of the self. In this way it can be said that the inner world is the seat not only of the struggle and the balance between benign and persecutory elements but also between impulse and control. This corresponds to what is called the growth of a "superego" in the classical Freudian theory.

2. The Area of Illusion

It can easily be seen that the transition from the state of absolute dependence to that of relative dependence corresponds in many ways to Freud's idea of the transition from the pleasure principle to the reality principle. While Winnicott found that what Freud implied by the phrase "pleasure principle" was insufficient to explain the psychic processes of early infancy, he nevertheless acknowledged and used in his theory the idea that the transition is potentially painful. This was especially true for him in so far as he regarded "the Real" as emanating primarily from the inner reality, fantasy being "more primary" than shared reality (21). "The Reality Principle is the fact of the existence of the world whether the baby creates it or not," he wrote. It is "arch-enemy of spontaneity, creativity and the sense of Real" (80). "The Reality Principle is an insult" (82).

Maturity, however, involves an acceptance of a "not-me" world and a relationship to it; only in this way can autonomy and viability be achieved. There is therefore a need to explain how the infant copes with the insult of the reality principle, or, in other words, how he bridges the gap between fantasy and reality without falling into a too sudden abyss of disillusionment.

It was Winnicott's thesis that a statement of human nature in terms of inner psychic reality and outer shared reality is not enough.

> If there is a need for this double statement, there is also need for a triple one: the third part of the life of a human being, a part that we cannot ignore, is an intermediate area of *experiencing*, to which inner reality and external life both contribute . . . It is usual to refer to "reality-testing," and to make a clear distinction between apperception and perception. I am here staking a claim for an intermediate state between a baby's inability and his growing ability to recognize and accept reality. I am therefore studying the substance of *illusion*, that which is allowed to the infant, and which in adult life is inherent in art and religion, and yet becomes the hallmark of madness when an adult puts too powerful a claim on the credulity of others (27).

The illusion allowed to the infant is, of course, the illusion of omnipotence—of having created what is there to be found. Maximal adaptation to the baby's needs, within a context of ego-relatedness, allows him a brief experience of omnipotence: omnipotence that is actual for him but an illusion from the point of view of the observer. Winnicott went so far as to say that without a modicum of such experience "It is not possible for the infant to begin to develop a capacity to experience a relationship to external reality or even to form a conception of external reality (27)."

From the very beginning, then, according to Winnicott's theory of the development of self, there is "some thing, some activity or sensation in between the infant and the mother" (27) (the mother at this stage being the subjective object). In health, it is in this area or space that fantasy and reality meet and are one and omnipotence is experienced. By means of this area the inner and outer world continue to overlap, so that what the infant discovers in the outer world, as it becomes "not me," he also creates. The illusion of omnipotence is thus to some extent retained and the insult of factual reality can be met and dealt with by the infant.

Here is a way of living in the world which, though based upon illusion, does not involve a betrayal of the self in compliance and imitation.

3. Transitional Objects and Transitional Phenomena

It was in terms of the area of illusion or, as he also called it, the "potential space" that Winnicott's most original contribution to the study of human nature was made. This part of his theory owed its evolution to sensitive and simple direct observation. He saw that very often the first special possession adopted by an infant has a particular importance that is allowed for by the parents. He called this the "first 'not-me' possession," tracing its origin to very primitive forms of relating and playing.

> Sooner or later in an infant's development there comes a tendency on the part of the infant to weave other-than-me objects into the personal pattern . . . In the case of some infants the thumb is placed in the mouth while fingers are made to caress the face by pronation and supination movements of the forearm. The mouth is then active in relation to the thumb, but not in relation to the fingers. The fingers caressing the upper lip, or some other part, may be or may become more important than the thumb engaging the mouth. Moreover, this caressing activity may be found alone, without the more direct thumb-mouth union.
>
> In common experience one of the following occurs, complicating an autoerotic experience such as thumb-sucking:
>
> (i) with the other hand the baby takes an external object, say a part of a sheet or blanket, into the mouth along with the fingers; or
>
> (ii) somehow or other the bit of cloth is held and sucked; or not actually sucked; the objects would naturally include napkins and (later) handkerchiefs, and this depends on what is readily and reliably available, or
>
> (iii) the baby starts from early months to pluck wool and to collect it and use it for the caressing part of the activity, less commonly the wool is swallowed, even causing trouble; or

(iv) mouthing occurs, accompanied by sounds of "mum-mum," bab-
   bling, anal noises, the first musical notes, and so on.

One may suppose that thinking, or fantasying, gets linked up with these
functional experiences.

All these things I am calling *transitional phenomena*. Also, out of this,
if we study any one infant, there may emerge some one thing or some
phenomenon—perhaps a bundle of wool or the corner of a blanket or
eiderdown, or a word or tune, or a mannerism—that becomes vitally
important to the infant for use at the time of going to sleep, as is a defence
against anxiety, especially anxiety of depressive type. Perhaps some soft
object or other type of object has been found and used by the infant, and
thus then becomes what I am calling a *transitional object*. This object
goes on being important. The parents get to know its value and carry it
around when travelling. The mother lets it get dirty and even smelly,
knowing that by washing it she introduces a break in continuity in the
infant's experience, a break that may destroy the meaning and value of
the object to the infant.

I suggest that the pattern of transitional phenomena begins to show at
about four to six to eight to twelve months. Purposely I leave room for
wide variations (27).

There are special qualities to be observed in the relationship of the
baby to the transitional object:

1. The infant assumes rights over the object, and we agree to this
   assumption. Nevertheless, some abrogation of omnipotence is a feature from the start.
2. The object is affectionately cuddled as well as excitedly loved and
   mutilated.
3. It must never change, unless changed by the infant.
4. It must survive instinctual loving, and also hating and, if it be a feature, pure aggression.
5. Yet it must seem to the infant to give warmth, or to move, or to have
   texture, or to do something that seems to show it has vitality or reality
   of its own.
6. It comes from without from our point of view, but not so from the
   point of view of the baby. Neither does it come from within, it is not a
   hallucination.

7. Its fate is to be gradually allowed to be decathected, so that in the course of years it becomes not so much forgotten as relegated to limbo. By this I mean that in health the transitional object does not "go inside" nor does the feeling about it necessarily undergo repression. It is not forgotten and it is not mourned. It loses meaning, and this is because the transitional phenomena have become diffused, have become spread out over the whole intermediate territory between "inner psychic reality" and "the external world as perceived by two persons in common," that is to say, over the whole cultural field (27).

So the theoretical place of the transitional object is the area of illusion; it is neither "me" nor "not-me." "Of the transitional object it can be said that it is a matter of agreement between us that we will never ask the question: 'Did you conceive of this or was it presented to you from without?' The important point is that no decision on this point is expected. The question is not to be formulated" (27). Elsewhere Winnicott wrote that this paradox (me/not-me) "needs to be allowed, and allowed for in the care of each baby . . . It is not to be resolved. By flight to split-off intellectual functioning it is possible to resolve the paradox, but the price of this is the loss of the value of the paradox itself" (64).

Winnicott's original paper on *Transitional Objects and Transitional Phenomena* first saw the light of day thirty years ago in 1951, and it is perhaps not out of place to say a few words, in parenthesis, about its subsequent fate. Since its publication the idea of the transitional object has been used in many branches of child care; and it has been enlarged upon not only in psychoanalytic practice and literature, but has also become the subject of many observational studies—studies that Winnicott himself would particularly have welcomed. A review of much of this work in the United States and elsewhere is to be found in a paper by Sylvia Brody entitled *Transitional Objects: Idealization of a Phenomenon* (1980) (134). Not surprisingly it has been found that use of transitional objects is to some extent culturally determined both by nationality and social status, and also by such factors as the incidence and duration of breast-feeding. The use of a transitional object in its strictest sense turns out to be found in the minority rather than the majority of infants observed, and the relationship between an infant's addiction to certain objects and "backwardness" in development is often stressed.

It needs to be emphasized that the transitional object appears in Winnicott's theory as *one concrete example,* placed in a specific period of development, of the transition from being merged with the environment to being separate from it. Always fascinated by the interplay of the inner and outer worlds, and by the nature of illusion, Winnicott saw that babies came into his clinic attached not only to parents but also inseparably to blankets, rags and other soft objects, and that the attitude of the parents to these objects was also special. He made a synthesis—a joining up—backwards to the observed "complications" of autoerotic experiences such as thumb-sucking, and, most important, forward to the serious business of the imaginative playing of early childhood where the interweaving of the inner and outer worlds has reached a sophistication that makes possible its use in the understanding and in the psychotherapy of children. For him the transitional object was one indication that a relationship to the outside world, acceptable to the self, had begun.

It also perhaps needs to be stressed that Winnicott himself indicated in his original paper that the line between a positive and a negative use of such objects is thin—at least to the observer: that the study of the transitional object "widens out" not only into "that of play, and of artistic creativity and appreciation, and of religious feeling, and of dreaming" but also "of fetishism, lying and stealing, the origin and loss of affectionate feeling, drug addiction, the talisman of obsessional rituals, etc." (27).

The transitional object was singled out by Winnicott as the most easily observable and comprehensible of a range of transitional phenomena. He believed that most of these phenomena are usually observable as well, but that even so a sequence in the use of them "may be maintained in a hidden way." He would have been upset indeed at the thought that his idea had been so misunderstood that mothers actually try to bring about the use and extended duration of transitional objects because of "a popular assumption" that they are "desirable and necessary for sound emotional development" (134). Basic to the whole concept of the area of transition and illusion was his conviction that it is spontaneity attached to the innate creativity of the infant that makes the compromise between inner and outer reality acceptable, and that compliance in this respect is false to the self.

4. Playing

The preoccupied playing of young children was seen by Winnicott as a further step in a sequence of activities in the area of illusion or the potential space between the individual self and the environment that leads to a mature capacity for participation in and contribution to the world's cultural fertility. In an article written for those who have care of children he gave the following advice:

> Put a lot of store on a child's ability to play. If a child is playing there is room for a symptom or two, and if a child is able to enjoy playing, both alone and with other children, there is no very serious trouble afoot. If in this play is employed a rich imagination, and if also pleasure is got from games that depend on exact perception of external reality, then you can be fairly happy, even if the child in question is wetting the bed, stammering, displaying temper tantrums, or repeatedly suffering from bilious attacks or depression. The playing shows that this child is capable, given reasonably good and stable surroundings, of developing a personal way of life, and eventually of becoming a whole human being, wanted as such, and welcomed by the world at large. (13).

The following are some of the special qualities of playing to which Winnicott attached importance:

1. "*Preoccupation* characterizes the playing of young children. The content does not matter. What matters is the near withdrawal state, akin to the *concentration* of older children and adults.
2. "In playing, the child manipulates external phenomena in the service of the dream and invests chosen external phenomena with dream meaning and feeling.
3. "There is a direct development from transitional phenomena to play-

ing, and from playing to shared playing, and from this to cultural experiences.

4. "Playing implies trust in the environment' and the capacity to be alone in the presence of someone.

5. "Playing involves the body because of manipulation of objects and because certain types of intense interest are associated with certain types of bodily excitement" (65), but where instinctual arousal is excessive, or sensuality compulsive, playing becomes impossible. "We leave out something vital if we do not remember that the play of a child is not happy when complicated by bodily excitements with their physical climaxes" (50).

6. "Playing is essentially satisfying.

7. "Playing can be said to reach its own saturation point, which refers to the capacity to contain experience.

8. "Playing is inherently exciting and precarious" because of "the inter-play in the child's mind of that which is subjective and that which is objectively perceived" (65).

9. "Children make friends and enemies during play, while they do not easily make friends apart from play" (15).

It is interesting to compare Winnicott's ideas about playing with Piaget's description of "symbolic play":

> Obliged to adapt himself constantly to a social world of elders whose interests and rules remain external to him, and a physical world which he understands only slightly, the child does not succeed as we adults do in satisfying the affective and even intellectual needs of his personality through these adaptations. It is indispensable to his affective and intellec-tual equilibrium, therefore, that he have available to him an area of activ-ity whose motive is not adaptation to reality, but, on the contrary, assimilation of reality to the self, without coercions or sanctions. Such an area is play, which transforms reality by assimilation to the needs of the self, whereas imitation (when it constitutes an end in itself) is accommo-dation to external models (146).

It can be seen that Piaget is here describing in his clear and sober way the difficulties inherent in the transition from the pleasure principle to the reality principle, and that he is very close to Winnicott in conclud-ing that an area of activity, in which play is included, is indispensable for the transition to be made. The two are very close together also in their description of playing, as can be seen from Chapter VI of Piaget's book *Play, Dreams and Imitation in Childhood* (145).

Piaget recognized that the symbolic play of children is, in a sense, "a source of creative imagination," provided it loses its *distortion* by the establishment of an equilibrium in the thought processes between assimilation of the external world to the self and accommodation of the self to external models. For him the ludic symbols of early childhood persist in adult life mainly in dreams. For Winnicott, too, an equilibrium or compromise between inner and outer reality is a vital part of the integration of the individual; but in considering Winnicott's psychology we need to think of the play area being carried forward in waking life, as integration proceeds, *along with something of the distortion*. To live creatively the individual has to go on being able to find his own inner reality—that part of the self from which the dream emanates— through a personal way of experiencing external reality. For Winnicott, playing itself is the basis for "the whole of man's experiential existence" (66).

5. The Potential Space

In his later writing Winnicott referred to the intermediate area where playing takes place as the "potential space." In the light of the observed qualities in the use of transitional phenomena and in the playing of young children certain characteristics of the potential space become clear.

To begin with, it is far more than an area where omnipotence continues to be served:

> From the initial experience of omnipotence the baby is able to begin to experience frustration, and even arrive one day at the other extreme from omnipotence, that is to say, at having a sense of being a mere speck in a universe, a universe that was there before the baby was conceived of

and conceived by two parents who were enjoying each other. Is it not
from being God that human beings arrive at the humility proper to individuality (98)?

The illusion of omnipotence after all becomes *delusion* in the growing
child or adult, so that where the absolutely dependent infant's experience is preserved in consciousness we recognize madness. What is
therefore vital in the individual's journey towards independence is not a
continuation of the experience of omnipotence, but, rather, a continuation of the capacity for creativity.

Creativity involves the individual in spontaneous action. This is as
true of the individual *experiencing* as it is of the child playing. In fact,
Winnicott called playing an experience, and a satisfying experience,
playing. Both involve "creative apperception" which, alongside cognitive development, enables the individual reaching towards independence to "engage in a significant interchange with the world, a two-way
process in which self-enrichment alternates with the discovery of *meaning* in the world of seen things" (71).

Because of the continuing overlap of inner and outer worlds, the
intensity of feeling and of the sense of Real invested in infantile experience and in playing is carried over into adult life. Winnicott wrote,

> It will be observed that I am looking at the highly sophisticated adult's
> enjoyment of living or of beauty or of abstract human contrivance, and at
> the same time at the creative gesture of the baby who reaches out for the
> mother's mouth and feels her teeth, and at the same time looks into her
> eyes, seeing her creatively (70).

Elsewhere he emphasized that such experiences are a part of everyday
life, and include such things as sharing a joke, or dressing up for a special occasion (7). Any activity can come within this area insofar as it is
coloured by the individual's sense of being personally present.

> I am hoping that the reader will accept a general reference to creativ-
> ity, not letting the word get lost in the successful or acclaimed creation,
> but keeping it to the meaning that refers to a coloring of the whole atti-
> tude to external reality.
> It is creative apperception more than anything else that makes the
> individual feel that life is worth living. Contrasted with this is a relation-

ship to external reality which is one of compliance, the world and its details being recognized but only as something to be fitted in with or demanding adaptation. Compliance carries with it a sense of futility for the individual and is associated with the idea that nothing matters and that life is not worth living.

In a tantalizing way, many individuals have experienced just enough of creative living to recognize that for most of their time they are living uncreatively, as if caught up in the creativity of someone else, or of a machine (67).

To this we can add the following, which clearly defines Winnicott's use of the word "apperception":

It is in playing and only in playing that the child or adult is able to be creative and use the whole personality, and it is only in being creative that the individual discovers the self.

He added,

Bound up with this is the fact that only in playing is communication possible; except direct communication [merging] which belongs to psychopathology or to an extreme of immaturity (66).

Here potential space activity branches out into personal relationships between separate individuals. Communication takes place in the overlap of potential spaces: this overlap forms the common ground in affectionate relationships where instinct tension is not a main feature, relationships made possible by the experience of ego-relatedness in infancy. Here communication comes about through "mutuality in experience" or the overlap of potential spaces, and interpersonal relationships can "attain a richness and an ease which carries with it stability of a flexible kind which we call health" (127).

Winnicott's own clinical work became increasingly linked with the idea of communication in the potential space: "Psychotherapy is done in the overlap of the two play areas, that of the patient and that of the therapist. If the therapist cannot play, then he is not suitable for the work. If the patient cannot play, then something needs to be done to enable the patient to become able to play, after which psychotherapy may begin" (66). Teaching, if it is to be profitable, also takes place in this overlap of play areas. "Teaching aims at enrichment," Winnicott wrote. To him propaganda was an insult. "It is an insult to indoctrinate people, even for their own good, unless they have the chance by being present to react, to express disapproval, and to contribute" (115).

On a broader scale, the overlap of personal experience is what gives to social institutions and custom their character, stability and flexibility. The value to society of the potential space of each individual lies in the contribution that can be made in terms of personal creativity. This, of course, includes the creations of outstanding individuals in the arts and sciences who have so obviously enriched our culture, but equally significantly it includes a giving of the self in less spectacular areas of living and working.

The potential of the area of illusion lies, therefore, in the possibility of an infinitely variable exchange in which the individual can draw from "the common pool of humanity" and contribute to a culture that "provides the continuity in the human race that transcends personal existence." The realization of this potential depends upon the holding environment at the stage of absolute dependence. It cannot be realized where the line of life is too seriously interrupted by reaction to impingements or where its place is taken by antisocial acting out, which is really the search for a boundary or framework. In health, the area of illusion is that which "initially both joins and separates the baby and the mother, when the mother's love, displayed and made manifest as human reliability, does in fact give the baby a sense of trust in the environmental factor" (69).

In this way, for each individual emerging from the environment on the journey towards independence, "at the place where continuity is giving place to contiguity" (69), the separating out is softened. But more than that, the separating out becomes, to borrow two lines from John Donne, not

> A breach but an expansion
> Like gold to airy thinness beat.

6. The Use of an Object and the Roots of Aggression

To state that there is a practical necessity in the ability to regard people and things both as separated from oneself and as permanent in time and space is to state the obvious. Without such an ability we could scarcely achieve any degree of independence; we would be unable to cope in the world of shared reality. Moreover, there would be no such thing for us as a body of scientific knowledge. Conversely, Winnicott believed that (historically speaking) "a body of science was needed before men and women could become integrated in terms of time and space, who could live creatively and exist as individuals" (67).

Looking at object permanence from a cognitive point of view, within the context of modern experimental psychology, Dr. Tom Bower has written:

> The information provided by our senses stays relatively constant throughout development. The way we interpret it changes. Consider disappearance transitions. Objects can disappear in many ways, sometimes incomprehensibly. Disappearances like this are the whole basis of conjuring tricks. Note, though, that while we adults suffer, or enjoy, the illusions that a conjurer produces, we know perfectly well that what we are seeing are illusions and that reality is different. The baby is affected by disappearance transitions in the same way, but does not know the reality is different. This is something he has to learn, and, as far as we know, he learns it in the course of the first year of life (132).

Looking at the same process from the point of view of psychic functioning (from Winnicott's point of view cognitive development, it will be remembered, served the needs of the self), Winnicott wrote:

In the most primitive state, which may be retained in illness and to which regression may occur, the object (person or part person) behaves according to magical laws, i.e. it exists when desired, it approaches when approached, it hurts when hurt. Lastly it vanishes when not wanted . . . We often hear of the very real frustrations imposed by external reality, but less often hear of the relief and satisfaction it affords . . . In fantasy things work by magic: there are no brakes on fantasy and love and hate cause alarming effects. External reality has brakes on it, and can be studied and known, and, in fact, fantasy is only tolerable at full blast when objective reality is appreciated well (21).

The achievement of a sense of object permanence is thus of the greatest importance to the infant self, and a study of the process in terms of psychic functioning formed part of Winnicott's theory.

The following developmental sequence, leading to a sense of object permanence, can be extracted from Winnicott's writing:

1. At the very beginning there is a primary unintegration or total merging with the environment, out of which arise
2. moments of integration, in which the infant relates to specific objects not yet separated out from the "me" (subjective objects): "In object-relating the subject allows certain alterations in the self to take place, of a kind that has caused us to invent the term cathexis. The object has become meaningful" (68).
3. As the "I am" moments become more frequent, what is "not-me" is gradually felt to be separate. Here also is to be found the beginning of a sense of time. The mother enables the baby to *complete* experiences and there is a feeling for time arising out of the recurring sequence of the states of unintegration, need, climax, satisfaction (frustration) and their consequences.
4. Finally, there is the development which Winnicott called "the change from relating to usage . . . The thing that there is between relating and use is the subject's placing of the object outside the area of omnipotent control, that is, the subject's perception of the object as an external phenomenon, not as a projective entity, in fact recognition of it as an entity in its own right" (68).

The development of this recognition, which means that the individual is able to use an object, cannot be taken for granted. To understand this achievement Winnicott found it necessary to look at the roots of aggression and destructiveness.

There is much in psychoanalytic literature linking aggression (particularly aggression reactive to frustration, i.e., anger) with the reality principle, but here as elsewhere Winnicott used psychoanalytic theory in a particular and characteristic way. To begin with, he could not look at destructiveness in terms of a death instinct, as Freud did. He believed that "the concept of the death instinct could be described as a reassertion of the principle of original sin" (67). Nor could he accept the Kleinian view that it is envy of the good object (person or part-person) that leads to destructiveness from the beginning of life. He believed that aggression can be traced to the prenatal motility of the infant, "to the impulses of the fetus, to that which makes for movement rather than stillness, to the aliveness of tissues and to the first evidence of muscular erotism. We need a term here such as life force" (8). Again, "At origin aggressiveness is almost synonymous with activity; it is a matter of part-function" (25).

If, during the period of absolute dependence, instinct experiences are felt by the infant to be a part of himself because of the mother's ego-support, the aggressive element (which at this stage is "destructive by chance") becomes fused with these experiences, and contributes to their intensity. This is putting a complex matter crudely; more understanding of it may be gleaned from the following:

> . . . the important thing to note about this instinctual aggressiveness is that although it soon becomes something that can be mobilized in the service of hate, it is originally a part of appetite, or of some form of instinctual love. It is something that increases during excitement, and the exercise of it is highly pleasurable. Perhaps the word *greed* conveys more easily than any other the idea of original fusion of love and aggression, though the love here is confined to mouth-love (76).

It is relatively easy to understand how, at the very beginning, motility contributes to the separating out of the individual from the environment:

> In health the fetal impulses bring about a discovery of the environment, this latter being the opposition that is met through movement, and sensed during movement. The result here is an early recognition of a "not-me" world, and an early establishment of the "me." (It will be under-

stood that in practice these things develop gradually, and repeatedly come and go, and are achieved and lost) (25).

What is more difficult is to see how aggression contributes to object permanence. Winnicott himself found difficulty with this part of his theory, which was only stated at the end of his life. He postulated the following sequence:

1. Primitive motility fused with erotic impulses brings
2. destructiveness aimed at the object (though not at the beginning in anger, which to Winnicott was a relatively sophisticated emotion). This destructiveness, like any other experience, has its imaginative elaboration in fantasy.
3. The object is seen to survive the destruction, and thus to take on a quality of permanence.

In his words,

> This change (from relating to usage) means that the subject destroys the object. From here it could be argued by an armchair philosopher that there is no such thing in practice as the use of an object; if the object is external, then the object is destroyed by the subject. Should the philosopher come out of his chair and sit on the floor with his patient, however, he will find that there is an intermediate position. In other words he will find that after "subject relates to object" comes "subject destroys object" (as it becomes external); and then may come "*object survives* destruction by the subject." But there may or may not be survival. A new feature thus arrives in the theory of object-relating. The subject says to the object: "I destroyed you," and the object is there to receive the communication. From now on the subject says "Hullo, object!" "I destroyed you." "I love you." "You have value for me because of your survival of my destruction of you." "While I am loving you I am all the time destroying you in (unconscious) *fantasy* . . ." In these ways the object develops its own autonomy and life, and, if it survives, contributes-in to the subject according to its own properties (68).

It can be seen that Winnicott was here talking about object permanence in terms of a person, namely the mother or mother-substitute. She is the first "object" to be placed outside and to acquire permanence because she is, in part or in whole, the first cathected object, the object of primary creation arising out of basic need. She is also the recipient of *actual* excited attack. But the process of externalization and the sense of permanence come gradually to be extended. We could mention here the transitional object, which, while a special case in that it "antedates established reality-testing" and retains magical qualities until it is finally decathected, nevertheless has a permanence and life of its own, bound up with its survival value. Just here the idea of the use of an object can be seen as belonging to the sequence of environment seen as (i) "me," (ii) "me/not-me," (iii) "not-me," with the emphasis on "not-me" because the object survives what I do to it. On the basis of cathexis, destruction *in unconscious fantasy* and survival, a whole world of permanent objects, people and things, becomes available to use.

The idea of destruction in relation to permanence is perhaps easier to grasp if we consider that, from a purely perceptual point of view, when an infant shuts his eyes he has, in fact, destroyed that bit of the world that was within his vision. If he then opens his eyes, and things have remained unchanged, this no doubt contributes to the permanent quality of external reality. Infants in the second half-year of life notoriously enjoy experimenting in this realm; games of "peep-bo" fascinate them and so do hiding and finding things. Winnicott described how a baby of ten months playing with a spatula in his clinic would shove it "under the blotting pad and enjoy the game of losing it and finding it again" (8). The fact that he saw this as the sort of playing in which the spatula and blotter are used in the service of fantasy—perhaps to represent an elaboration of the digestive process and of "the mystery of the middle of the body where the food is lost" (8)—makes no difference to the fact that it is also an experiment in object permanence. This is just one example of cognitive development as an aspect of psychic functioning.

The change from relating to usage distinguishes dreaming from waking life; it is the point at which dreaming and imagination, as we understand them, can begin for the individual. Discovery of external world qualities can now also begin: the baby can start to be a scientist. He can measure his expectations against a world of shared and permanent phenomena.

In terms of personal relationships, with which Winnicott was here most particularly concerned, the change from relating to usage brings about the infant's first true interrelationship between himself and an object "objectively perceived"—between a "me" and a "you." The recognition of the other person as a living entity in his or her own right has its reciprocal in the recognition of the self as an individual—an individual, moreover, who can use the personality, character, experience and created world of the other to grow; and here is a basis for true learning. Furthermore, the survival of the person who has been destroyed means that this same person can with safety be hated, repudiated and rebelled against, which all the while leads to a strengthening of their being loved, accepted and relied upon. In other words, a person can be used in the way that children become able to "use their parents and their siblings and their homes" to grow up out of (68).

It needs to be understood that it is not only magical or fantasy destruction that can now be tolerated by the infant or child: he also becomes able to tolerate his own natural (or age-appropriate) aggressive behaviour. The object having survived and not retaliated, aggression is now something that can be "encompassed" and not something that can be "retained only in the form of a liability to persecution" (68). This links with Winnicott's statement made many years earlier (1950) that "if society is in danger, it is not because of man's aggressiveness but because of the repression of personal aggressiveness in individuals" (25).

In the course of time the child naturally (in health) brings his destructive behaviour under control and uses his aggressiveness, which carries so much of spontaneity and of the life force, not only in the service of hate (and therefore of love which is the other side of the coin) or against what truly threatens from the outside, but also to achieve his aims and his goals in life, and to continue to feel real. In the meantime it is the pattern of "developing personal aggressiveness that provides the backcloth of a continuous unconscious fantasy of destruction" (107) that leads to growth through the use of objects.

With the change from relating to usage the isolation of the infant (as Tennyson put it in *In Memoriam*) has grown defined. But the infant and the growing child and the adult (given a good enough beginning) still retain the ability to interrelate through the overlap of potential spaces. Moreover, there is now a growing capacity to relate to others through "cross-identifications": that is, through empathy or the ability to "stand in someone else's shoes"—a relationship that implies a "different-from-me" understanding. In these ways the sharp line between the "me" and the "not-me," which can be a painful part of the reality principle, is softened (72).

The environmental provision necessary for arrival at the capacity to use an object can be seen to include

1. Initial ego-support allowing for meaningful object relationships including an element of "destruction by chance."
2. Gradual de-adaptation to need by the mother, allowing for the introduction of the reality principle, and a lessening of the magical qualities attached to what is omnipotently controlled.
3. The actual survival of the mother, unchanged, when she has been "destroyed" or placed outside the infant's self. It is important here that "survive" means "not retaliate" (68).

7. Innate Morality and the Capacity for Concern

It was Winnicott's view that "we need to abandon absolutely the theory that children can be born innately amoral" (77). Along with an inborn continuity of the line of life there exists in each individual powerful forces towards the preservation of personal integrity. "The fiercest morality is that of early infancy, and this persists as a streak in human nature that can be discerned throughout an individual's life. Immorality for the infant is *to comply at the expense of a personal way of life.* For instance, a child of any age may feel that to eat is wrong, even to the extent of dying for the principle" (56). "Compared with these powerful forces (which appear in life and in the arts and in terms of *integrity*) the mores of local society are mere distractions" (77).

The implication here is that for the mature person there can be no true morality except insofar as it has become a part of the self. The exoskeletal morality based upon the imitation and compliance that characterizes the false self involves the sacrifice of integrity; when issues are crucial, or where there is stress, such morality is liable to break down.

Maturity, however, was seen by Winnicott in the ability of the individual to compromise, to feel and act responsibly, and to accept (as a part of the self) the mores of local society, as well as to have a hand in their evolution. The beginning of this process of socialization was described by him as the achievement of a capacity for concern. This part of his theory owes much to Melanie Klein. The conditions necessary for the development of this capacity, briefly put, are

1. Integration of the ego. There has to be a whole person, with an inside and an outside, who can contain anxiety within the self. "I am" has to come before "I am responsible." At this stage the ego is beginning to be "independent of the mother's auxiliary ego."
2. Object relationships in which there are elements of love and destruction, such as "I love you; I eat you," though there has come to be some "appreciation of the difference between fact and fantasy" (29).
3. The mother seen as a whole person, separate from the infant, and in the process of becoming permanent. The mother's reliable presence is essential.

Here is Winnicott's description of the process by which concern develops in the individual, a process which, in health, begins somewhere towards the second half of the first year of life, and is consolidated by about two years of age:

It is helpful to postulate the existence for the immature child of two mothers—shall I call them the object-mother and the environment-mother? I have no wish to invent names that become stuck and eventually develop a rigidity and an obstructive quality, but it seems possible to use these words "object-mother" and "environment-mother" in this context to describe the vast difference that there is for the infant between two aspects of infant care, the mother as object or owner of the part-object that may satisfy the infant's urgent needs [id-relation] and the mother as the person who wards off the unpredictable and who actively provides care in handling and in general management [ego-relation]. What the infant does at the height of id-tension and the use thus made of the object seems to me very different from the use the infant makes of the mother as part of the total environment.

In this language it is the environment-mother who receives all that can be called affection and sensuous co-existence; it is the object-mother who becomes the target for excited experience backed by crude instinct-tension. It is my thesis that concern turns up in the baby's life as a highly sophisticated experience in the coming together in the infant's mind of the object-mother and the environment-mother . . .

The fantasy that goes with full blooded id-drives contains attack and destruction . . . If the object is not destroyed, it is because of its own survival capacity, not because of the baby's protection of the object. This is one side of the picture.

The other side of the picture has to do with the baby's relation to the environment-mother, and from this angle there may come so great a protection of the mother that the child becomes inhibited or turns away. Here is a positive element in the infant's experience of weaning and one reason why some infants wean themselves.

In favorable circumstances there builds up a technique for the solution of this complex form of ambivalence. The infant experiences anxiety, because if he consumes the mother he will lose her, but this anxiety becomes modified by the fact that the baby has a contribution to make to the environment-mother. There is a growing confidence that there will be an opportunity for contributing-in, for giving to the environment-mother, a confidence which makes the infant able to hold the anxiety. The anxiety held in this way becomes altered in quality and becomes a sense of guilt.

Instinct-drives lead to ruthless usage of objects, and then to a guilt sense which is held, and is allayed by the contribution to the environment-mother that the infant can make in the course of a few hours . . .

When confidence in this benign cycle and in the expectation of opportunity is established, the sense of guilt in relation to the id-drives becomes further modified, and we need a more positive term, such as "concern." The infant is now becoming able to be concerned, to take responsibility for his own instinctual impulses and the functions that belong to them. This provides one of the fundamental constructive elements of play and work. But in the developmental process, it was the opportunity to contribute that enabled concern to be within the child's capacity (54).

Psychoanalytic theory has always emphasized that tolerance of ambivalence towards both parents and other loved people is inherent in growing up, and here we have an explanation of the origins of this tolerance, woven in with the concept of reparation. Winnicott, perhaps more than most writers, emphasized the continuing need for tolerance of ambivalence towards loved people throughout life as the basis of social responsibility and of the performance of the day to day work of the world, including the care of the next generation of children. "Social activity," he wrote, "cannot be satisfactory except it be based on a feeling of personal guilt in respect of aggression" (29).

It can be seen that Winnicott held it as crucial during this period when ambivalence can be reached that the actual person (at first mother or mother-substitute) who has been loved and attacked should be reliably present. Although the infant may now no longer be her sole preoccupation, her presence is needed to give opportunity for, and to acknowledge the effort behind, acts of reparation. Unless she is available, the "benign cycle" is incomplete, and the result can be a loss of the capacity to feel responsible—a loss of a sense of guilt—and its replacement by a cruder form of anxiety concerning loss of the mother herself. This can lead to "crude defences, such as splitting, or disintegration." Less drastically, the lack of opportunity to mend can result in a "depressed mood." The depressed mood involves a damping down, or inhibition, of the instincts because of fear of harm done through aggression. This is partly what Winnicott meant when he called depression "the illness of valuable people." The corollary to this is that a continual repetition of the benign cycle of attack and reparation "frees the instinctual life" and allows the individual to take risks. Winnicott linked successful development at this stage with adult potency (54).

With the development of the capacity for concern there comes a new step in the integration of the infant, for to the sequence mentioned above of unintegration, need, climax, satisfaction (frustration) and anxiety there is now added a working through of the results of the experiences followed by reparation. The mother's care thus enables the infant to "catch hold of time," which is "the fourth dimension in integration" (122), joining the present with the past and the future. The psychic and intellectual ability to hold the idea of the mother as a whole person through this sequence (which depends on the physical presence of the mother at first) is an essential step towards independence. It means that physical union, the actual holding of the infant, can become less, and weaning, which to Winnicott meant the whole process of disillusionment or of the introduction of reality, has a firm foundation (54).

The presence of the mother is also needed at this time because of her strictness:

> At first the mechanics of self-control are crude like the impulses themselves, and the strictness of the mother helps by being less brutal and

more human; for a mother can be defied, but the inhibition of an impulse from within is liable to be total. The strictness of the mother has an unexpected significance, therefore, in that it produces compliance gently and gradually, and saves the infant from the fierceness of self-control. By natural evolution, if the external conditions remain favorable, the infant sets up a "human" internal strictness, and so manages self-control without too great a loss of that spontaneity which alone makes life worth living (33).

From this point we can return to the question of a sense of values. Without the development of a capacity for concern or the arrival of the stage at which self-control has meaning, "training" and later moral education can only bring "sanctions and the implantation of social values *apart from* the child's inner growth and maturation"—morality false to the self. On the other hand, Winnicott pointed out, "it is no answer to the problem of moral values to expect a child to have his or her own, and for the parents to have nothing to offer that comes from the local social system . . . The parents provide the children with an example, not better than they really are, not dishonest, but tolerably decent" (56). With the parents' humanizing strictness, and with the infant's desire to please and to make amends, there comes a natural acceptance of values, first with regard to personal habits, then to living with others and to contribution to society as a whole.

It can be seen that the concept of the development of a capacity for concern is similar in many ways to that of the capacity to use an object. In the history of Winnicott's ideas the acceptance of the former concept (based on Klein's work, though somewhat altered) antedated by many years his final statement of the use of an object and was undoubtedly a part of the understanding that led to it.

Both statements involve the instinctual backing of destructiveness "which partly shows in the baby's behavior and which is partly a matter of the infant's own elaboration of the physical function" (29). In both the survival of the object is of the greatest importance, and both result in the toleration of ambivalence and the acceptance of personal aggressiveness. But while the earlier concept explains the beginnings of social responsibility, it does not explain how the infant (child, adult, patient) can use "other-than-me substance" for personal growth. The capacity for concern is based on a fantasy of the object as destroyed, consumed, depleted; by the infant's reparative actions in relation to the real (differentiated) object, who is reliably present, the fantasy object becomes whole once more. In the later concept, however, the survival of the object makes it permanent, *a part of external reality* and not simply "a bundle of projections" (68). It is the fact that it is understood as an entity in its own right that cannot be destroyed that makes its use for personal growth possible. Both statements were necessary in Winnicott's theory of development.

8. The Antisocial Tendency

A consideration of the result of environmental failure at the stage of relative dependence involves the concept of deprivation. *Privation* was the word used by Winnicott to refer to failure at the earliest stages, when the infant has "no means of knowing about the maternal care." *Deprivation* refers to good-enough environment experienced and lost: "Things went well enough and then they did not go well enough" (85). The loss takes place at a stage when the infant or child can know about dependence, that is, when his development has "made it just possible for him to perceive the nature of the environment's maladjustment" (62). By this Winnicott did not mean, as he pointed out to a conference of Borstal Governors, "that the child could come here and give a lecture on himself or herself but, given suitable conditions, the child is able to remember in terms of material produced in playing or in dreaming or in talking, the essential features of the original deprivation" (85).

It was Winnicott's thesis that "the antisocial tendency is linked inherently with deprivation" (85). This tendency was described by him as that which has its clinical manifestations in a range of behaviour including "bed wetting, stealing, telling lies, aggressive behaviour, destructive acts and compulsive cruelty, and perversion" (56). The link is clarified in the following sequence:

> (a) "Things went well enough for the child" (77). Ego-support allowed integration to take place.
> (b) "Something disturbed this." Ego-support was withdrawn, and "the withdrawal extended over a period longer than that over which the child

could keep the good experience alive" (32). In talking about the antisocial tendency Winnicott distinguished two relevant sorts of deprivation:

(i) The loss of the mother's adaptation to ego needs at an age in the period of relative dependence. (The mother could become ill, for example, or there could be a new baby).
(ii) The (rather later) loss of an indestructible environment that enabled the child to explore destructive activities relating to instinctual experience. (This could be due to the family ceasing for a time to be a "going concern") (85).

(c) "The child was taxed beyond capacity" of the ego to stand the strain (77). "Crude anxieties and confusion relating to object loss" were experienced; unthinkable anxiety could be revived (85).
(d) "The child reorganized on the basis of a new pattern of ego-defence, inferior in quality" (77). This meant that "a reaction in the child took the place of simple growth. The maturational processes became dammed up" (62). Again, there are two aspects to this damming up:

(i) "Loss of contact with objects [people]" and of "the capacity creatively to find anything" (85) and
(ii) A taking over of the control which was lost with the indestructible environment. Winnicott gave this example: "When a deprivation occurs in terms of a break-up of the home, especially an estrangement between the parents, a very severe thing happens in the child's mental organization. Suddenly his aggressive ideas and impulses become unsafe. I think that what happens is that the child takes over the control that has been lost and becomes identified with the framework, the result being that he loses his own impulsiveness and spontaneity. There is too much anxiety now for experimentation which could result in his coming to terms with his own aggression" (85).

It can be seen here that a sense of guilt, insofar as it has developed, has been lost. Guilt becomes an intolerable burden where ego-support is withdrawn and the environment fails to survive unchanged. At this stage in the sequence, the child can be "in a fairly neutral state" and seem untroublesome and amenable to those who have care of him, but the deprived child is, in fact, "complying because there is nothing else that he is strong enough to do" (85). He is "hopeless, hapless and harmless" (56).

(e) The child, because of an improvement in environmental conditions, "begins to become hopeful again, and organizes antisocial acts in hope" (77). Here again Winnicott distinguished two trends:

(i) "The staking of claims on people's time, concern, money, etc. (manifested by stealing).

(ii) The expectation of that degree of structural strength and organization and 'comeback' that is essential if the child is to rest, to relax, unintegrate, feel secure (manifested by destruction which provokes strong management)" (62).

The hope in the antisocial act is that the child can "get back behind the moment of deprivation, and so undo the fear of the unthinkable anxiety or confusion that resulted before the neutral state became organized" (87); or that "the environment may acknowledge and make up for the specific failure that did the damage" (62). At this point, the child regains the capacity to suffer and so to be helped. Spontaneity returns and the sense of guilt is recovered, but, as Winnicott pointed out, antisocial acts of this nature are compulsive, and it will not be guilt of which the child is aware. Paradoxically, it is at this point that onlookers say "This boy or girl has no moral sense—no clinical sense of guilt" (77).

(f) If the right sort of help is at hand, the child can "reach back before the moment of deprivation and rediscover the good object and the good human controlling environment, which by existing originally enabled him or her to experience impulses, including destructive ones" (77). The two aspects of help needed are

(i) "The allowance of the child's claims to rights in terms of a person's love and reliability" and

(ii) "The provision of an ego-supportive structure that is relatively indestructible" (62).

Help can be found in psychotherapy, or in an institution where people sensitive to needs are available, but Winnicott believed that the vast majority of deprived children are helped to recovery within their own families. "The parents or the family or the guardians of the child recognize the fact of 'let down' (so often unavoidable) and by a period of special management, spoiling, or what could be called mental nursing, they see the child through to a recovery from the trauma" (62). Again ". . . in fact any parent with several children knows how over and over again the mending by the employment of special and temporary adaptive techniques does actually take place and is successful" (77). Within this kind of environmental context, the relative deprivations which so often occur in the early history of individuals and become mended can turn out to be of value in the establishment of trust and in the enrichment of inner reality.

If no help is offered at the time of the antisocial "acting-out," then it is possible that the acts themselves can take on added importance for the individual in terms of secondary gains. "The secondary gains quickly take over, lessen the suffering, and interfere with the drive of the individual to seek help or accept help offered." The sense of guilt is lost again, and the result can be recidivism or psychopathy, conditions which were described by Winnicott as "uncured delinquency" (62).

9. Adolescence

Winnicott saw in adolescence a time when a new adaptation to reality has to be made and when the vulnerability of the self causes a new necessity for dependence.

It is a commonplace in literature concerning the adolescent to find reference to the difficulty of dealing with new-found potency. Winnicott expressed the psychoanalytic point of view when he wrote

> Even when growth at the time of puberty goes ahead without major crises, one may need to deal with acute problems of management because growing up means taking the parent's place. *It really does . . .* In the total unconscious fantasy belonging to growth at puberty and in adolescence, there is *the death of someone . . .* In the psychotherapy of the individual adolescent (and I speak as a psychotherapist), there is to be found death and personal triumph as something inherent in the process of maturation and in the acquisition of adult status. This makes it difficult enough for parents and guardians. Be sure it makes it difficult for the individual adolescents themselves who come with shyness to the murder and triumph that belong to maturation at this critical stage (72).

In terms of the self, the problem that arises is "how shall the ego orga-

organization meet the new id advance? How shall the pubertal changes be accommodated in the personality pattern that is specific to the boy or girl in question? How shall the adolescent boy or girl deal with the new power to destroy and even to kill, a power which did not complicate feelings of hatred at the toddler age? It is like putting new wine into old bottles" (41).

The personality pattern *is* an old bottle in the sense that "the boy or girl comes up to puberty with all patterns pre-determined, because of infantile and early childhood experiences," but (and this is an important but) "there is much that is unconscious, and much that is unknown because it has not yet been experienced" (39). Bound up with the problem of whether the self can contain the murder and triumph of the unconscious fantasy is the fact that at this time of great strain the individual is immature in the sense that he or she has only partly discovered the self and confidence in the self. Winnicott found that new light was cast upon adolescence looked at in this way: the problems of the adolescent boy or girl could be said to centre round the statement "I am" and the question "What am I?" Without an answer to this question it is difficult to feel real, for the capacity to feel real is itself a result of self-discovery.

The dilemma is obviously exacerbated by the fact that the body in which the self dwells, and which the self informs, changes rapidly at puberty. The experience of a child who suddenly discovers, on looking in the mirror, that his nose no longer belongs to him, or on buying a new pair of shoes, that his feet seem to stretch from here to eternity, can indeed be disconcerting. The body shape has altered and so has body function; here again there is uncertainty, because in early adolescence "the boy or girl does not yet know whether he or she will be homosexual, heterosexual, or simply narcissistic" (41).

Uncertainty about the self brings about a return of "the fierce morality on the basis of the real and the false" (41) that belongs to infancy. For the adolescent, any false solution to the problem of personal identity is usually "out" (77).

> Once the adolescent can tolerate compromise, he or she may discover various ways in which the relentlessness of essential truths can be softened. For instance, there is a solution through identification with parent-figures; or there can be a prematurity in terms of sex; or there can

be a shift of emphasis from sex to physical prowess in athletics, or from the bodily functions to intellectual achievement. In general, adolescents reject these helps, and instead they have to go through a sort of *doldrums area*, a phase, in which they feel futile and in which they have not found themselves. We have to watch this happening. But a total avoidance of these compromises, especially the use of identifications and vicarious experience, means that each individual must start from scratch, ignoring all that has been worked out in the past history of our culture. Adolescents can be seen struggling to start again as if they had nothing they could take over from anyone . . . Young people can be seen searching for a form of identification which does not let them down in their struggle, *the struggle to feel real*, the struggle to establish a personal identity, not to fit into an assigned role, but to go through whatever has to be gone through. They do not know what they are going to become. They do not know what they are, and they are waiting. Because everything is in abeyance, they feel unreal, and this leads them to do certain things which feel real to them, and which are only too real in the sense that society is affected (41).

Defiance as well as dependence is thus a characteristic of adolescence.

Those looking after adolescents will find themselves puzzled as to how boys and girls can be defiant to a degree and at the same time so dependent as to be childish, even infantile, showing patterns of infantile dependence that date from their earliest times. Moreover, parents find themselves paying out money to enable their children to be defiant against themselves. This is a good example of the way in which those who theorize and write and talk are operating in a layer that is different from the layer in which adolescents live, and in which parents or parent-substitutes are faced with urgent problems of management (41).

Rejection of the false solution means that adolescents are, by and large, isolates. They are unable to feel that "I am here, I exist here and now, and on this basis I can enter into the lives of others, and without a sense of threat to my own basis for being myself" (125). This statement belongs to maturity. Relating in terms of cross-identification is dangerous to the un-established self, and instead young adolescents can be seen "attempting by various means to form an aggregate through the adoption of an identity of tastes"; here uniformity can be seen to be

important in such departments as dress, music, football team supported, etc. (41).

It is the attempt to feel real that Winnicott saw also as the cause of the
antisocial acts of adolescents. As we have seen, aggression is inherent in
the statement "I am" and in the act of growing up. Aggressive action has
value to the adolescent in binding him or her together, psyche and
soma. "I am" can become "I am the (murderous and triumphant) king of
the castle." Aggression can be used in this way in rebellion against parents and parent-figures. But also, it will be remembered, in immaturity
the statement of "I am" brings with it, in fantasy or inner reality, an
expectation of persecution. The feeling of real is particularly to be found
where the expectation is fulfilled and thus aggression "turns up in the
form of a search for persecution" (72).

> In the group that the adolescent finds to identify with, or in the aggre-
> gate of isolates that forms into a group in relation to a persecution, the
> extreme members of the group are acting for the total group. All sorts of
> things in the adolescents' struggle—the stealing, the knives, the break-
> ing out and the breaking in, and everything—all these have to be con-
> tained in the dynamic of this group . . . And, if nothing happens, the
> individual members begin to feel unsure of the reality of their protest,
> and yet they are not in themselves disturbed enough to do the antisocial
> act which would make things right. But if in the group there is an antiso-
> cial member, or two or three, willing to do the antisocial thing which pro-
> duces a social reaction, this makes all the others cohere, makes them feel
> real, and temporarily structures the group. Each individual member will
> be loyal and will support the one who will act for the group, although not
> one of them would have approved of the thing that the extreme antisocial
> character did (41).

This, however, is not the whole picture. Winnicott believed that out
of the struggle for self-discovery in new and uncompromising ways, that
is, out of the immaturity of the adolescent, there comes also an idealism
that can benefit society.

> Immaturity is a precious part of the adolescent scene. In this is con-
> tained the most exciting features of creative thought, new and fresh feel-
> ing, ideas for new living. Society needs to be shaken by the aspirations of
> those who are not responsible. If the adults abdicate, the adolescent

becomes prematurely, and by false process, adult . . . The adolescent's idea of an ideal society is stimulating and exciting, but the point about adolescence is its immaturity and the fact of not being responsible. This, its most sacred element, lasts only a few years, and it is a property that must be lost to each individual as maturity is reached.

I constantly remind myself that it is the state of adolescence that society perpetually carries, not the adolescent boy or girl, who, alas, in a few years becomes an adult, and becomes only too soon identified with some kind of frame in which new babies, new children, and new adolescents may be free to have vision and dreams and plans for the world (72).

So the immaturity of the adolescent needs to be recognized and allowed. "There is only one cure for immaturity, and that is the *passage of time*." In the meantime, *understanding* is of no help to the adolescent. If adults go around saying, "The exciting part of you is your immaturity!" or "Look at these dear little adolescents having their adolescence; we must put up with everything and let our windows get broken," they are guilty of a "gross example of failure to meet the adolescent challenge." "The phrase 'a meeting of the challenge,'" Winnicott wrote, "represents a return to sanity, because *understanding* has become replaced by *confrontation* . . . Confrontation belongs to containment that is non-retaliatory, without vindictiveness, but having its own strength." It means that "a grown-up person stands up and claims the right to have a personal point of view, one that may have the backing of other grown-up people" (72).

D. THE ENVIRONMENTAL PROVISION

"One half of the theory of the parent-infant relationship," Winnicott wrote, "concerns the infant and the infant's journey from absolute dependence, through relative dependence, to independence. The other half of the parent-infant relationship concerns maternal care, that is to say the qualities and changes in the mother that meet the specific and developing needs of the infant towards whom she orientates" (51). When stating his theoretical position in relation to other psychoanalysts, as he was doing here, Winnicott found a particular need to emphasize the actual nature of the concrete environment, especially at the stage of absolute dependence:

> We know that the infant (at the beginning) is not aware of the environment as environment, especially when the environment is good or good-enough. The environment induces reactions indeed when it fails in some important respect, but what we call a good environment is taken for granted. The infant in the early stages has no knowledge of the environment, knowledge, that is, which could be brought forward and presented as material in analysis. . . . If a formulation of a complete child psychology is being made, one that can be tested by direct observation, the analyst must imaginatively clothe the earliest material presented by the patient with the environment, the environment *that is implied* but which the patient cannot give in analysis because of never having been aware of it. . . . There is no emotional or physical survival of an infant minus environment. The infant who is held or who is lying in a cot is not aware of being preserved from infinite falling. In analysis a patient may report a sense of falling, dating from earliest days, but can never report being held at this early stage of development (57).

86

For this reason he found that "certain (psychoanalytic) concepts ring true from my point of view when I am doing analysis, and yet ring false when I am looking at infants in my clinic" (57), and he believed a study of the environment in its own right to be crucial to our understanding of the journey from dependence to independence.

1. Mothering and Biology

The question is often asked: is the natural mother of an infant necessarily his best caretaker? In other words, is there something that makes parents, and particularly first mothers, best able to provide the special environment needed at the beginning of life? One answer to these questions has appeared in a recent book on *Mothering* by Professor Rudolf Schaffer. We give it here because it expresses a view that has increasingly been voiced over the last decade or so.

> Whom a child chooses to become attached to depends on the adult's behaviour in interaction—on subtle qualities like sensitivity, responsiveness, emotional involvement, and probably others we know little about as yet.
>
> What we can say with confidence, though, is that it is these personality attributes (whatever they may turn out to be) that are the essential adult contribution to bonding—and not kinship. Mother need not be the biological mother: *she can be any person of either sex.* The ability to rear a child, to love and cherish and care for him, is basically a matter of personality: the so-called blood bond is a complete myth. There is nothing at all to suggest that firm attachments cannot grow between children and unrelated adults who take over the parental role—by fostering or adoption, for instance. The notion that the biological mother, by virtue of being the biological mother, is uniquely capable of caring for her child is without foundation.
>
> There is, for that matter, no reason why the mothering role should not be filled as completely by males as females. The human male's relative lack of involvement in child rearing is essentially a cultural

rather than a biological phenomenon. Originally, of course, biological factors were involved, in particular the fact that it is the mother who gives birth to the child and that it was she who subsequently had to suckle it for many months to come. Child care of necessity thus used to be women's business. Add to that the need to use the superior strength of the male to hunt, work the fields, and make war, and one finds sufficient reasons for the division of labor almost universal in former times and still prevalent today. Yet technological progress, in this respect as in so many others, can free mankind from biological constraints and make possible new patterns of social living. Technology has perfected milk formulas and the feeding bottle so that anyone, of either sex, can satisfy a baby's hunger. That same technology has provided us with so many mechanical aids that sheer physical strength is now rarely needed: women can just as well press the button that starts an agricultural harvester or fires a nuclear rocket. And, finally, biologists give us reason to think that even the process of birth, in its natural form, is not sacrosanct—that it may eventually be possible to grow a fetus not in a womb but in an artificial environment from which it is delivered in due course. Thus all the original reasons for confining child care to women are disappearing: *mother need not be a woman* (149).

The author does say elsewhere, with regard to an infant and his mother, that "some minimum period of togetherness is required, but there is nothing absolute about how much" (149).

In certain aspects Winnicott's theory contrasts sharply with these views. For one thing, his approach to the study of human nature was evolutionary rather than revolutionary. It was influenced by Darwin as it was by Freud, this influence being taken for granted and largely implicit in his writing. The evolutionary approach meant that new patterns of social living came about not through avoiding the biological provision or being freed *from* it by technology or other means but by using it as a source of vitality and energy; for him the instincts in mothers and in all human beings are the carriers of spontaneity and creativity, and constraints upon our freedom come as much through denying or ignoring the instincts as through allowing them to run away with us.

"It is likely," he wrote, "that true strength belongs to the individual's experience of development along *natural* lines, and this is what we hope for in individuals" (95). To him the word "natural" implied the idea of instinctual freedom.

It will be remembered that the "line of life" begins with the beginning of body functioning and is inseparable from it. The fantasy of the infant, as well as the inner psychic reality that subsequently develops around the self and determines the personality of the individual, is founded on "somatic parts, feelings and functions." While Winnicott held, in common with Freud and others, that there are "male and female elements" in each individual, which both enrich and complicate the instinctual life, he nevertheless not surprisingly assumed that *in general* the bisexuality of the individual is naturally loaded on the side of his or her anatomy. In other words, "most males become men, and most females become women" (90). Environment and culture of course play a part in the determination of male and female identification within the personality of men and women, but it is worth repeating that for Winnicott the optimum state of affairs was "one in which the environment can evolve according to the inherited [or inborn] pattern of the individual" (95).

Applied specifically to the subject of maternal care all this means that:

> (a) A woman is *likely* to make the best mother on account of her greater "female element potential" which enhances her capacity to identify with the female element in her boy or girl baby. This capacity is a part of the development of primary maternal preoccupation (discussed below) and underlies the ability to "hold" and to provide ego support at the very beginning of life. It is only in illness or in the extreme of immaturity that the male and female elements in individuals are dissociated or unmixed, but Winnicott believed that the "pure" female element in the infant establishes "what is the simplest of all experiences, the experience of *being*." The "pure" male element, per contra, establishes "doing and being done to"—both the active and passive of id-driven impulse (67). Without a capacity on the mother's part to allow her baby the sense of identity arising out of the continuity of "being," "doing and being done to" are not experiences within the competence of the ego, do not carry the "feeling of real," and cannot be the basis for creative living.
>
> (b) The "natural" mother has in her favor the fact that her function *is* natural: It involves her body and therefore involves the self in a special way; it connects her baby with her own line of life so that she becomes able to identify with her particular infant.

Having said all this, however, we must also emphasize Winnicott's concern that the study of the mother should be "rescued from the purely biological" (31). Here his views correspond more closely to Professor Schaffer's. He considered the term "maternal instinct" far too crude to comprehend the myriad personal subtleties of the mother-infant relationship. "When thinking of a *maternal instinct,*" he wrote, "we get bogged down in theory, and we get lost in a mix up of human beings and animals. Most animals do in fact manage this early mothering pretty well, and at the early stage of the evolutionary process reflexes and simple instinctual responses sufficed. But somehow or other human mothers and babies have human qualities and these must be respected. They also have reflexes and crude instincts, but we cannot satisfactorily describe human beings in terms of that which they share with animals" (34). The specifically human qualities are dependent on the human being's greater capacity to accumulate and to use *experience,* to build up riches in the inner world and in the personality, and to use these in combination with the biological provision—the maternal instincts and the reflexes—to start the infant on the journey to independence and maturity.

2. The Accumulation of Experience in the Mother and in the Parents

It is possible from Winnicott's writings to make a list of the personal experiences of parents and of mothers which he considered particularly important in contributing to the pattern and the quality of infant care.

(a) First there is the experience of having been born, of having been an infant, and the elaboration of such experience in fantasy. It will be remembered that Winnicott believed that no experience is lost, even if it is inaccessible to consciousness. The quality of experiences in infancy thus has a bearing on the quality of mothering. Of the mother he wrote, "She was a baby once, and she has in her memories of having been a baby; she also has memories of having been cared for, and these memories either help or hinder her in her own experience as a mother" (94). Again, "The mother and father do really carry round with them hidden memories of having been babies themselves and of having been cared for in terms of reliability, shielding from unpredictability, opportunity to get on with this highly individual matter of personal growth" (116).

(b) As a result of good-enough early mothering, there develops a capacity to create a live child in fantasy. "The beginning of children is when they are conceived of. They turn up in the play of many different children after the age of two years. It is part of the stuff of dreams and many occupations" (96).

(c) In playing, as we have seen, the child "gathers objects or phenomena from external reality and uses these in the service of some sample derived from inner or personal reality" (65). This means that any experience the growing child has of "watching parents with babies" or of "taking part in the care of siblings" can enrich the playing and become a part of the assimilation of the world of shared reality to the self. Through the *information* thus gathered a mother of the future becomes "deeply affected by local custom," which she may later either accept or seek to change (97).

(d) The experience of the actual conception of the child is an important factor in the nature of the parents' attachment to him or her. Winnicott wrote "We hear it said that it is strange that children can be so different from each other when they have the same parents and are brought up in the same house and in the same home. This leaves out of account the whole of the imaginative elaboration of the important function of sex, and the way that each child fits specifically, or fails to fit, into a certain imaginative and emotional setting, a setting which can never be the same twice, even when everything else in the physical environment remains constant." Specifically, Winnicott singled out as important that part of the total fantasy of sex that has to do with "the sense of concern or guilt that arises out of the destructive elements (largely unconscious) that go along with the love impulse when expressed physically." There is a connection here with the infantile sequence of "I love you, I eat you, I am concerned, I make amends." Winnicott continued:

It can be readily conceded that this sense of concern contributes a good deal to the need of each parent, and of the parents together, for a family. The growing family, better than anything else, *neutralizes the frightening ideas of harm done* . . . The very real anxieties of the father at the time of the mother's parturition reflect as clearly as anything else the anxieties that belong to the fantasy of sex and not just the physical realities. Surely a great deal of the joy that the baby brings into the parents' life is based on the fact that the baby is whole and human, and, furthermore, that the baby contains something that makes for living—that is to say, living apart from being kept alive; that the baby has an innate tendency towards breathing and moving and growing. The child *as a fact* deals, for the time being, with all the *fantasies* of good and bad, and the innate aliveness of each child gives the parents a great sense of relief as they gradually come to believe in it; relief from ideas that arise from their sense of guilt or unworthiness (37).

Thus it can be said that the parents "*need the actual children* in the development of their relation to each other." The need has consequences for the children's development, because "the positive drives generated in this way are very powerful. It is not enough to say that parents love their children. They often do get around to loving them, and they have all sorts of other feelings. Children need more of their parents than to be loved; they need something that carries over when they are hated and even hateful" (37).

Winnicott here made particular mention of adoption within the context of marriage: "Those who have adopted children will know how such children can fill the gap in the imaginative needs arising out of a marriage. And married people with no children can and do find all sorts of other ways in fact of having a family; they may be found sometimes to have the largest families of all" (37). Nevertheless, he believed that the richest relationships, both for parents and children, are those that come about when love expressed physically results in a physical fact. It is a matter of body involvement and the unconscious fantasy that accompanies body function and body experience, linking up with experience in early infancy.

(e) Body involvement is, of course, particularly the lot of a mother carrying a child. Winnicott believed that the baby in the womb becomes specifically linked in fantasy with the "good internal object" (34)—that is, with a good-enough mother of the expectant mother's own early infancy, with the subjective mother and the reliable care which, in metapsychological terms, she, as an infant, has created. This good environment becomes internalized and is maintained within and is felt to be part of the self: it constitutes her "inner reserve." The result of this is that the mother shows an "increasing identification with the infant" (34) which is characteristic of the state that Winnicott called "primary maternal preoccupation." If the internalized early environment is poor, the mother has difficulty in producing a whole live child in *fantasy*, and this can lead to difficulties in her relationship to her baby at the very beginning (105).

(f) In the weeks before and after the birth of the baby, the mother and baby share certain experiences. These strengthen the mother's identification with the baby and result for both in the "experience of mutuality" (108). Such experiences are usually quiet, having to do with the crude evidences of life such as breathing movements and heart beat. A more dramatic example is the experience of birth itself: "Among features typical of the true birth memory," Winnicott wrote, "is the feeling of being in the grips of something external, so that one is helpless. You will note that I am not saying that the mother is gripping. This would not be talking in terms of the baby at this stage. . . . There is a very clear relation here between what the baby experiences and what the mother experiences in being confined, as it is called. There comes a state in the labor in which, in health, a mother has to be able to resign herself to a process almost exactly comparable to the infant's experience at the same time" (23).

3. Primary Maternal Preoccupation

Primary maternal preoccupation is the name given by Winnicott to the special psychological condition of the mother in the weeks before and after the birth of the baby. It comes about through body involvement and through the (largely unconscious) imaginative elaboration of body involvement using all the accumulated experience of the past that has built up within the self. He set out the characteristics of the condition thus:

> It gradually develops and becomes a state of heightened sensitivity during, and especially towards the end of, the pregnancy.
> It lasts for a few weeks after the birth of the child.
> It is not easily remembered by mothers once they have recovered from it.
> I would go further and say that the memory mothers have of this state tends to become repressed.
>
> This organized state (that would be an illness were it not for the fact of the pregnancy) could be compared with a withdrawn state, or a dissociated state, or a fugue, or even a disturbance at a deeper level such as a schizoid episode in which some aspect of the personality takes over temporarily . . . I do not believe that it is possible to understand the functioning of the mother at the very beginning of the infant's life without seeing that she must be able to reach this state of heightened sensitivity, almost an illness, and to recover from it. (I bring in the word "illness" because a woman must be healthy in order to develop this state and to recover from it as the infant releases her. If the infant should die, the mother's state suddenly shows up as illness. The mother takes this risk.) (31).

Other observers have come to similar conclusions about the state of the mother at this time. In the words of T. Berry Brazelton (1975):

> Fifteen years ago . . . we were studying young women weekly in psychoanalytic interviews, to try to understand what their personalities were like before they had their baby . . . These were women who turned out to be normal mothers later on and who had already mothered a previous child successfully. Then we made predictions . . . that is, at the end of each stage one makes a prediction to see what is wrong with it . . . The predictions made by their therapists at the end of these women's pregnancies were that all of them were likely to be psychotic when they got their babies . . . When the predictions turned out to be wrong, we had to reorganize our thinking about the anxiety that normally occurs in pregnancy. It is something like this: anxiety and disruption of old concepts, through dreams, become part of a normal process, a kind of unwiring of all the old connections to be ready for the new role. As I began to look at

what happened to these women as they assumed their new roles it became apparent that the mother's prenatal anxiety helped her to shape herself in a very powerful way around the individuality of the particular baby she had (133).

This view is close to that of Winnicott when he wrote that primary maternal preoccupation "gives the mother her special ability to do the right thing. She knows what the baby could be feeling like. No one else knows. Doctors and nurses may know a lot about psychology, and of course they know all about body health and disease. But they do not know what a baby feels like from minute to minute because they are outside this area of experience" (34).

There are, of course, "maternal disorders" which affect this aspect of mothering. Winnicott drew attention to two sorts:

(a) "There are certainly many women who are good mothers in every other way and who are capable of a rich and fruitful life but who are not able to achieve this 'normal illness' which enables them to adapt delicately and sensitively to the baby's needs at the very beginning; or they achieve it with one child but not with another . . . It may be supposed that there is a 'flight to sanity' in some of these people. Some of them certainly have very big alternative concerns which they do not readily abandon or they may not be able to allow this abandonment until they have had their first babies. When a woman has a strong male identification she finds this part of her mothering function most difficult to achieve . . .

"In practice the result is that such women, having produced a child, but having missed the boat at the earliest stage, are faced with the task of making up for what has been missed. They have a long period in which they must closely adapt to their growing child's needs and it is not certain that they can succeed in mending the early distortion. Instead of taking for granted the good effect of an early and temporary preoccupation they are caught up in the child's need for therapy, that is to say, for a prolonged period of adaptation to need, or spoiling. They do therapy instead of being parents" (31).

(b) At the other extreme is "the mother who tends to be preoccupied in any case; the baby now becomes her *pathological* preoccupation. This mother may have a special capacity for lending her own self to her infant, but what happens at the end? It is part of the normal process that the mother recovers her self-interest and does so at the rate at which her

infant can allow her to do so. The pathologically preoccupied mother not
only goes on being identified with her baby too long, but also she
changes suddenly from preoccupation with the infant to her former preoccupation" (34).

It can be seen that mentally ill mothers—the schizoid and the
depressive, for instance—are likely to fit into this last category. Winnicott believed that a mother severely ill in these ways fails her infant
except insofar as "recognizing her deficiency, she hands her child over
to the care of someone else" (40). He gave an interesting summary
of a case history which throws light on these considerations. It is the
case history of "Esther," his patient, who turned out to be a deprived
child.

> Esther's real mother was said to be a very intelligent woman, who was
> at ease in several languages; but her marriage came to grief, and then
> she lived with a "tramp-type." Esther was the illegitimate result of this
> union. In her early months, therefore, Esther was left with a mother who
> was entirely on her own. The mother was the last but one of many chil-
> dren. During her pregnancy, it was recommended to the mother that
> she should have treatment as a voluntary boarder, but she did not accept
> this suggestion. The mother nursed the child herself from birth, and she
> is described, in the social worker's report, as idolizing her baby.
> This state of affairs continued until Esther was five months old when
> the mother began to behave strangely, and to look wild and vague. After
> a sleepless night she wandered in a field near a canal, watching an
> ex-police constable digging. She then walked to the canal and threw the
> baby in. The ex-police constable rescued the infant immediately,
> unharmed, but the mother as a result of this was detained, and was sub-
> sequently certified as a schizophrenic with paranoid trends. So Esther
> was taken into the care of the local authority, and later was described
> as "difficult" in the nursery, where she stayed till fostered out at two years
> and a half . . .
> A very ill mother like Esther's real mother may have given her baby
> an exceptionally good start; this is not at all impossible. I think Esther's
> mother not only gave her a satisfactory breast-feeding experience, but
> also that ego-support which babies need in the earliest stages, and which
> can be given only if the mother is identified with her baby. This mother
> was probably merged in with her baby to a high degree. My guess would

be that she wanted to rid herself of her baby that she had been merged in with, that she had been at one with, because she saw looming up in front of her a new phase, which she would not be able to manage, a phase in which the infant would need to become separated from her. She would not be able to follow the baby's needs in this new stage of development. She could throw her baby away but she could not separate herself from the baby. Very deep forces would be at work at such a moment and when the mother threw the baby into the canal (first choosing a time and place that made it almost certain that the baby would be rescued), she was trying to deal with some powerful unconscious conflict (40).

In sum, the very best in infant care is to be had from the ordinary devoted mother, the natural mother, who can "reach this special state of primary maternal preoccupation without being ill" (31). But while Winnicott's theory was stated in terms of the very best—of what could make for the richest quality in life—and not simply in terms of normality, he was also a practical man engaged in medical and psychiatric consultation and, as we have seen, he knew about casualties. "In my practice," he wrote, "I have always recognized the existence of a type of case in which it is essential to get a child away from a parent" (40). He had much to say also about the difficulties and the rewards of adopting children, believing that "an adoptive mother, or any woman who *can* be ill in the sense of 'primary maternal preoccupation,' may be in a position to adapt well-enough, on account of having some capacity for identification with the baby" (31).

4. Holding

The mother's capacity to identify with her baby allows her to fulfill the function summed up by Winnicott in the word "holding." Holding is "the basis for what gradually becomes a self-experiencing being" (94). From the time the line of life begins, reliable holding has to be a feature of the environment if the line is not to be broken. It starts with, and is a

continuation of, "the physiological provision that characterizes the prenatal state" (97). The function of holding in psychological terms is to provide ego-support, in particular at the stage of absolute dependence
before integration of the ego has become established. The establishment of integration and the development of ego-relatedness both rely
upon good-enough holding.

At the very beginning, when "physiology and psychology have not
yet become distinct, or are only in the process of doing so," holding
includes "especially the physical holding of the infant which is a form of
loving." It also, however, stretches to include the "total environment
provision prior to the concept of living with," that is, prior to the emergence of the infant as a separate person relating to other separate people. "In other words," Winnicott wrote, "it refers to a three dimensional
or space relationship with time gradually added. This overlaps with, but
is initiated prior to, instinctual experiences that in time would deter-
mine object relationships. It includes the management of experiences
that are inherent in existence, such as the *completion* (and therefore the
non-completion) of processes, processes which from the outside may
seem to be purely physiological but which belong to the infant and take
place in a complex psychological field, determined by the awareness
and empathy of the mother" (51).

A more concrete description of holding is also given:

> Holding
>
> Protects from physiological insult.
>
> Takes account of the infant's skin sensitivity—touch, temperature, audi-
> tory sensitivity, visual sensitivity, sensitivity of falling (action of gravity)
> and of the infant's lack of knowledge of the existence of anything other
> than the self.
>
> It includes the whole routine of care throughout the day and night, and it
> is not the same with any two infants because it is part of the infant, and no
> two infants are alike.
>
> Also, it follows the minute day-to-day changes belonging to the infant's
> growth and development, both physical and psychological (51).

In his broadcast talks to mothers and to parents, designed to show
ordinary parents the importance of what they were naturally doing all

Here is one passage on the subject, describing the way a mother picks up her baby girl:

> Does she catch hold of her foot and drag her out of her pram and swing her up? Does she hold a cigarette with one hand and grab her with the other? No. She has quite a different way of going about it. I think she tends to give the infant warning of her approach, she puts her hands round her to gather her together before she moves her; in fact she gains the baby's co-operation before she lifts her, and then she lifts her from one place to another, from cot to shoulder . . .
>
> The mother does not involve her baby in all her personal experiences and feelings. Sometimes her baby yells and yells till she feels like murder, yet she lifts the baby up with just the same care, without revenge—or not very much. She avoids making the baby the victim of her impulsiveness. Infant care, like doctoring, is a test of personal reliability.
>
> Today may be one of those days when everything goes wrong. The laundry man calls before the list is ready; the front door bell rings, and someone else comes to the back door. But a mother waits till she has recovered her poise before she takes up her baby, which she does with the usual gentle technique that the baby comes to know as an important part of her. Her technique is highly personal, and is looked for and recognized, like her mouth, and her eyes, her colouring and her smell. Over and over again a mother deals with her own moods, anxieties, and excitements in her own private life, reserving for her baby what belongs to the baby. This gives a foundation on which the human infant can start to build an understanding of the extremely complex thing that is a relationship between two human beings (10).

Although the "holding phase" in Winnicott's theory is equivalent to the stage of being merged or of absolute dependence, ego-support continues to be a need of the growing child, the adolescent, and at times of the adult, whenever there is a strain which threatens confusion or disintegration. Here is a simple example involving physical holding:

> A child is playing in the garden. An aeroplane flies low overhead. This can be hurtful even to an adult. No explanation is valuable for the child. What is valuable is that you hold the child close to yourself, and the child uses the fact that you are not scared beyond recovery, and is soon off and away, playing again (116).

The important aspects of child care that include the strictness of the parents and their survival can also be seen as a continuation of crucial ego-support.

Winnicott found the concept of holding particularly useful in describing the case work of social work. In a talk given to the Association of Social Workers in 1963, he said:

> Your function can logically be reviewed in terms of infant care, that is in terms of the facilitating environment, the facilitation of the maturational processes. Integration is vitally important in this connection, and your work is quite largely counteracting disintegrating forces in individuals and in families and in localized social groups . . .
>
> Social work always has as its aim not a directing of the individual's life or development but an enabling of the tendencies that are at work within the individual, leading to a natural evolution based on growth (63).

5. Handling

As can be seen from Winnicott's description of picking up a baby given above, the handling of an infant is an important aspect of the holding environment at the beginning of life. Through adequate handling, the infant comes to accept the body as part of the self, and to feel that the self dwells in and throughout the body. The boundaries of the body, moreover, provide the limiting membrane between what is "me" and what is "not-me." As we have mentioned, this process was called by Winnicott "personalization."

Behind the concept of personalization was Winnicott's belief that "at the beginning the child has a blueprint for normality which is largely a matter of shape and functioning of his or her own body" (109). Good-enough handling involves an implicit understanding of this on the part of the mother.

Almost every child has been accepted in the last stages before birth, but love is shown in terms of the physical care which is usually adequate when it is a matter of the fetus in the womb. In these terms, the basis for what I call personalization, or an absence of a special liability to depersonalization, starts even before the child's birth, and is certainly very much a matter of significance once the child has to be held by people whose emotional involvement needs to be taken into account, as well as their physiological response. The beginning of that part of the baby's development which I am calling personalization, or which can be described as an indwelling of the psyche in the soma, is to be found in the mother's ability to join up her emotional involvement, which originally is physical and physiological (109).

These ideas are shown up clearly where Winnicott talked about work with physically handicapped children. He found that psychological problems could sometimes arise because of loss of contact with the body or dissociation from it. Where this happens the child fails in some degree to adapt to reality in the sense of accepting his physical limitations as real. Winnicott saw the genesis of this state of affairs in the attitude of the mother who cannot accept and love the infant as he has started.

Distortions of the ego come from distortions of the attitude of those who care for the child. A mother with a baby is constantly introducing and reintroducing the baby's body and psyche to each other, and it can readily be seen that this easy but important task becomes difficult if the baby has an abnormality that makes the mother feel ashamed, guilty, frightened, excited, hopeless. Under such circumstances she can do her best, and no more (109).

It is worth noting that Winnicott believed a woman can more easily accept and love a handicapped child for what he is if she herself has been able to create a whole child in fantasy, that is, if her own early environment, now internalized, has been good-enough (74, 105).

In general, then, adequate handling is a part of a mother's natural technique. She is able "to hold the baby in a natural way," so that the baby does "not have to know about being made up of a collection of parts. The baby is a belly joined on to a chest and has loose limbs and particularly a loose head: all these parts are gathered together by the mother who is holding the child and in her hands they add up to one"

(114). This oneness, so necessary for ego integration, is the basis for body coordination and grace, and for pleasure in bodily activity where the individual, through his personal organization of motility, is constantly able to discover the self.

Jean Liedloff, who in her book *The Continuum Concept* described the lives of the Yequena Indians living in the rain forest of southeastern Venezuela, was struck by the fact that "they did not distinguish work from other ways of spending time." Hard physical work was done at their own pace, with economy of force and with much pleasure. Her description of Yequena women bathing themselves and their babies comes as no surprise:

> Once a day each woman put her gourds and her clothing . . . on the bank and bathed herself and her baby. However many women and children participated, the bath had a Roman quality of luxuriousness. Every move bespoke sensual enjoyment, and the babies were handled like objects so marvelous that their owners felt constrained to put a mock-modest face on their pleasure and pride (143).

Winnicott believed that adequate handling, like other aspects of the holding environment, can be reinforced by social provision—by "translating the needs of infants into language that is appropriate at all ages":

> When we provide a swimming pool and all that goes with it, the provision links with the care with which a mother baths her infant, and with which she generally caters for the infant's need for bodily movement and expression, and for muscle and skin experiences that give satisfaction. It also links with the provision that is appropriate in the therapeutics of certain illnesses. On the one hand it links with the occupational therapy that has great value at certain stages in the treatment of the mentally ill; and, on the other, it links with the physiotherapy that is appropriate, for instance, in the care of spastic children.
>
> In all these cases—the normal child, the infant, the mentally ill person, and the spastic or handicapped—the provision is facilitating the child's innate tendency to inhabit the body and to enjoy the body's functions and to accept the limitation that the skin provides, a limiting membrane, separating me from not-me (53).

6. Object Presenting

Object presenting can be said to embrace not only the initiation of inter-personal relationships, but also the introduction of the whole world of shared reality to the baby and growing child. It is therefore a vast sub-ject. At the very beginning, however, it needs to be stated in terms of the mother's presentation of herself. "The baby's use of the non-human environment," Winnicott wrote, "depends upon the previous use of a human environment" (98).

The most primitive of all relationships is that which takes place in the weeks before and after the birth of the baby and is referred to by Win-nicott as relating in terms of the pure female element, an aspect of hold-ing. This relationship characterizes the merged state, "when the baby and the mother are not yet separated out in the baby's rudimentary mind" (67). It is through this relationship that the infant experiences a sense of being. The infant's sense of being relies on the capacity of the mother (who is a part of the infant) to be someone "who *is*" and not someone "who *does*," until the infant is ready to initiate the doing. Out of these primitive beginnings comes object relating in terms of the infant's creation of the mother and the mother's care, made possible by the mother doing the right thing at the right time—that is, when the infant is ready for it (67).

In the section on object relating above (II B3), we have quoted one of Winnicott's descriptions of infant feeding. At the risk of being repeti-tious, we here take some similar lines from a broadcast talk entitled "Close-Up of Mother Feeding Baby," with the emphasis this time on the mother's presentation of herself in this common situation.

> When I see in what a delicate way a mother who is not anxious manages the situation I am always astounded. You see her there, making the baby comfortable, and arranging a *setting* in which the feeding may happen, if all goes well. The setting is part of a human relationship. If the mother is feed-

ing by the breast we see how she lets the baby, even a tiny one, have the hands free so that as she exposes her breast the skin can be felt, and its warmth—moreover the distance of her breast from the baby can be measured, for the baby has only a little bit of the world in which to place objects, the bit that can be reached by mouth, hands and eyes. The mother allows the baby's face to touch the breast. At the beginning babies do not know about breasts being part of mother. If the face touches the breast they do not know whether the nice feeling comes in the breast or in the face. In fact babies play with their cheeks, and scratch them, just as if they were breasts, and there is plenty of reason why mothers allow for all the contact that a baby wants. No doubt a baby's sensations in these respects are very acute, and if they are acute we can be sure they are important.

The baby first of all needs all these rather *quiet* experiences which I am describing, and needs to feel held lovingly, that is, in an alive way, yet without fuss, and anxiety, and tenseness. This is the setting. Sooner or later there will be some kind of contact between the mother's nipple and the baby's mouth. It does not matter what exactly happens. The mother is there in the situation and part of it, and she particularly likes the intimacy of the relationship. She comes without preconceived notions as to how the baby ought to behave.

This contact of the nipple with the baby's mouth gives the baby ideas!— "perhaps there is something there outside the mouth worth going for." Saliva begins to flow; in fact, so much saliva may flow that the baby may enjoy swallowing it, and for a time hardly needs milk. Gradually the mother enables the baby to build up in imagination the very thing that she has to offer, and the baby begins to mouth the nipple, and to get to the root of it with the gums, and bite it, and perhaps to suck.

And then there is a pause. The gums let go of the nipple, and the baby turns away from the scene of action. The idea of the breast fades.

Do you see how important this last bit is? The baby had an idea, and the breast with the nipple came, and a contact was made. Then the baby finished with the idea and turned away, and the nipple disappeared. This is one of the most important ways in which the experience of the baby we are now describing differs from one placed in a busy institution.

How does the mother deal with the baby's turning away? The baby does not have a thing pushed back into the mouth in order that sucking movements shall be started up again. The mother understands what the baby is feeling, because she is alive and has an imagination. She waits. In the course of a few minutes, or less, the baby turns once more towards where she is all the time willing to place the nipple, and so a new contact is made, just at the right moment. These conditions are repeated time and again and the baby drinks not from a thing that contains milk, but from a personal possession lent for a moment to a person who knows what to do with it. (6).

Something that emerges clearly from this sequence of events is that the mother is in charge from start to finish. For Winnicott there was no such thing as a human relationship between a baby and his mother unless the mother *managed* the situation—there had to be a holding environment. This seems so obvious as to be hardly worth repeating, yet, since Winnicott wrote these words in 1949, our knowledge of the minutiae of mother-infant interaction has been vastly increased by the fascinating results of frame-by-frame analysis of film, and observers have often found it useful to place these minutiae within an ethological framework. Sequences in parent-infant interaction are thus often written about in terms of biological programming, stimuli and rewards leading to parent-infant "bonding"; and even though the mother's management may be taken for granted, the impression is given that both partners in interaction are being stirred by forces outside themselves.

Winnicott never disputed the need for or the value of such a framework, nor indeed did he minimize the fact that nature has allowed for the mother and the baby to be attracted to each other through live interaction. Nevertheless, he found such terms insufficient for describing the development of the whole nascent person where they fail to take into account the fact that the mother is *using* her innate capacities and her instincts to adapt to her infant. It was his view that, without the mother's personal management of the situation, the innate abilities of the infant cannot be brought within the competence of the infant's self. A baby's cheek may be touched, and he will automatically turn his head in the direction of the touch. If a nipple is put into his mouth he will suck and take in milk. The rooting and sucking reflexes will have been elicited by stimulation. But the baby will be feeding from a *thing*; to him this sequence of events will be a seduction, not becoming integrated into the personal pattern unless there is ego-support given by the mother. As Winnicott put it, "the reflex has betrayed its owner. It almost owns the infant" (117).

External stimuli outside the context of ego-support imply *reactions*. Writing about the origins of creativity, Winnicott said: "It is possible to show that in some people at certain times the activities that indicate that the person is alive are simply reactions to stimulus. A whole life may be built on the pattern of reacting to stimuli. Withdraw the stimuli and the individual has no life. But in the extreme of such a case the word *being* has no relevance. In order to be and so have the feeling that one *is*, one must have a predominance of impulse-doing over reactive doing" (82). In the extreme of such a case, defences in the ego against primitive agony would have arisen which could be described in terms of psychosis—of a nearly total false self.

These were the considerations that led to Winnicott's insistence that, when discussing the relationship between mother and baby at the very beginning of life, account should be taken of "very great *psychological* differences between, on the one hand, the mother's identification with her infant, and, on the other, the infant's dependence on the mother" (31). "The mother has of course been a baby. It is all in her somewhere, the experiential conglomerate, with herself dependent and gradually achieving autonomy . . . But the baby has never been a mother. The baby has not even been a baby before. It's all a first experience. There are no yardsticks" (98).

Through the repetitive nature of the one mother's management and technique, and through her near complete adaptation to need, the baby acquires a yardstick made from expectation and its near perfect fulfilment (experience of omnipotence). Later he can use the yardstick to measure the world of shared reality and by reality-testing arrive at a *modus vivendi* as he moves towards independence. But for viability to be achieved in the world of shared reality, this world needs to be presented in small doses. "Only on the basis of monotony can a mother profitably add richness" (21)—meaning that when something new is added to the infant's life it needs to be added within a framework of predictability. Where the mother or mother-substitute is herself present, it is easier to add richness in the shape of wider opportunity for experience, because the mother, grown familiar to her infant through her person and through the way she goes about things, provides the necessary framework.

In fact, the infant's familiarity with his natural mother begins before he is born. As Winnicott pointed out in a broadcast talk to mothers, "the baby . . . has shared your meals. His blood has flowed more quickly when you drank a cup of tea in the morning, or when you ran to catch a bus. To some extent he must have known whenever you were anxious or excited or angry. If you have been restless he has become used to movement, and he may expect to be jogged on your knee or rocked in his cradle. If, on the other hand, you are a restful sort of person he has known peace, and may expect a quiet lap and a still pram" (3). During the remainder of the period of absolute dependence, after birth, the mother becomes more and more familiar to the baby, and her own personal technique is essential:

> The whole procedure of infant care has as its main characteristic a steady presentation of the world to the infant. This is something that cannot be done by thought, nor can it be managed mechanically. It can only be done by continuous management by a human being who is consistently herself. There is no question of perfection here. Perfection belongs to machines: what the infant needs is just what he usually gets, the care and attention of someone who is going on being herself. This of course applies to fathers too (55).

When the stage is reached at which the infant begins to "know in his mind" that the mother is necessary, the need for the actual mother to be available becomes "fierce and truly terrible, so that mothers do really hate to leave their children" (55). By the age of about two, however, Winnicott believed that, in health, the child has developed the equipment to deal with loss. In the meantime there will be others besides the mother with whom he will have become familiar—friends or relations perhaps—"who by their constant presence qualify as mother-substitutes" (55).

Familiarity is not only the framework for the fruitful presentation of what is new but is also essential for the avoidance of traumatic muddle. "I know a baby who was cared for by two people, one left-handed and the other right-handed," Winnicott wrote. "This was too much" (117). At a later stage, perhaps, confusion can be caused by such things as "the mother having one set of don'ts and the helpful grandmother another set" (118), before the baby has acquired the mental capacity to cope with this. Sometimes the mother herself can be the cause of the muddle, especially if she is ill in a way that makes her use chaos as a defence against the threat of her own disintegration. Such a mother can "muddle everything up with distractions, and unpredictable and therefore traumatic actions" (40). Winnicott's emphasis on the avoidance of coincidence during infancy also fits into this context. Examples he mentioned were "handing a baby over to someone else's care at the same time as weaning, or introducing solids during an attack of measles, and so on" (7). He believed that adoptive parents sometimes have an especially difficult task in sorting out (largely unavoidable) muddles which have occurred before they take over the baby's care (123).

Presentation of the world in small doses continues to be a need of the growing child. As the child grows, the mother is still "sharing a specialized bit of the world" with him or her, "keeping that bit small enough so that the child is not muddled, yet enlarging it so that the growing capacity of the child to enjoy the world is catered for" (7). Of great importance is the preservation of a certain amount of illusion—an avoidance of too sudden insistence on the reality principle.

> The child of two, three, and four is in two worlds at once. The world that we share with the child is also the child's own imaginative world, and so the child is able to experience it intensely. The reason for this is that we do not insist, when we are dealing with a child of that age, on an exact perception of the external world. A child's feet need not be all the time firmly planted on the earth. If a little girl wants to fly we do not just say "Children don't fly." Instead of that we pick her up and carry her around above our heads and put her on top of the cupboard, so that she feels to have flown like a bird to her nest.
>
> Only too soon the child will find that flying cannot be done magically. Probably in dreams magical floating through the air may be retained to some extent, or at any rate there will be a dream about taking rather long steps. Some fairy story like the one about the Seven-League Boots, or the Magic Carpet, will be the grown-ups' contribution to this theme. At ten years or so the child will be practicing long-jump and high-jump, trying to jump farther and higher than the others. That will be all that remains, except dreams, of the tremendously acute sensations associated with the idea of flying that came naturally at the age of three.
>
> For the little child it is legitimate for the inner world to be outside as well as inside, and we therefore enter into the imaginative world of the child when we play the child's games and take part in other ways in the child's imaginative experiences (7).

While it is valuable for the child when an adult can use imagination to enter the imaginative world of the child, it is necessary that adults caring for small children keep a clear distinction between fact and fantasy in themselves. Winnicott, as we have seen, believed that "fantasy is only tolerable at full blast when objective reality is appreciated well" (21). The parents, particularly the mother or mother-substitute, need to provide for the small child a framework of well-appreciated objective reality in order that his or her imaginative life can be lived to the full. This is yet another way in which muddle is avoided.

> When your little boy turns away from the milk pudding you have specially prepared with the very best ingredients, and makes a face intended to convey the idea that it is poisonous, you are not upset, because you know perfectly well that it is good. You also know that just for the moment he feels that it is poisonous. You find ways round the difficulty, and quite possibly in a few minutes the pudding will be eaten with relish. If you had been uncertain of yourself you would have got all fussed up, and would have tried to force the pudding into the child's mouth to prove to *yourself* that it was good.
>
> In all sorts of ways your clear knowledge of what is real and what is not real helps the child, because the child is only gradually getting to the understanding that the world is not as imagined, and that imagination is not exactly like the world. Each needs the other (7).

This task of keeping things separate all the time, of being prosaic, so to speak, so that the child may be a poet, relies on the continuing capacity of the mother to identify with the child: to find the poet that is in herself in him. It is certainly a help when cultural activities and friendship with other adults provide a resting place.

Object presenting can also be said to include the provision of opportunity needed if the infant or child is to develop a capacity for concern, as well as the implicit understanding of parents and teachers of such a need, so that there will be acceptance and acknowledgment, an "appreciation not so much of talent as of the struggle behind all achievements, however small" (78). It includes also the handing on of the values of the parents themselves and of society, by both parents and teachers, in a way that allows for immaturity in the child and does not stifle spontaneity. As the playing of the child gives way to other pursuits—academic, sporting or artistic, for instance—the principle of allowing the child to "come at things creatively" is still important. It is a matter of timing, and the provision of opportunity. Winnicott wrote:

Give a child Mozart and Haydn and Scarlatti from the beginning and you may get precocious good taste, something that can be shown off at parties. But the child probably has to start with noises blown through toilet paper over a comb, and then graduate to drumming on a saucepan and blowing into an old bugle; the distance from screaming and vulgar noises to *Voi che Sapete* is vast, and an appreciation of the sublime should be a personal achievement, not an implant. Yet no child can write or perform his or her Mozart. You must help him find this and other treasures (56).

In sum, the environment was seen by Winnicott as having

a kind of growth of its own, being adapted to the changing needs of the individual. The individual proceeds from absolute dependence to relative dependence towards independence. In health, the development takes place at a pace that does not outstrip the development of complexity in the mental mechanisms, this being linked to neurophysiological development (101).

7. De-adaptation and Failure

"It has often been noted," Winnicott wrote, "that, at five to six months, a change occurs in infants which makes it more easy than before for us to refer to their emotional development in terms that apply to human beings generally." He added, "In specifying five to six months we need not try to be too accurate" (21).

This is the change that marks the passage of the infant from absolute to relative dependence, when he becomes "aware of the details of maternal care and can to a growing extent relate them to personal impulse" (51). It will be remembered that the achievements of this stage of development include the emergence of a relationship between the infant and his mother "as between whole persons," and also the infant's increasing use of and pleasure in intercommunication. At this point, too, the baby becomes able to play with *things*. "To some extent it is an affair of physical development, for the infant at five months becomes skilled to the extent that he grasps an object he sees, and can soon get it to his mouth" (21). This achievement was important to Winnicott, because in playing with things (as, for example, in the Spatula Game) it is possible to see the beginning of an infant's capacity to "gather objects or phenomena from external reality and use these in the service of some sample derived from inner or personal reality" (65).

These achievements in the infant—this passage from the merged to the separated state—require a particular facilitation on the part of the mother which Winnicott described as "de-adaptation" or graduated failure in adaptation. This is "the second part of the maternal function," the first being the near perfect adaptation which gives "opportunity to the infant for an actual experience of omnipotence. Normally adaptation leads on to a graduated adaptive failure . . . The infant's sense of the 'not-me' depends on the fact of the mother's operation in this field of maternal care" (102).

De-adaptation is thus the same thing as the introduction of the reality principle. The result is not traumatic because de-adaptation is graduated according to the needs of the infant, and occurs "within a framework of adaptation," which is supplied by "the mother's capacity to sense the baby's capacity, moment by moment, to employ new mental mechanisms" (102).

As we have seen (II B7), the mother uses the baby's developing intellectual powers to help her in the baby's care, so that she is increasingly released from the need for near perfect adaptation to his needs, and can "gradually acquire a life of her own" (33).

It can therefore also be said that the ability of the mother to fail in adaptation corresponds to her "recovery" from the state of primary maternal preoccupation. She is able to return to a normal attitude towards life and the self. When mothers are for some reason unable to make this recovery, the increasing abilities of the baby cannot be put to use for furthering his journey towards independence. In such cases,

> . . . the infant who has begun to become separate from the mother has no means of gaining control of all the good things that are going on. The creative gesture, the cry, the protest, all the little signs that are supposed to produce what the mother does, all these things are missing, because the mother has already met the need just as if the infant were still

merged with her and she with the infant. In this way the mother, by being a seemingly good mother, does something worse than castrate the infant. The latter is left with two alternatives: either being in a permanent state of regression and of being merged with the mother, or else staging a total rejection of the mother, even of the seemingly good mother.

We see therefore that in infancy and in the management of infants there is a very subtle distinction between the mother's understanding of her infant's need based on empathy, and her change over to an understanding based on something in the infant or small child that indicates need. This is particularly difficult for mothers because of the fact that children vacillate between one state and the other; one minute they are merged with their mothers, and require empathy, while the next they are separated from her, and then if she knows their needs in advance she is dangerous, a witch.

It is a very strange thing that mothers who are quite uninstructed adapt to these changes in their developing infants satisfactorily and without any knowledge of the theory (51).

We could refer here again to the story of Esther's mother, quoted above, who, because of her illness, could not cope with her baby as a separate individual.

Quite different from the graduated failure in adaptation that facilitates the baby's increasing independence are the universal relative failures that occur because the mother is "human, and not mechanically perfect" (98). Even at the earliest stages, as Winnicott pointed out, "it is impossible to think of a child who was so well cared for that there was no occasion for overstrain of the personality as it was integrated at a given moment" (103); also, in the care of children of all ages he was aware that "the human beings who are the facilitating environment have their own private lives, their moods, their phases of tiredness or exasperation, their weaknesses." Thus, there are bound to be times when for one reason or another "the mind has dropped the baby" (125).

Winnicott believed, however, that these relative (not gross) human failures are themselves necessary for the mother's reliability to be communicated to her infant.

The baby does not know about the communication except from the effects of *failure* of reliability. This is where the difference comes in between mechanical perfection and human love. Human beings fail and fail; and in the course of ordinary care a mother is all the time mending her failures. These relative failures with immediate remedy undoubtedly add up eventually to a communication, so that the baby comes to know about success. Successful adaptation thus gives a sense of security, a feeling of having been loved. . . . It is the innumerable failures followed by the sort of care that mends that build up into a communication of love, of the fact that there is a human being there who cares. Where failure is not mended within the requisite time, seconds, minutes, hours, then we used the term deprivation. A deprived child is one who, after knowing about failures mended, comes to know about failure unmended. It is then the lifework of the child, to provoke conditions in which failures mended once more give the pattern to life (98).

Elsewhere Winnicott wrote "Perfection has no *meaning*" (77).

8. Ego-relatedness and Communication

As we have mentioned in writing about integration of the ego, Winnicott used the term "ego-relatedness" to describe the relationship between mother and baby that arises specifically from the holding environment. His concept goes beyond what is generally understood by object relating in strictly Freudian terms, that is, in terms of erotic or id-driven impulse, with its attendant tensions, satisfactions and frustrations. Winnicott once wrote about Freud, 'In his early theoretical formulations he was concerned with the id, by which he referred to the instinctual drives, and the ego, by which he referred to that part of the whole self that is related to the environment. The ego modifies the environment in order to bring about id-satisfactions, and it curbs id-impulses in order that what the environment can offer can be used to best advantage, again for id-satisfaction" (49). Winnicott, among others, found these formulations insufficient for describing human relationships. He believed not only that ego-relatedness is an essential ingredient in the total "in love" relationship, but also that highly satisfactory experience is to be derived from relating in terms of the ego alone, apart from id considerations (50). He acknowledged a correspondence here between his own work and Fairbairn's concept of "object-seeking" (136). In the first relationships between the infant and the environment-mother he saw the root of affection and of friendship between individuals (50).

In order for there to be meaningful relationships between individuals there needs to be communication. This is a statement of the obvious and it is perhaps doubly obvious to psychoanalysts, because insofar as psychoanalysis is effective as therapy it *is* communication. A study of the means of communication is, to the analyst, a study of his own technique; his technique is also closely linked to the theory of emotional development. In the last decade of his life, Winnicott became particularly interested in stating his own theory of early psychic functioning in terms of communication between the infant and the environment-mother. It is not altogether easy to extract the main points of what he said and make something coherent, but it is worth trying because there seems to be a link between this work and the remarkable findings of those who have recently been engaged in observational studies of mothers and their newborn babies (as summarized, for example, in Klaus and Kennell (1976)) (142).

In 1962 Winnicott gave a paper in which he contrasted "silent" or "direct" communication with "indirect communication." It was his thesis that direct communication is the "most primitive and fundamental" of interactions. It is only possible with a subjective object and belongs essentially to the state of being merged. "In so far as the object is subjective," Winnicott wrote, "so far is it unnecessary for communication to be explicit. In so far as the object is objectively perceived, communication is either explicit or dumb" (60). At the very beginning the baby is able to communicate silently with the mother because he is merged with her; the mother, because of the temporary state of primary maternal preoccupation, is also in a special way both physically and psychologically merged to a high degree with the baby, though in health she retains her own identity as well.

Silent communication has to do with the very core of the self—with going-on-being and with the fulfilment of inborn processes. What the mother is able to communicate to her infant (because of the fulfilment of her capacity to care for him) is her *reliability*. What the infant communicates to the mother is his vitality and growth (60, 98).

It can be seen that where silent or direct communication continues beyond the merged state, it is a cul-de-sac in the sense that it involves only the self communicating with the subjective objects, that is, with aspects of the self. It takes place *in isolation*. It belongs to psychopathology (for example, to autism) and to people who are able, as Winnicott put it, to look for "infinity at the centre of the self"—a capacity which he linked with mysticism (70). It has value because, being concerned with the core of the self, it carries "all the sense of real." But except in the merged state it cannot become a two-way exchange (60).

In order for there to be a relationship between separate individuals, therefore, it is necessary for communication to be to some extent indirect, explicit and deliberate. Indirect communication is pleasurable and involves "extremely interesting techniques, including that of language" (60). Like creativity itself, it grows out of the needs of the infant—id-needs and ego-needs. "The mother communicates with her baby by knowing what is needed before the need is expressed in a gesture. From this follows naturally the gesture that expresses the need, and the parent can meet this communication by appropriate response. Out of this comes deliberate communication of all kinds" (99).

Of course it is true to say that no (indirect) communication is possible at all except in terms of what is shared and that external reality itself is described in terms of how far our conception of it is shared with others. But this is taking us in another direction away from the "highly satisfactory experience" that Winnicott believed was to be derived from interpersonal relationships. What is germane here is the communication of feeling and attitude, whether there is verbalization or not. We all know the expression "we have nothing to say to each other," and we know that this can be used by people who have spent the last half-hour talking to (or at) each other. Perhaps there is room here for the idea that if communication were totally explicit it would also be totally meaningless.

Against this background it is possible to pick out three aspects of ego-relatedness that allow for (silent) communication between infant and mother and that also allow for the development of a capacity for meaningful communication between separate individuals.

(a) *Mended failures*. It will be remembered from the last section that

Winnicott believed that mended failures in holding amount to a communication of being well held. As the infant separates out from the
mother, this becomes the basis of his trust in other people and of his
capacity for affection.

(b) *Mutuality in Experience.* Another "language" for the communication of reliable holding is "mutuality in experience." At the very beginning this is particularly related to the handling of the infant; it is body
experience, realized "in terms of the anatomy and physiology of live
bodies," of "the crude evidences of life, such as heart beat, breathing
movements, breath warmth, movements that indicate a need for change
of position, etc.." Winnicott mentioned as an example rocking movements performed by mother and baby together, "with the mother
adapting her movements to those of the baby"—that is, not imposing a
pattern from without (108).

There is no doubt that innate capacities enter into such experiences
and also that the baby has learned something of the mother before he is
born, perhaps from her heart beat, perhaps from her characteristic
movements in various occupations. From this point of view the beginning of the mother's adaptation could be seen in the way she cares for
herself, and carries herself, when she is carrying a child before birth.
Nevertheless, there is a difference when the baby is outside the body in
the mother's arms; Winnicott believed that mutuality relies upon the
mother's continued unthinking preoccupation with the needs of her
infant, while at the same time being an experience for *both* the mother
and the baby and therefore also reinforcing the mother's capacity to
identify with him.

Early experiences of mutuality contribute to the experience of
omnipotence; they become part of the stuff of fantasy and of the infant's
creation of the mother. As the baby begins to have moments of relating
to a mother who is "not-me," so his creation of the mother begins to
include the idea of the mother being like, or doing like, himself. He
begins to realize that experiences of mutuality are *shared* experiences.
This is the beginning of empathy between individuals. Winnicott gave
the following example:

> Although normal babies vary very much in their rate of development
> (especially measured by observable phenomena) it can be said that at
> twelve weeks they are capable of the following play: settled in for a

[breast] feed the baby looks at the mother's face and his or her hand reaches up so that in play the baby is feeding the mother by means of a finger in her mouth.

It may be that the mother has played a part in the establishment of this play detail, but if this is true it does not invalidate the conclusion that I draw from the fact that this kind of communication can happen.

I draw the conclusion from this that whereas all babies take in food there does not exist a communication between the baby and the mother except in so far as there develops a mutual feeding situation. The baby feeds and the baby's fantasy includes the idea that the mother knows what it is like to be fed . . .

In this way we actually witness a *mutuality* which is the beginning of a communication between two people; this (in the baby) is a developmental achievement, one that is dependent on the baby's inherited process leading towards emotional growth, and likewise dependent on the mother and her attitude and her capacity to make real what the baby is ready to reach out for, to discover, to create.

Babies feed, and this may mean much to the mother, and the ingestion of food may give the baby gratification in terms of drive satisfactions. Another thing however is the communication between the baby and the mother, something that is a matter of experience and that depends on the mutuality that results from cross-identifications (108).

When the mother has reached to the full status (as far as the infant is concerned) of being a person in her own right, with an inside and an outside, and also permanence in the world of shared reality, the infant who has experienced mutuality in the merged state is able to go over from being *the same as* to being *at one with*. In other words, the earliest experiences of mutuality, by becoming part of the baby's creation of the mother, lead to more sophisticated relationships between separate individuals that are characterized by empathy.

(c) *Reflecting Back*. For Winnicott a very important facet of mutuality was the "reflecting back" of the infant's nascent self. His main statement about reflecting back was made in terms of mutual gaze between mother and infant.

Observational studies over the course of some years have shown that a newborn infant is particularly attracted to, and fascinated by, the sight of a human face, especially by the eyes. It is known that babies' eyes focus best on objects around eight to ten inches away, and it has been

pointed out that the mother's eyes are likely to be at the appropriate distance when she is feeding her baby. Eye-to-eye contact with their new
born babies seems also to be very important to the mothers (142).

In Winnicott's theory of the "mirror-role of the mother" (which was
influenced by the work of Jacques Lacan), the mother who is identified
with her baby looks into the baby's eyes "and what she looks like is
related to what she sees there." Thus the baby, looking into the mother's
face, "sees himself or herself" (71). Winnicott underlined the importance of this kind of contact by showing what happens when it is absent.
In doing so he indicated that such intercommunication is an urgent
need for the baby.

> Of course nothing can be said about the single occasions on which a
> mother could not respond. Many babies, however, do have to have a long
> experience of not getting back what they are giving. They look and they
> do not see themselves. There are consequences. First, their own creative
> capacity begins to atrophy, and in some way or other they look around for
> other ways of getting something of themselves back from the environ-
> ment. They may succeed by some other method, and blind infants need
> to get themselves reflected through other senses than that of sight.
> Indeed a mother whose face is fixed may be able to respond in some
> other way. Most mothers can respond when the baby is in trouble or is
> aggressive, and especially when the baby is ill. Second, the baby gets set-
> tled into the idea that when he or she looks, what is seen is the mother's
> face. The mother's face is not then a mirror. So perception takes the place
> of apperception, perception takes the place of that which might have
> been the beginning of a significant exchange with the world, a two-way
> process in which self-enrichment alternates with the discovery of mean-
> ing in the world of seen things.
>
> Naturally, there are half-way stages in this scheme of things. Some
> babies do not quite give up hope and they study the object and do all that
> is possible to see in the object some meaning that ought to be there if
> only it could be felt. Some babies, tantalized by this type of relative
> maternal failure, study the variable maternal visage in an attempt to pre-
> dict the mother's mood, just exactly as we all study the weather. The baby
> quickly learns to make a forecast: "Just now it is safe to forget the mother's
> mood and to be spontaneous, but any minute the mother's face will
> become fixed or her mood will dominate and my own personal needs
> must then be withdrawn otherwise my central self will suffer insult."
>
> Immediately beyond this in the direction of pathology is predictability

which is precarious, and which strains the baby to the limits of his or her own capacity to allow for events. This brings a threat of chaos, and the baby will organize withdrawal, or will not look except to perceive as a defence. A baby so treated will grow up puzzled about mirrors and what the mirror has to offer. If the mother's face is unresponsive, then a mirror is a thing to be looked at but not to be looked into (71).

Winnicott brought home his point by quoting one of his patients, who had said, "Wouldn't it be awful if the child looked into the mirror and saw nothing!" (71).

For the infant who is fortunate in being reflected back there is this sequence:

> When I look I am seen, so I exist,
> I can now afford to look and see.
> I now look creatively and what I apperceive I also perceive.
> In fact I take care not to see what is not there to be seen (71).

In the course of time, "as the child develops and the maturational processes become sophisticated, and identifications multiply, the child becomes less and less dependent on getting back the self from the mother's and father's face and from the faces of others who are in parental or sibling relationships" (71). The reflecting back of the mother at the very beginning becomes to some extent a part of the internalized environment or "inner reserve." But in sophisticated relationships, reflecting back continues to be an important part of the interplay of communication, with the use of the eyes, voice and body to express attitude. Where words are used in communication, the attitude can be conveyed in "the nuances and in the timing and in a thousand ways that compare with the infinite variety of poetry" (98).

As Winnicott suggested, there seem to be other means, apart from mutual gaze, open to mothers for reflecting back the infant's self. It appears that eye-to-eye contact is more a feature in our society than elsewhere. We quote from Marshall Klaus and John Kennell in their book, *Maternal-Infant Bonding:*

> Hearing and vision assume greatly enhanced importance in Western industrialized nations, where mother and baby are separated for many hours of the day . . . A woman in Africa who carries her baby on her back

or side is identified as a poor mother if her baby wets or soils her after the seventh day—that is, if she cannot anticipate these elimination behaviours and hold the baby away before they occur. This finely tuned awareness of the movements of the baby is almost inconceivable to those in nations where mother and baby are kept apart much of the day and sleep separately at night (142).

This brings us back to the experience of mutuality in terms of live bodies.

It will be seen that much of what has been quoted here could be stated in language more conventional in psychoanalytic theory. The concept of cross-identification in particular usually involves a consideration of the mechanisms of introjection and projection first postulated by Freud and developed especially by Melanie Klein. Winnicott does, in fact, often make use of these concepts, referring to them occasionally directly but more often in language of his own. Examples are "human internal strictness" (introject) and "the child becomes able to populate the world with samples of his or her own inner life" (projection). When describing communication during the stage of absolute dependence, however, Winnicott did not find these concepts adequate. In his words, "At the beginning the word 'internal' cannot be used in the Klein sense since the infant has not yet properly established an ego boundary and has not yet become master of the mental mechanisms of projection and introjection. At this early stage 'inner' only means personal, and personal insofar as the individual is a person with a self in process of becoming evolved. The facilitating environment, or the mother's ego-support to the infant's immature ego, these are still essential parts of the child as a viable creature" (60).

In finding different terms to describe communication at this very early stage, Winnicott illuminates not only the subject of early psychic functioning but also the subject of the origin of the mature capacity for meaningful relationships. For although a two-way exchange can be explained in terms of introjection and projection, and though these terms can cover the source of our feeling for other people, and how we are able to identify with them, and indeed our conduct towards them, something is still left unsaid about the vehicle of inter-communication—about the simultaneous or near simultaneous reciprocity that is so often a feature in meaningful and pleasurable exchange. Here the concepts of mutuality and reflecting back come into their own as something to be added to the necessary ingredients of trust and empathy and here the theory joins up with direct observations—naturally with Winnicott's own observations and also with the observational studies that point to the importance of early sensuous contact between a mother and her newborn baby for the future of their relationship to each other, as well as with the studies that have shown extraordinary abilities in the newborn to relate to other human beings, such as the following with eyes and head of a human face and the capacity to move in synchrony with the speech of adults (142).

Finally, it is possible to say something here about Winnicott's statement that "only in playing is communication possible; except direct communication . . ." (64), for it can be seen that within his theory of development it is the potential space that allows the individual to communicate at once directly and indirectly, that is, to discover the self, including the innate potential and all the sense of "real" *and* to be in touch with what is "other-than-me."

In his example of the three-month-old baby putting his finger in his mother's mouth, Winnicott indicated that the baby is both experiencing and communicating mutuality. The baby is, in fact, playing, and the playing belongs to the place of transition "where continuity is giving way to contiguity" (69); it belongs to one of the moments of separateness that arise out of being merged. In separate individuals it is in the overlap of potential spaces that mutuality is experienced and expressed.

9. The Ordinary Devoted Mother

It is important to emphasize that not only are good-enough mothers not perfect, but in Winnicott's view they are *ordinary* people doing ordinary things. "We must assume," he wrote, "that the babies of the world, past and present, have been and are born into a human environment that is good enough, that is adaptive in just the right way, appropriately, according to the baby's needs" (98). It is worth looking at his account,

given in a lecture to the Nursery School Association in 1966, of how the
phrase "ordinary devoted mother" came into being.

> I was walking, in the summer of 1949, to have drinks with the B.B.C.
> Producer, Miss Isa Benzie, who has retired and whose name I like to
> remember, and she was telling me that I could give a series of nine talks
> on any subject that might please me. She was, of course, on the lookout
> for a catchphrase, but I did not know this. I told her that I had no interest
> whatever in trying to tell people what to do. To start with, I didn't know.
> But I would like to talk to mothers about the thing that they do well, and
> that they do well simply because each mother is devoted to the task in
> hand, namely the care of one infant, or perhaps twins. I said that ordinar-
> ily this just happens, and it is the exception when a baby has to do with-
> out being cared for at the start by a specialist. Isa Benzie picked up the
> clue in a matter of twenty yards, and she said: "Splendid! The Ordinary
> Devoted Mother." So that was that.
>
> You can imagine that I have been ragged somewhat on account of this
> phrase, and there are many who assume that I am sentimental about
> mothers and that I idealize them, and that I leave out fathers, and that I
> can't see that some mothers are pretty awful, if not in fact impossible. I
> have to put up with these small inconveniences because I am not
> ashamed of what is implied by these words (94).

Of his idea of "devotion" he went on to write

> . . . women are not all the time fussing around thinking they ought to be
> looking after a baby. They play golf, they have a job that they lose them-
> selves in, they quite naturally do all sorts of male things like being irre-
> sponsible, or taking everything for granted, or motor racing . . .
>
> Then one day, they find they have become hostess to a new human
> being who has decided to take up lodgings, and like Robert Morley in *The
> Man Who Came to Dinner*, to exercise a crescendo of demands till some
> date in the far-extended future when there will once again be peace and
> quiet; and they, these women, may return to self-expression of a more
> direct kind. [During this time] they have been in a phase of self-
> expression through identification with what with luck grows into a baby,
> and becomes autonomous, biting the hand that fed it . . .
>
> Any parent here will know what I mean when I say that although you
> subjected your baby to the most awful frustrations, you never once let
> him (or her) down . . . (94).

If the mother's devotion was not idealized, still less was mother love. "You all know the kind of person," Winnicott wrote, "who goes about saying 'I simply *adore* babies.' But you wonder, do they love them? A mother's love is a pretty crude affair. There's possessiveness in it, appetite, even a 'drat the kid' element; there's generosity in it, and power, as well as humility. But sentimentality is outside it altogether and is repugnant to mothers" (2).

Sentimentality, according to Winnicott, is a quality born of the repression of hate—of the inability of an individual to admit anywhere in himself or herself that he or she is capable of hating. He was very well aware of the reasons mothers have for hating their babies, and at one point he gave a list of these reasons, beginning with "The baby is not her own (mental) conception," and ranging through a series of what must be familiar sentiments, including

> The baby is an interference with her private life.
> He treats her as scum, an unpaid servant, a slave.
> His excited love is cupboard love, so that having got what he wants he throws her away like an orange peel.
> At first he does not know at all what she does or what she sacrifices for him. Especially he cannot allow for her hate.
> He is suspicious, refuses her good food, and makes her doubt herself, but eats well with his aunt.
> After an awful morning with him she goes out, and he smiles at a stranger who says "Isn't he sweet?" (24).

In a broadcast talk and discussion with mothers of small children entitled "What Irks?" Winnicott gave an elaboration of how the baby, grown beyond the stage of absolute dependence, interferes with the privacy of his mother.

> Probably you won't find anything worse than the way children invade your innermost reserve . . . At the very beginning there is no difficulty, because the baby is in you and part of you. Although only a lodger, so to speak, the baby in the womb joins up with all the ideas of babies you ever had, and at the beginning the baby actually is the secret. The secret becomes a baby. [But when the time comes for the end of the merged state,] there starts a tremendous struggle—the baby, no longer being the secret, makes a claim on all your secrets . . . The onlooker can easily

remember that it is only for a limited time that his mother is a free-house
to her children. She had her secrets once and she will have them again.
And she will count herself lucky that for a while she was infinitely bothered by the infinite claims of her own children.

For the mother who is right in it there is no past and no future.
For her there is only the present experience of having no unexplored
area, no north or south pole but some intrepid explorer finds it, and
warms it up, no Everest but a climber reaches to the summit and
eats it. The bottom of her ocean is bathyscoped, and should she have
one mystery, the back of the moon, then even this is reached, photo-
graphed, and reduced from mystery to scientifically proven fact.
Nothing of her is sacred (119).

There are things a mother can do about her resentment; she can talk
to other people about it, for instance. She can even talk to the baby
about it, as Winnicott once wrote, saying, "'Damn you, you little bug-
ger', so that she feels better and the baby smiles back pleased to be
burbled at" (98). By and large she accepts her resentment and carries
on as usual, having within her the ability to hate "without paying the
child out" and the ability to "wait for rewards that may or may not come
at a later date" (24).

Hate acknowledged leaves room for enjoyment of "the great feelings
of pleasure that belong to the intimate body and spiritual bond that can
exist between a mother and her baby" (5), and of "the signs that gradually appear that the baby is a person" (4). Moreover, as Winnicott put
it, "Just as a writer is surprised by the wealth of ideas that turn up when
he puts pen to paper, so the mother is constantly surprised by what
she finds in the richness of her minute to minute contact with her own
baby" (4). In fact, a mother, by doing what she "naturally" knows how
to do, discovers herself and *becomes* herself in a way that was hitherto
only potential. And for the baby, the mother's pleasure is "like the sun
coming out" (4).

The word "natural" when applied by Winnicott to a mother's care of
her infant has a particular significance: it carries with it the idea that
instruction and formal education in this field are useless, or worse than
useless, to the ordinary devoted mother. "A great deal happens in the
dark interstices of your aspidistra, if you have one," he wrote, "and you
may be completely ignorant of biology; yet you may be famous in your

street for your aspidistra and its clean green leaves, with no brown edges" (116).

Information about such things as diet or how to deal with infection is useful; instruction about the details of management is not. In a lecture given to medical practitioners he said:

> It is true that some mothers are able to get help of a limited kind from books but it must be remembered that if a mother goes to a book or to someone for advice and tries to learn what she has to do we already wonder whether she is fitted for the job. She has to know about it from a deeper level and not necessarily from the part of the mind which has words for everything. The main things that a mother does with the baby cannot be done through words. This is very obvious but it is also a very easy thing to forget. In my long experience I have had a chance to know many doctors and nurses and teachers who thought they could tell mothers what to do and spent a lot of their time giving parents instruction, and then I have watched them when they became mothers and fathers and have had long talks with them about their difficulties, and I have found they have had to forget all they thought they knew, and, in fact, had been teaching. Quite frequently they found that what they knew in this way interfered so much at the beginning that they were not able to be natural with their own first child. Gradually they managed to shed this useless layer of knowledge that is intertwined with words and settle down to involvement with this one baby (97).

In fact, Winnicott believed that is is when parents feel that things are going wrong that they sometimes need to be able to step back and take an objective look at the care they provide. In general, however, he found that the unsophisticated and uninstructed of the world are more likely to get things right at the very beginning.

Finally, he felt that no blame can be apportioned when an infant is not started off well enough in respect of ordinary maternal devotion, nor can it be said that there is a debt owed when things go well. In his words,

> . . . there are all manner of reasons why some children do get let down before they are able to avoid being wounded or maimed in personality by the fact . . .
> It is necessary for us to be able to look at human growth and devel-

opment, with all its complexities that are internal or personal to the child, and we must be able to say: here the ordinary devoted mother factor failed, without blaming anyone. Mothers and fathers blame themselves, but that is another matter . . .

I have one special reason why I feel we must be able to apportion aetiological significance (not blame), and that is that in no other way can we recognize the positive value of the ordinary devoted mother factor—the vital necessity for every baby that someone should facilitate the earliest stages of the processes of psychological growth, or psycho-somatic growth, or shall I say the growth of the most immature and absolutely dependent human personality.

In other words, I do not believe in the story of Romulus and Remus, much as I respect wolf bitches. Someone who was human found and cared for the founders of Rome, if we are to allow any truth at all to this myth. I do not go further and say that we as men and women *owe* anything to the woman who did this for each one of us severally. We owe nothing. But to ourselves we owe an intellectual recognition of the fact that at first we were (psychologically) absolutely dependent, and that absolutely means absolutely. Luckily we were met by ordinary devotion (94).

10. Dependence and Domination

It was Winnicott's belief that there are certain social consequences stemming from the fact that "every man and woman grew in a womb" and "at first everyone was absolutely dependent on a woman, and then relatively dependent . . . The more this is examined," he wrote, "the more it becomes necessary to have a term WOMAN that makes possible a comparison between men and women . . . WOMAN is the unacknowledged mother of the first stages of the life of every man and woman." Insofar as absolute dependence on a woman remains unacknowledged, "all individuals (men and women) have in reserve a certain fear of WOMAN" (90).

It can be seen that there is a connection here with the maternal function of de-adaptation for, once the infant becomes *aware* of the fact of dependence, merging has to cease and autonomy begin. The emerging self has to be kept inviolate and the mother who continues to penetrate a sacred area by knowing beforehand what the baby or growing child wants is indeed a fearful figure—a witch. But even in health there is a residual fear of the dependence which is not acknowledged because not consciously remembered by the infant. Perhaps this is what is so eloquently expressed in Ted Hughes' poem *Revenge Fable*:

> There was a person
> Could not get rid of his mother
> As if he were her topmost twig.
> So he pounded and hacked at her
> With numbers and equations and laws
> Which he invented and called truth.
> He investigated, incriminated
> And penalized her, like Tolstoy,
> Forbidding, screaming, condemning
> Going for her with a knife,
> Obliterating her with disgusts
> Bulldozers and detergents
> Requisitions and central heating
> Rifles and whisky and bored sleep.
> With all her babes in her arms, in ghostly weepings,
> She died.
>
> His head fell off like a leaf . . .

It is possible for both men and women (because of the female element in both) to deal with the fear of WOMAN by identification with her. In general, however, this is easier for women than for men. Women can become mothers themselves; even if they do not they are usually better able to make an imaginative identification with the "infinite series of girl baby, mother and mother's mother." They thus have a capacity for being "merged in with the race" which a man is unlikely to have, because "the development of motherliness as a quality in his character does not get far enough" and such merging can be a violation of his nature (90).

In men especially, therefore, Winnicott believed that fear of dependence will "sometimes take the form of a fear of WOMAN, or fear of a woman," and at other times will take "less easily recognized forms, always including the fear of domination" (1). He believed this fear to be responsible for the fact that "in very few societies does a woman hold the political reins" and also for the "immense amount of cruelty to women, which can be found in customs that are accepted by almost all civilizations" (47). The fear of domination can also lead people "towards a specific or chosen domination. Indeed, were the psychology of the dictator studied one would expect to find that, among other things, he in his own personal struggle is trying to control the woman whose domination he unconsciously fears, trying to control her by encompassing her, acting for her, and in turn demanding total subjection and 'love'" (1). A result of these social phenomena is a reinforcement of feminism in women, which Winnicott defined as the denial of the difference between men and women (90).

Winnicott saw one solution to these problems in the study and the intellectual acknowledgment of the role of the mother at the beginning of life. Fear of WOMAN is a first stage in such an acknowledgment; an objective study can do much to remove the fear (47). This leads us back to Winnicott's idea that where "living things can be examined scientifically . . . gaps in knowledge and understanding need not scare us" (120). This is why he wrote that, while we owe nothing to our good-enough mothers, "to ourselves we owe an intellectual recognition of the fact that at first we were absolutely dependent, and that absolutely means absolutely" (94).

11. The Father

When Winnicott talked about the role of the father, it was with the assumption that the father is necessary in his own right and not as a reduplication of the mother. He was, of course, aware that "there has been a change in orientation in this country in the last fifty years so that fathers become real to their infants more in the role of duplicated mothers than they did, it would seem, a few decades ago" (88). He was also aware that "there are some fathers who really would make better mothers than their wives" (12) and that "maternal males can be very useful. They make good mother-substitutes, which is a relief to the mother when she has several children, and when she is ill, or if she wants to get back to her job" (90). Nevertheless, it was his view that when fathers become mothers this interferes to a greater or lesser extent with their function as fathers. Of the father of one of his patients he wrote, "One could say that he is so maternal that one wonders how he will manage when he becomes used as a male and as a true father" (124).

Winnicott believed that when the mother becomes preoccupied with the baby in the last months of pregnancy, a change occurs in the father, too. Because of this change he is able to become "the protecting agent who frees the mother to devote herself to the baby" (47). This "protective covering" supplied by the father is needed when the mother is "carrying, bearing and suckling his infant" (87), for she is thereby "saved from having to turn outwards to deal with her surroundings at the time when she is wanting so much to turn inwards" (4). It is just now especially that she is vulnerable to impingement and interference from without (34).

If there is no father, then someone else is needed to take this protective role—to take over the paternal function. Winnicott believed that puerperal illnesses could "to some extent be brought about by failure of the protective covering" at this time (34).

When the infant emerges from the stage of absolute dependence and begins to relate to separate whole people, the father becomes important to him as a person; part of the importance lies in the fact that, though the father is a familiar figure, he is essentially different from the mother out of whom the infant has grown. The relationship to the mother takes on a new dimension when merging ceases, it is true; however, to the infant and small child the mother retains a subjective quality, for it is part of her function to be available for a return to the merged state at moments when the child needs this. It is from the father that the child can first learn about a human being different from himself and different from other human beings—in a word, unique. Here is a pattern that he can use for his own further integration. Winnicott believed that children are lucky when they can get to know their fathers "even to the extent of finding them out" (12), for from the father as a separate individual, known for what he is, the child can learn about relationships that include love and respect without idealization.

In our culture and in its history the father has also represented the "indestructible environment." As Winnicott put it, certain valued qualities of the mother, such as her punctuality and her strictness and sternness with her infant (when these become appropriate), "gradually group together in the infant's mind, and these qualities draw to themselves the feelings which the infant at length becomes willing to have towards father . . . Much of the arranging of a child's life," Winnicott wrote, "must be done by mother, and children like to feel that mother can manage the home when father is not actually in it. Every woman has to be able to speak and act with authority; but if she has to be the whole thing, and has to provide the whole of the strong or strict elements in her children's lives as well as the love, she carries a big burden indeed. Besides, it is much easier for children to be able to have two parents; one parent can be felt to remain loving while the other is being hated, and this in itself has a stabilizing influence" (12).

So the father's support not only enables the mother to fulfil her own function without having to have conflicting qualities in herself at the same time, but it also allows for destructiveness in the child, for it is safe to be destructive when there is something indestructible to kick against. And if the father's role is partly to continue the disillusionment begun by the mother's adaptive failure, such disillusionment is carried on within a context of a rich—and increasingly rich—relationship. The father "opens up a new world to the children" (12) as they begin to understand and learn the details of his work, his interests and his views. When he joins in the play of the children he adds valuable new elements, and when he takes them out they see the world through a new pair of eyes. If to the mother belongs "the stability of the house," then to the father belongs "the liveliness of the street" (116).

In Winnicott's description of the father's part in the child's life the idea of the child's *use* of an object can clearly be seen.

12. The Family

"It would be a truism," Winnicott wrote, "to say that the family is an essential part of our civilization. The way we arrange our families practically shows what our culture is like, just as a picture of the face portrays the individual" (37).
    Everyone needs a family.

> I know that our relations are often a nuisance, and that we are liable to grumble because of the burden of them. We may even die of them. Yet they are important to us. One has only to look at the struggles peculiar to men and women with no relations at all (as, for instance, in the case of some refugees and some illegitimate children) to see that the absence of relations to grumble about, to love, to be loved by, to hate, and to fear, constitutes a terrible handicap; it leads to a tendency to suspect even quite friendly neighbors (37).

Of the role of the family in individual development he wrote:

> . . . each individual needs to make the long road from being merged in with mother to being a separate person, related to mother, and to mother and father together; from here the journey goes through the territory known as the family, with father and mother as the main structural features. The family has its own growth, and the individual small child experiences the changes that belong to the family's gradual expansion and to its troubles. The family protects the child from the world. But gradually the world begins to seep in. The aunts and uncles, the neighbors, the earliest sibling groups, leading on to schools. This gradual environmental seeping in is the way in which a child can best come to terms with the wider world, and follows exactly the pattern of the introduction to external reality by the mother (37).

The basis of the family is the relationship between the parents themselves, including their "deep rooted wish to be like their own parents in the sense of being grown up," and their attachment to each other in terms of "overlap of cultural interests and pursuits." Most important of all, the relationship "involves the meaning of each child in terms of the parents' conscious and unconscious fantasy around the act that produced the conception." As we have mentioned elsewhere, the powerful forces generated by this fantasy mean, in health, a deep and continuing sense of responsibility for each child—a dimension in caring that belongs to a child's parents alone, arising out of their own fundamental needs (37).

Of course, Winnicott realized that parents have their difficulties and that while having a family they are still in the process of growing up themselves. Some parents are unable to continue making personal sacrifices until their children have attained the necessary degree of true independence. He wrote:

> We should not, I think, despise those who were not very mature at the time of their marriage and who cannot afford to wait indefinitely, and for whom the time comes when they must make new spurts forward in personal growth or else degenerate. Difficulties occur in the marriage, and the children then have to be able to adapt themselves to the family disruption. Sometimes parents are able to see children through to a satisfactory adult independence in spite of the fact that they themselves have found a necessity for breaking up the framework of a marriage, or perhaps have found a need for remarriage.

Nevertheless he believed that usually "enough maturity exists in the parents for them to be able to make sacrifices themselves, as their parents did for them, in order to establish and maintain their family, so that the children may not only be born into a family but may grow and reach adolescence in the family, and may in relation to the family pass right through to achieving an independent and perhaps married life, each one" (37).

The parents' ability to relate to the society in which they live is also important—a family cannot develop in a vacuum. "What the parents can 'contribute in' to the family that they are building up depends a great deal on their general relationship to the wider circles around them, their immediate social setting" (37).

If the parents' relationship to each other and to society provides the basis for the family, its continuity as a unit also depends on the integration of each child.

> It cannot be too strongly emphasized that the integration of the family derives from the integrative tendency of *each individual child* . . . The contributing in from each individual child may be forgotten until one experiences the shock of a child who is ill or defective, and who for one reason or another is not contributing in. One then observes how the parents and family suffer in consequence. Where the child is not contributing in the parents are burdened with a task which is not altogether a natural one—they have to supply a home setting and to maintain this setting, and try to keep up a family and a family atmosphere *in spite of the fact that there is no help to be derived from the individual child.* There is a limit beyond which parents cannot be expected to succeed in this task (37).

In health,

> . . . each individual child, by healthy emotional growth and by the development of his or her personality in a satisfactory way, promotes the family and the family atmosphere. The parents, in their efforts to build a family, benefit from the sum of the integrative tendencies of the individual children. It is not just simply a matter of the lovableness of the infant or child; there is something more than that, for children are not always sweet. The infant and the small child and the older child flatter us by *expecting a degree of reliability and availability* to which we respond, partly I suppose because of our capacity to identify with them. This capacity to identify with the children again depends on our having made a good-enough growth in our own personality development when we were at the same age. In this way, our own capacities are strengthened and are brought out, developed, by what is expected of us from our children. In innumerable and very subtle ways, as well as in obvious ways, infants and children produce a family around them, perhaps by needing something, something which we give because of what we know about expectation and fulfilment. We see what the children create when playing at families, and we feel that we want to make real the symbols of their creativeness (37).

Here the description of what the family *is* links up with the description of what it *does*. Winnicott believed that one of its crucial functions in the emotional development of the infant and small child is to provide "a length of time in which steady experiences in relationships can be used for the development of intermediate areas in which transitional or play phenomena can become established for that particular child" (88). Not only does each child actually help to create the family through his expectations and personal contribution, but he also imaginatively creates the family by himself. As Winnicott said,

> It is not simply that there is a father and a mother and that perhaps new children come along and then there is a home with parents and children enriched by aunts and uncles and cousins. This is just an observer's statement. For the five children in a family there are five families. It does not require a psychoanalyst to see that these five families need not much resemble each other, and are certainly not identical (88).

When the child has had time to create and recreate the family in play, so that it becomes assimilated into the inner reality, he is ready to use the family in its function as a road towards a relationship with wider social groups. This kind of relating was described by Winnicott as "excursions and returns" (88). "The individual in the course of emotional growth is going from dependence to independence, and in health retains the capacity for shifting to and fro, from one to the other" (42). There is a parallel here between the child's use of the family and a smaller child's use of the mother.

> The child needs to be able to experience the various kinds of object relating all in the same day or even at one moment; for instance, you may see a small child enjoying relationships with an aunt or a dog or a butterfly and the observer may see not only that the child is making objective perceptions but is enjoying the enrichment that comes from discovery. This does not mean, however, that the child is ready to live in a discovered world. At any moment the child merges in again with a cot or the mother or the familiar smells and is re-established in a subjective environment (88).

Thus, in going away from the family, when the individual "breaks through whatever is around him or her, giving security," the excursion is only profitable if there is a return ticket.

The individual needs to find a wider circle ready to take over, and this is almost the same thing as saying that what is needed is the capacity to return to the situation that has been broken up. In a practical sense the little child needs to break away from the mother's arms and lap, but not to go into space, the breaking away has to be to a wider area of control, something that is symbolical of the lap from which the child has broken away. A slightly older child runs away from home, but at the bottom of the garden has finished running away. The garden fence is now symbolical of the narrower aspect of holding which has just been broken up, shall we say the house. Later, the child works out all these things in going to school and in relation to the other groups that are outside the home. In each case these outside groups represent a getting away from the home, and yet at the same time they are symbolical of the home that has been broken away from and in fantasy broken up.

It is the ability to "get back to the parents and back to the mother, back to the centre or back to the beginning" that makes the getting away from them "a part of growth instead of a disruption of the individual's personality" (42).

The process of breaking out into ever wider circles is greatly facilitated by the continued existence of the actual family.

It is the child's family pattern more than anything else that supplies the child with relics of the past so that when the child discovers the world there is always a return journey that makes sense. If it is the child's own family then the return journey does not put a strain on anyone because it is of the essence of the family that it remains oriented to itself and the people within it (88).

The orientation of the family to its own members accounts for the fact that "the vast bulk of psychotherapy is and always has been done in the family, by the family, and without psychiatric intervention" (102).

When the family has remained intact, even when its individual children become adult, they are more easily able to retain the way back.

As long as the family is intact then everything relates ultimately to the individual's actual father and mother. In the conscious life and fantasy the child may have got away from the father and mother, and may have gained great relief from doing so. Nevertheless the way back to the father and the mother is always retained in the unconscious. In the unconscious fantasy of the child it is always on his or her own father and mother that a claim is made fundamentally. The child gradually comes to lose much or nearly all of the direct claim on the actual father and mother, but this is conscious fantasy. What has happened is that gradually displacement has taken place from the actual parents outwards. The family exists as something which is cemented by this fact, that for each individual member of the family the actual father and mother are alive in the inner psychic reality (42).

III. Boundary and Space

Underlying Winnicott's writing is a sense of balance and proportion—an aesthetic sense that often seems to take a visual form, just as his favorite method of communication in his work with children took a visual form in the Squiggle Game. From him therefore we borrow the concepts of boundary and space to give coherence to this last part of our essay, which touches upon some implications of his theory of development—implications for the individual and for the society in which the individual lives, which he maintains, and which he creates anew.

1. Form and Content

In fact, the balance and proportion apparent in Winnicott's work are not
due only to his facility in expressing his ideas. They lie at the heart of his
belief about human nature, as, for instance, conveyed in this sentence
from his first book, *Clinical Notes on Disorders in Childhood* (1931):
"The great difference between the human being and other mammals is,
perhaps, the much more complicated attempt on the part of the former
to make the instincts serve instead of govern" (19). When this sentence
is considered in conjunction with the following passage from a broadcast
talk to parents entitled "The Innate Morality of the Baby" (1949), the
link between his work and sense of proportion that he believed natural
in human beings becomes clear:

> I am still talking about infants, but it is so very difficult to describe
> what is happening in the first months in infant terms. To make it easier,
> let us look now at a boy of five or six drawing. I shall pretend he is con-
> scious of what is going on, though he is not really. What does he do? He
> knows the impulse to scribble and make a mess. This is not a picture.
> These primitive pleasures have to be kept fresh, but at the same time he
> wants to express ideas, and also to express them in such a way that they
> may be understood. If he achieves a picture he has found a series of con-
> trols that satisfy him. First of all there is a piece of paper of a particular
> size and shape which he accepts. Then he hopes to use a certain amount
> of skill that has come of practice. Then he knows that the picture when it
> is finished must have balance—you know, the tree on either side of the
> house—this is an expression of the fairness which he needs and probably
> gets from the parents. The points of interest must balance, and so must
> the lights and shades and the color scheme. The interest of the picture
> must be spread over the whole paper, and yet there must be a central
> theme which knits the whole thing together. Within this system of

accepted, indeed self-imposed, controls he tries to express an idea, and
to keep some of the freshness of feeling that belonged to the idea when it
was born. It almost takes my breath away to describe all this, yet your
children get to it quite naturally if you give them half a chance (11).

Here we can understand the space to be the place where the content
of the picture exists—where the primitive pleasures and the freshness
of feeling have room to turn up in the idea that is expressed. And we can
take the boundary of this space to be the self-imposed controls that
make the pleasures and feelings serve in the expression of the idea, that
give it form and therefore meaning. Elsewhere Winnicott wrote,
"Spontaneity only makes sense in a controlled setting. *Content is of no
meaning without form*" (79, our italics).

All of Winnicott's work can be looked at from this point of view. His
psychiatric practice itself was given form by the boundary of his theory
of emotional development as it happened to be at any given moment in
its development—as it altered according to what he observed. This was
true in a double sense, because the theory informed both diagnosis and
therapy, which came to be the same thing. Here is one of his descriptions of what happened in psychotherapy:

What we do together is always quite a natural thing: something limited
is taken from the natural procedures of child care and home life or of
being a child growing or failing to grow in the setting that obtains. If we
find we are doing something or behaving in a way that has no counterpart
in ordinary life and living, then we pull ourselves up and think again.

What we do is arrange a professional setting made up of time and space
and behaviour, which frames a limited area of child or child care experience, and we see what happens. This is the same as form in art. Religious
people of the Christian persuasion use the phrase: "whose service is pre-
fect freedom," which is the same as the sonnet form accepted by Shake-
speare or Keats which allows of spontaneous impulse, and the
unexpected creative gesture. This is what we wait for and value highly in
our work and we even hold back our own bright ideas when they come
for fear of blocking the bright ideas that might come from the adult or
child client (128).

The form that develops naturally (in health) within is thus always
seeking correspondence without. In all departments of life Winnicott

stressed the importance of the setting. It was to be found in the shape
and size of the drawing paper that the little boy used and accepted; in
the stage that holds the play so that we may experience it without
trauma because it is contained *over there* and our feelings are therefore
bearable; even in the sea that surrounds the British Isles and has
allowed their character to develop. He once gave a lecture in a hall
which appalled him by its size and unsuitability for the purpose of making contact with his audience, and so began the lecture by mentioning
this and talking of his regrets for the old Regent Street, which was so
much better suited to the human beings who had business there than
the new grandiose one. And then there was his own house, a tall thin
terrace house with two rooms or so on each floor, the floors somehow
corresponding with layers of meaning within his view of human nature:
at the top, a place for the unintegration of sleep and for dreams; on the
next floor down, the kitchen and sitting room, a place for relaxing, for
friends and for occupations of pleasure, lower down a more formal room
with books and cupboards, but containing his piano, and a door to the
roof garden; and at the bottom, down to earth, the work space: his con-
sulting room, waiting room and office. In different places there were
mirrors to look into and in one in particular a reflection could be seen of
stairs: of the way down to work and to the street door and of the way up,
"back to the centre and back to the beginning." For one of his Christmas
cards, he made a drawing of this mirror reflecting the stairs, linking his
life and his life's work together. It gives a visual form to the fact that
paradox is inherent in living—something that human beings have
acknowledged at least since Heraclitus, who pointed out that the road
up is the same as the road down.

2. Security and Risk

To return to the picture drawn by the small boy: Winnicott saw this as
an achievement in terms of control from within giving room for spontaneity which found expression without. On the basis of what he wrote,

we can equate autonomy with self-control—that is, with the compromise between boundary and space achieved within the inner reality of each individual, corresponding to a lessening need for control from without. We can roughly summarize this idea, and at the same time recapitulate what we have written, by drawing two sets of circles, as in the Figure.

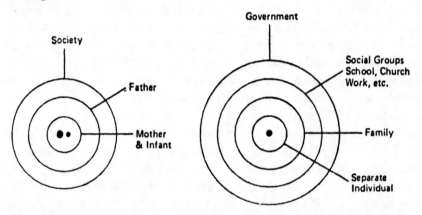

We know that, according to Winnicott's theory, it is not possible to talk about self-control or internal boundaries until there is an integrated self which makes sense of the terms "inner reality" and "shared reality." The fundamental boundary is, therefore, the limiting membrane between the "me" and the "not-me" which corresponds to the skin of the body; the fundamental space is the place within this boundary where growth takes place along "natural" lines according to the maturational processes, and where the self and the inner psychic reality begin to be. Until integration is achieved, the father supplies the circle around the mother and infant that protects them, and society is arranged so that this can happen.

In health, as the "me" becomes separate from the "not-me," the mother's care becomes internalized, and the individual sets out on the road to independence. The infant's fierce morality, arising from his awareness of the need for maternal care, and thus of the need to protect his caregiver from his uncontrolled impulses carrying the fantasy of destruction, makes him accept control from without—control, that is, which is adult and personal, and which gradually humanizes his own morality and gives it the quality of fairness. The survival of the mother who does not retaliate, together with the father who comes to represent the indestructible environment, allows for freedom of the instinctual life—the source of spontaneity—within the family circle. Parental control itself becomes internalized, and the child can identify with widening groups, which rely more and more on the autonomy of their members and less and less on control or management from without. Within the ethos of the group, each individual is free to grow and to contribute personally, so that new patterns can evolve. But each circle of society has *meaning* for the individual only insofar as he can identify with it on the basis of his own good-enough internalized environment. Winnicott believed that there is a limit to the width of the environmental groupings with which individuals can identify (47, 72).

It can easily be seen that almost the same statement about boundary and space can be made in terms of security and risk. The first and greatest risk comes with the first moments of integration—of I AM—which carry aggression and the fear of persecution, and are only possible within the circle and security of the mother's arms. Parental care, which protects the child from both impingement and the consequences of his own impulses, provides security for him. Once this security has become established within, there comes a need to take the risk of breaking out—of struggling against the boundary. This, in individuals reaching towards independence, is the same as the need to "establish themselves as themselves." In Winnicott's words,

> Children need to go on finding out whether they can still rely on their parents, and this testing may continue till the children are themselves ready to provide secure conditions for their own children, and after. Adolescents quite characteristically make tests of all security measures and of all rules and regulations and disciplines. So it usually happens that children do accept security as a basic assumption. They believe in good early mothering and fathering because they have had these. They carry with them a sense of security and this is constantly being reinforced by their tests of their parents and family, of their schoolteachers and friends, and of all sorts of people they meet. Having found the locks and bolts securely fastened, they proceed to unlock them and to break them open; they burst out . . . Healthy children do need people to go on being in control, but the disciplines must be provided by persons who can be loved and hated, defied and depended upon; mechanical controls are of no use, nor can fear be a good motive for compliance. It is always a living relationship

between persons that gives the elbow room which is necessary for true growth. True growth gradually, and in the course of time, carries the child or adolescent on to an adult sense of responsibility, especially responsibility for the provision of secure conditions for the small children of a new generation.

We can see all this going on in the work of creative artists of all kinds. They do something very valuable for us, because they are constantly creating new forms and breaking through these forms only to create new ones. Artists enable us to keep alive, when the experiences of real life often threaten to destroy our sense of being alive and real in a living way. Artists best of all people remind us that the struggle between our impulses and a sense of security (both of which are vital to us) is an eternal struggle and one that goes on inside each one of us as long as our life lasts.

In health, then, children develop enough belief in themselves and in other people to hate external controls of all kinds, controls have changed over into self-control. In self-control the conflict *has been worked through within the person* in advance. So I see it this way: good conditions in the early stages lead to a sense of security, and a sense of security leads on to self-control, and when self-control is a fact, then security that is imposed is an insult (36).

3. The Individual and Democracy

If we take the widest circle on our diagram and give to it the name "democracy," the name that we give to the political system of our society at the present time, we can see on the basis of what we have written above why Winnicott held that democracy is "the exercise of freedom." On the one hand, the democratic society allows freedom for growth and contribution in the space that it creates by administering the law and by keeping in being the political institutions, which include the "provision of a certain degree of stability for the elected rulers" that could not be maintained through "direct voting on every point." In this way democracy can be seen as an "extension of family facilitation." On the other hand, it keeps in being "democratic machinery . . . for the election of leaders by free vote, the true secret ballot . . . and for the people to get rid of leaders." In this way there is room for the breaking through of boundaries, the law itself becoming subject to evolution through the participation of the electors. In a dictatorship, per contra, "the definition of good and bad belongs to the dictator and is not a matter for discussion among the individuals that compose the group and is therefore not constantly in revision in regard to meaning" (47). In a dictatorship suppression of spontaneity from without and indoctrination are therefore both likely to occur. "There is a limited value to inner freedom," Winnicott wrote elsewhere, "if it is only consciously experienced in circumstances of persecution" (92).

He believed that a democratic society relies upon the individuals within it at any one time who are mature enough to identify with the wide circle that comprises the whole of that society, as well as being able to identify with narrower groups bound by (for instance) similarity of religion, of political views, of cultural interests or of work. This mature social sense comes from a balance between boundary and space within the individual, which means that there has already been a working through of the conflict between impulse and control, so that the individual is able to "find the whole conflict within the self as well as being able to see the whole conflict outside the self in external (shared) reality" (47).

Winnicott saw the main threat to democracy as coming from antisocial individuals, that is from those who are not able to contain the conflict within themselves. The antisocial individual cannot make use of boundaries in the world of shared reality (such as the law, for example) as a representation of those within himself, because control has not yet become internalized. He is thus forced (where there is hope) to provoke actual strong management from society. Alternatively, the antisocial tendency can take the form of identification with *authority*—something quite different from identification with a social group. In Winnicott's words,

> this is unhealthy, immature, because it is not an identification that arises out of self-discovery. It is a sense of frame without sense of picture, a sense of form without retention of spontaneity. This is a pro-society tendency that is anti-individual. People who develop in this way can be

called "hidden antisocials." Hidden antisocials are not "whole persons" any more than manifest antisocials, since each needs to find and control the conflicting force in the world outside the self (47).

It was his firm belief that "the basis for a society is the whole human personality . . . It is not possible for persons to get further in society building than they can get with their own personal development" (47).

For this reason he held that "Of a true democracy one can say: In this society at this time there is sufficient maturity in the emotional development of a sufficient proportion of the individuals that comprise it for there to exist an innate tendency [i.e. coming from within the mature individuals] towards the creation and recreation and maintenance of the democratic machinery"; from this follows naturally his definition of democracy as "society well adjusted to its *healthy* individual members." It also follows that "It would be possible to take a community and impose on it the machinery that belongs to democracy, but this would not be to create democracy. Someone would be needed to continue to maintain the machinery (for secret ballot, etc.) and also to force people to accept the results" (47).

But even within a society where there are enough autonomous or mature individuals to maintain a democracy—a society where freedom can be exercised—Winnicott believed that there is inevitably strain and stress. "The experience of freedom is tiring, and at intervals the free seek a rest from responsibility . . . Freedom puts a strain on the individual's whole personality" (91). This is because the individual has no logical outlet in public life for ideas of being persecuted or feelings of anger or aggression; he must take responsibility for these within himself. In a dictatorship these feelings can attach themselves to the dictator, and in a war they can attach themselves to the enemy. Thus, according to Winnicott's theory, there are bound to be, and indeed need to be, "periods when the political scene [within the delimited society] is in a state of turmoil," just as there are bound to be periods of turmoil within the individual (93). He attached particular importance to the periods of sorting out and working through prior to an election, when for each individual "the external scene is internalized and so brought into association with the interplay of forces in his own personal inner world." The vote then expresses the outcome of the struggle within himself—the inner struggle, that is, between security and risk, represented without in the character and views of those who seek election. This is why Winnicott considered the secret ballot to be "the essence of democratic machinery": It "ensures the freedom of the people to express deep feelings *apart from conscious thoughts* . . . If there is doubt about the secrecy of the ballot, the individual, however healthy, can only express by his vote his *reactions*" (that is, compliance or rebellion with regard to what is expected) (47). "Parliamentary government," he wrote, "is the attempt to make freedom possible through the willingness of individuals to tolerate their opinion's eclipse if they are outvoted. The willingness to put up with not getting one's way if one cannot get the support of the majority is a remarkable human achievement involving much strain and pain. It can only be possible if the gratification is allowed of a periodical illogical riddance of the leader" (91). During periods of uncertainty Winnicott saw the monarchy as providing continuity and representing the indestructible environment (91, 93).

4. The Broken Boundary

Continuing on the lines suggested by the concepts of boundary and space, it is possible to say that distortion in the boundary brings about distortion in the space (and therefore in the maturational processes). Boundary can be distorted in itself in the sense of being too weak, or fractured, or even absent when needed. Such distortion takes away form, so that what occurs in the space has no meaning. Failure in the holding environment, perhaps because of illness in, or accident to, the mother, can mean that the infant's line of life is interrupted and his development hindered by the need for defence against primitive anxiety. But it can also be seen that failure of the father to protect the mother in the crucial weeks after the infant's birth can contribute to this state of affairs: If the circle made by the father, or by some person fulfil-

ling the father's function, is broken, the mother cannot abandon herself
without anxiety to her infant's needs.

The father's strength is also, as we have seen, of great importance in
the family circle. The antisocial tendency that is manifest in delinquency (where there is hope) arises from deprivation at an early age,
and the deprivation often consists in the absence of an indestructible
environment that makes impulsive behaviour possible. The set of circles belonging to the delinquent's relationship to society thus includes a
weakness in the one representing the family—the continuing paternal
or maternal provision—with all the subsequent social circles being
used to provoke strong management or to find a reliable person who can
be used. As Winnicott vividly puts it:

> What happens if the home fails the child before he has got the idea of a
> framework as part of his own nature? The popular idea is that finding
> himself 'free' he proceeds to enjoy himself. This is far from the truth.
> Finding the framework of his life broken, he no longer feels free. He
> becomes anxious, and if he has hope he proceeds to look for a framework
> elsewhere than at home. The child whose home fails to give a feeling of
> security looks outside his home for the four walls; he still has hope, and
> he looks to grandparents, uncles and aunts, friends of the family, school.
> He seeks an external stability without which he may go mad. Provided at
> the proper time, this stability might have grown into the child like the
> bones in his body, so that gradually in the course of the first months and
> years of his life he would have passed on to independence from depend-
> ence and a need to be managed . . . Children deprived of home life must
> either be provided with something personal and stable when they are yet
> young enough to make use of it to some extent, or else they must force us
> later to provide stability in the shape of an approved school or, in the last
> resort, four walls in the shape of a prison cell (18).

Winnicott felt that these ideas could usefully be carried over into the
provision of schooling. It was his view that there is difficulty in having a
universal type of school, as opposed to a variety of institutions, not
because of difference in I.Q.—"most teachers feel that it is natural for
their classes to contain both clever and less clever children, and they
naturally adapt themselves to the varying needs of their pupils in so far
as the classes are not too big for them to be able to do individual work"
(17)—but because of difference in home security. Within the range of

normal children he believed there are those "whose parents have managed well and are managing well. These children will be the rewarding ones, able to show and cope with all kinds of feelings." They "come to school for something to be added to their lives; they want to learn lessons." Also within this range are those whose homes for some reason are less secure, who come to school not so much to learn as to "find a home from home. This means that they seek a stable emotional situation in which they can exercise their own emotional lability, a group of which they can gradually become a part, a group that can be tested out as to its ability to withstand aggression and to tolerate aggressive ideas." Ideally he believed there should be specific provision for both these groups of children (17).

The weakened boundary can also show up in the lives of adolescents, where the absence of personal confrontation means that they have either to become immaturely responsible—that is, to supply the frame themselves before they are ready to do so, and hence to miss out on the achievement of true maturity—or else they have to provoke society into supplying the framework for them. Adolescents seeking management can align themselves temporarily with the true antisocials amongst them, with the result that there is a danger in the reaction of society producing controls that lessen the opportunity for fulfillment and contribution of its healthy individual members.

There is a link between failure to provide the boundary of adequate management and what is often called permissiveness. Winnicott was well aware that there can be a general attitude in society which affects this and which can swing back and forth like a pendulum. "The phase of Truby King," he wrote, "is still being lived down by adults trying to give their babies the right to discover a personal morality, and we can see this in a reaction to indoctrination that goes to the extreme of extreme permissiveness" (72). Such attitudes are bound in some degree to affect society in the next generations. But in the private lives of the ordinary good-enough mother and her infant, and the ordinary good-enough parents and their children, he believed that, especially among the unsophisticated, the balance between boundary and space is *naturally* adjusted within the range of health.

What can, however, weaken the secure boundary supplied by parents and by society is the conjunction of sentimentality with the sort of permissive reaction that Winnicott describes. Sentimentality, as we have mentioned, was seen by Winnicott as arising from the denial of personal awfulness. "The truly responsible people of the world," he wrote, are "those who accept the fact of their own hate, nastiness, cruelty, things which co-exist with their capacity to love and to construct. Sometimes their sense of their own awfulness gets them down" (38). It is this sense of awfulness, so often reflected in the awfulness of things in the world of shared reality, that leads to the ordinary depression of valuable people. Individuals who are unable to take responsibility for this side of their nature (because somewhere in their history there was a relative failure in boundary) are forced to deny its existence, and hence to deny the actual depressing things in the world around them. They escape into make-believe (93).

Permissiveness that has sentimentality at its root can turn up in a mother's reluctance to allow her baby to cry or to frustrate him by the de-adaptation to his needs, roughly covered by the word 'weaning'. "A wish to wean must come from the mother. She must be brave enough to stand the baby's anger and the awful ideas that go with anger" (9). This kind of permissiveness can also turn up in an idea in society or its representatives that a child should *never* be separated from his parents, or in an acceptance of the idea of offenders as ill people being allowed to undermine the function of those who administer the law. In a talk to magistrates Winnicott expressed the opinion that "there would be danger in the adoption of a purely therapeutic aim on the magisterial bench" (78). Such an attitude would ignore the fact that people need to see justice done. Winnicott acknowledged that many people are unwilling to believe that a need for retributive justice is a part of individual makeup; nevertheless, he could not avoid the conclusion that "crime produces public revenge feelings." He continues:

> Public revenge would add up to a dangerous thing were it not for the law and those who implement it. First and foremost in court work, the magistrate gives expression to public revenge feelings, and only by so doing can the foundation be laid for the humane treatment of the offender . . . There is a real danger lest those who want to see offenders treated as ill people (as they are indeed) will be thwarted just as they are seeming to succeed, through not taking into account unconscious revenge potential (78).

In sum, it can be seen that Winnicott believed that where firm boundaries are needed to give meaning to content and control to spontaneity, and do not hold, there will be an increase in the number and power of antisocial individuals, tipping the balance against the mature in society. The end result of this process could be a dictatorship, because *actual management* of the individuals in society would have to come from somewhere. A democracy can only be maintained if the vast majority of individuals in the society are prepared to obey its laws and a substantial proportion are prepared to participate in their evolution by constitutional means.

5. The Oppressive Boundary

If a threat to the freedom of individuals and society can come from broken boundaries because of their own insufficiency, it can also come from impingement from without that lessens the space and impoverishes the content. In a political boundary, for instance, the threat of invasion or the necessity to fight an external aggressor will cause a tendency away from the freedom that a government can allow in peacetime. During the Second World War, in 1940, Winnicott wrote:

> The war period provides us not only with a temporary relief from the strain of being free, but also it gives opportunity for dictators to have their little day. We have dictators all over the place, and they often do wonderful things which could never have been done in a Parliamentary way (91).

We can take this idea back through the circles of society. Poverty, bad housing, accidental death or injury can all be threats to the family as a going concern, and can reduce the space for freedom of the children to grow and to flourish within. There is an obvious need for such factors to be minimized wherever possible by social provision. As Winnicott said, "Provision for the ordinary home of a basic ration of housing, food, clothing, education, and recreation facilities, and what could be called cultural food, has first claim on our attention" (45).

What he believed to be not quite so obvious is that the maintenance of a democratic and creative society also involves freedom for ordinary good-enough families and for ordinary devoted mothers from interference in the name of society's capacity to *care*—in the name of the benevolent society. In a broadcast talk entitled "Support for Normal Parents" he said:

> It may be asked: Why trouble to talk to people who are doing well? Surely the greater need comes from those parents who are in difficulties? Well, I try not to be weighed down by the fact that much distress undoubtedly exists here in England, in London, in the district immediately around the hospital where I work. I know only too well about this distress, and about the anxiety and depression that prevail. But my hopes are based on the stable and healthy families which I also see building up around me, families that form the only basis for the stability of our society for the next couple of decades.
>
> It may also be asked: Why concern yourself with healthy families which you say exist, and on which you base your hopes? Can they not manage for themselves? Well, I have a very good reason for giving active support here, which is this: there exist tendencies towards destruction of these good things . . . liable to appear in the form of interferences, petty regulations, legal restrictions, and all manner of stupidities.
>
> I do not mean that parents are ordered about or cramped by official policy. The State in England takes pains to leave parents free to choose, and to accept and to refuse what the State offers . . .
>
> The trouble is that those who actually administer the public services are by no means uniformly confident in the mother's ability to understand her child better than anyone else can. Doctors and nurses are often so impressed with the ignorance and stupidity of some of the parents that they fail to allow for the wisdom of others. Or perhaps the lack of confidence in mothers that is so often to be noted arises out of the specialized training of the doctors and nurses, who have expert knowledge of the baby in sickness and in health, but are not necessarily qualified to understand the parents' whole task. [The mother] is a specialist in this matter of her own children, and if she is not overawed by the voice of authority, she can be found to know well what is good and what is bad in the matter of management.
>
> Whatever does not specifically back up the idea that parents are

responsible people will in the long run be harmful to the very core of society (16).

The voice of authority that removes personal choice can diminish the natural responsibility that parents feel for each individual child. It is this 24-hour-a-day responsibility that sees the child through and Winnicott believed that "we must see that we never interfere with a family that *is a going concern*, not even for its own good" (45). Of the children brought to his clinic for psychiatric help he found that "in the great majority of cases we manage to help the child in the setting which already exists. This is of course our aim, not only because it is economical but because when the home is good-enough the home is the proper place for the child to grow up in" (45).

Sometimes the home is not good-enough, and cannot "maintain itself, either because of defects in the field of reliability, or because the strains and provocations of the growing individual child (and then of the children) ask too much of the human beings who collectively form the emotional environment, so that the innumerable hurts and moments of agony in the child's life are not all the time being mended"; here, if the "wobbly environment" cannot be helped to acquire stability, it is necessary to provide "specialized child care," which "often means temporary or permanent alternative management" (128). But universal provisions made because of what turns up in ill-health were seen by Winnicott as destructive. It is sometimes forgotten that in the majority of known cases where parents have failed in some respect—even where they have failed grossly and have become criminally responsible for neglect or harm—it is they themselves, who, on one pretext or another, come for help. In 1968 Winnicott wrote in a footnote a list of "common persecutions" to which the less fortunate in society are vulnerable. They are "overcrowding, starvation, infestation, the constant threat from physical disease and disaster *and from the laws promulgated by a benevolent society*" (72, our italics).

Winnicott applied the same principles to mothers and infants during that all-important period of absolute dependence in the first weeks of the infant's life. Talking of the period around birth, he wrote:

> Administrative tidiness, the dictates of hygiene, a laudable urge towards the promotion of bodily health, these and all sorts of other things

get between the mother and her baby, and it is unlikely that mothers
themselves will rise up in concerted effort to protest against interference.
Someone must act for the young mothers who are having their first and
second babies, and who are necessarily themselves in a dependent state.
It can be assumed that no mother of a newborn baby will ever go on
strike . . . because she is otherwise engaged (1).

These words were written twenty-odd years ago. In the last decade
or two there has been an increasing awareness of the importance of the
mother's continuing physical union with her baby after birth—an
awareness that has grown with the range of observational studies of
mother–infant interaction. These studies have themselves been given
impetus by statistical evidence that failure to thrive without organic
cause and actual physical injury done to infants are linked to separation
of the mother and infant in the days after birth (142). There is now a
growing tendency to allow mothers physical contact with and a share in
looking after even premature and ill newborn babies. Nevertheless, it is
perhaps fair to say that even in this area there sometimes remains a
tendency to control from without, and that in the process of childbirth
itself there is much that is not well-adjusted to the healthy individual
mother, whose emotional and even physical well-being can take a second place to negative considerations of safety or efficiency. It is a matter
of allowing parents the responsibility of sharing decisions—of a balance
between security and risk. As Winnicott pointed out, "With reference
to the natural process of childbirth one thing can seldom be forgotten,
the fact that the human infant has an absurdly big head." But he also
added, "It would be terrible if adaptation to ill health should ever
swamp a natural procedure adapted not to illness but to life" (44).
   In subtler ways, advice, education or propaganda can impinge upon
the freedom of the mother with her infant. We can take as an example
the subject of infant feeding, because Winnicott used this so often to
illustrate his ideas. It can be seen that he considered breast-feeding to
be preferable to feeding by the bottle; in fact, going through his writing
one can extract a long list of reasons for this preference. Among these is
the richness of the experience, both for mother and baby: "Although the
feeding of a baby can be very satisfactory, however it is done, the satisfaction is of a different order altogether for the woman who is able to use
a part of her body in this way" (95). For the baby the experience means

the engagement of the total nascent personality, which includes his capacity for "sensuous coexistence" (54). Winnicott said he thought that, if a baby fed by the bottle could think things out, he would be unable to believe that "the capacity he is born with for sensuous experience has to be wasted on stuff like rubber" (95). Furthermore, in Winnicott's theory of development, the survival of the mother after an excited feeding experience is, as we have seen, a vital factor in the transition from absolute to relative dependence—the transition "which is so important in the life of every child and enables the child to be a part of the world and to use the world and to contribute to the world." He believed that the "survival of the breast, which is part of the mother, has a significance which is entirely of a different order from the significance of the survival of a glass bottle, a thing" (95). The survival of the mother enhances the capacity of the individual to take risks.

Nevertheless, when giving a lecture on the subject of breast-feeding to members of the National Childbirth Trust, Winnicott said:

> What I want to do first is dissociate myself from a sentimental attitude towards breast-feeding. There is no doubt whatever that a vast number of individuals in this world today have been brought up without having had the experience of breast-feeding. This means that there are other ways by which an infant may experience physical intimacy with the mother . . .
>
> I have seen a great number of children who were given a very bad time with the mother struggling to make the breast work, which of course she is completely unable to do because it is outside her conscious control. The mother suffers and the baby suffers. Sometimes great relief is experienced when at last bottle feeding is established and at any rate something is going well in the sense that the baby is getting satisfied by taking in the right quantity of suitable food. Many of these struggles could be avoided if religion were taken out of this idea of breast-feeding. It seems to me the ultimate insult to a woman who would *like* to breast-feed her child, and who comes naturally to do so, if some authority, a doctor or a nurse, comes along and says "You must breast-feed your baby." If I were a woman this would be enough to put me off. I would say: "Very well then I won't" (95).

Knowing him, one can well believe it. But his words show up how easily the spontaneous gesture can be crushed, and how pleasure can be removed from this area where there is so great an opportunity for richness in experience, because the mother may simply be forced to *react*, either by rebellion or compliance. Winnicott continues by pointing out that someone in authority cannot "*get* a mother and baby into relationship with each other" because this is a "matter of intimacy" between the two. In any such matter, "telling people what to do is to be deplored" (95). "We even find mothers," he wrote elsewhere, "(not, I hope, in this country) being told that they *must mother* their infants, this being the most extreme degree of denial that 'mothering' grows naturally out of being a mother" (1).

What is needed at the very beginning is "an environmental provision which fosters the mother's belief in herself" (8). Information (as opposed to advice) given by experienced people is often essential to mothers, and can help in building up confidence. For instance, in Winnicott's words, "It would be helpful to point out to mothers that sometimes mothers do not love their babies at first, or to show why mothers often find themselves unable to feed the baby at the breast, or to explain why loving is a complex matter, and not just an instinct" (115).

These principles are to be found wherever Winnicott talked about education in matters of living. Discussing his own experience and aims in broadcasting, he said,

> Almost every bit of advice that one gives over the air gives distress somewhere. Recently I spoke about telling adopted children that they are adopted. I knew of course that I was in danger of causing distress. No doubt I did upset many, but one mother who had listened came to me from a long way away and told me exactly why it would be very dangerous *in the circumstances* to tell her adopted child that she was adopted. I had to agree, although in principle I know that it is right to tell adopted children that they are adopted, and to do so as soon as possible (115).

He suggested that the useful alternative in health education to advice or propaganda is

> . . . to attempt to get hold of ordinary things that people do, and to help them to understand why they do them. The basis for this suggestion is the idea that much that people do is really sensible in the circumstances. It is astonishing how, when one listens over and over again to the descriptions mothers give of the management of a child at home, in the end one comes down to the feeling that one cannot tell these parents

what to do; one can only see that one might have done the same, or one might have done worse in the circumstances.

What people do like is to be given an understanding of the problems they are tackling, and they like to be made aware of things that they do intuitively. They feel unsafe when left to their own hunches, to the sort of things that come to them at the critical moment, when they are not thinking things out. It may be that parents gave the child a smack or a kiss or a hug or they laughed. Something appropriate happened. This was the right thing, nothing could have been better. No one could have told these parents what to do in the circumstances, because the circumstances could not have been described in advance. Afterwards, however, the parents find themselves talking over things and wondering, and often they have no notion what they have been doing and feel confused about the problem itself. At such a moment they tend to feel guilty, and they fly to anyone who will speak with authority, who will give orders (115).

Even when things are going well, he believed that parents "very easily get pushed sideways or backwards by any person with some kind of conviction which must be spread or a religion to which people must be converted. It is always the natural things that get spoiled" (92).

Applying this theme to the freedom of individuals at large, Winnicott wrote:

Serenity does not know how to fight for itself, but the anxious drive to push forward and to progress seems to contain all the dynamic. This idea is contained in the phrase of John Maynard Keynes "The Price of Freedom is Eternal Vigilance," adopted as its motto by the New Statesman.

There is a threat to freedom, therefore, and to all natural phenomena, simply because they do not contain the propaganda drive, and natural phenomena find themselves over-ridden, by which time is too late (92).

The desire to control others was seen by Winnicott as emanating from those individuals in society who could not feel free:

The majority of people are comparatively healthy and they enjoy their health without being too self-conscious about it or without even knowing that they have it. All the time, however, there are the people in the community whose life is dominated by some degree of psychiatric disorder or an unhappiness that they cannot account for, or a lack of certainty that they are glad to be alive, or that they want to go on living . . . It is not always realized that there is something that goes deeper even than class distinction. It goes deeper even than the distinction between poverty and riches, although the practical problems associated with either of these two extremes produce such powerful effects that these effects dominate the scene only too easily.

When the psychiatrist or the psycho-analyst looks at the world he cannot help seeing that there is this terrible contrast between those who are free to enjoy life and who live creatively and those who are not free in this way because they are all the time dealing with the threat of anxiety or a breakdown or the threat of a behavior disorder which makes sense only if the whole be known.

. . . I am suggesting that while all other kinds of class distinction have validity and produce their own resentments, this one may turn out to be the most significant of all. It is true that a great number of individuals who have done exceptionally well or who have moved the world or who have contributed in an exceptional way have been as we know them at great cost, as if they were on the borderline between the haves and the have nots. One can see how they have made some exceptional contribution out of unhappiness, or driven by a sense of threat from within. This, however, does not alter the fact that there are two extremes in this area, those who have it in them to fulfill themselves and those who because of environmental failures in the early stages are not able to fulfill themselves. It must be expected that the latter resent the existence of the former. The unhappy will try to destroy happiness. Those who are caught up in the prison of the rigidity of their own defences will try to destroy freedom. Those who cannot enjoy their bodies to the full will try to interfere with the enjoyment of the body even in the case of their own children whom they love. Those who cannot love will try to destroy the simplicity of a natural relationship by cynicism; and (over the border) those who are too ill to take revenge and who spend their lives in mental hospitals make those who are sane feel guilty to be sane and to be free to live in society and to take part in local or world politics (92).

In sum, Winnicott believed that freedom to grow and to create and to contribute—the same freedom that is the essence of the democratic tendency—needs conscious support from society:

> The most valuable support is given in a negative way by organized non-interference with the ordinary good mother-infant relationship, and with the ordinary good home. For more intelligent support, even of this nega-

tive kind, much research is needed on the emotional development of the
infant and the child of all ages, and also on the psychology of the nursing
mother and of the father's function at various stages (47).

To repeat what we have already written: it was his deeply held conviction that "true strength belongs to the individual's experience of
development along natural lines, and this is what we hope for in individuals. In practice this kind of strength becomes easily lost sight of
because of the comparable strength that can come from fear and resentment and deprivation and the state of never having had" (95). Development along natural lines includes the development of an internal system
of boundary and space "grown into the individual like the bones in his
body" (78).

6. Space Without Boundary

The question arises, where in the scheme of boundaries and spaces
does Winnicott's concept of the potential space come in? It is not an
easy question to answer, because he used this concept of his as a kind of
working-out place for various ideas right up until the time of his death.
He was, in fact, working on the proofs of his book *Playing and Reality* on
the evening when he died, and had been saying that he still had not
quite got it right. This, of course, does not alter the fact that he has left
us a marvelously stimulating book.
    The development for each individual of a potential space requires the
same room to grow along natural lines that we have been describing
above, particularly the room given by the boundary of the holding environment in the first weeks and months of life during which the infant
comes to trust the mother. Nevertheless, it is not the *same thing* as
room to grow along natural lines; it is something that *may happen* if
there is room to grow. It is a "hypothetical area" (70) given a visual form
by Winnicott as a way of gathering together certain related phenomena
that have practical and theoretical importance—phenomena that have

to do with the individual's experience of *living* as opposed to merely functioning, with the quality of life and the value of life to the individual. These phenomena, which are given the collective name of "playing," include cultural activities *apart from* immediate considerations of the balance between impulse and control.

We can say that the small boy drawing a picture in Winnicott's description (see Section III 1) is engaged in potential space activity, and when we say this we are looking at him not merely from the point of view of his innate morality, but also from the point of view of the pleasure that self-discovery gives him and of the possibilities of what he *may* draw—that is, of the manifest content of the picture—because of his unique personality, including his experience of life. The issue is complicated by the fact that playing is spontaneous, and spontaneity depends upon freedom of the instinctual life; nevertheless, in Winnicott's words, "the special feature of this place where play and cultural experience have a position is that *it depends for its existence on living experiences, not on inherited tendencies*" (70).

The potential space is concerned with the question:

> What are we doing when we are listening to a Beethoven symphony or making a pilgrimage to a picture gallery or reading *Troilus and Cressida* in bed, or playing tennis? What is a child doing when sitting on the floor playing with toys under the aegis of the mother? It is not only: what are we doing? The question also needs to be posed: where are we (if anywhere at all)? . . . Where are we when we are doing what in fact we do a great deal of our time, namely, enjoying ourselves? (70).

For Winnicott the answer to these questions is that we are neither inside in the world of dream and fantasy nor outside in the world of shared reality. We are in the paradoxical third place that partakes of both these places at once. So while the boundary between the "me" and the "not-me" is of fundamental importance in the attainment of integration, health and indeed sanity, the potential space, "the place where we live," transcends this boundary.

In another sense (which is almost the same sense), the potential space is concerned with symbols—with the complex matter of the meaning of meaning. It is the place where symbols are used. Its point of origin is at the very beginning of life when the mother through adaptation to need "superimposes external reality on what the infant conceives of" (88). This allows the infant, emerging from the state of being the same as the environment, to superimpose what is conceived of on external reality—on what is found and discovered (see Section II C1).

Transitional phenomena are thus at the root of the individual's ability to use symbols. An example of the importance of this ability in the theory of development can be seen in the idea that "for each individual the widening circles of social contact in some way or another represent or symbolize the mother's or the parents' care"—the environment that has become a part of the inner psychic reality. This gives form and therefore meaning to each wider circle within which there is "increased freedom of ideas and functioning" (42). As Winnicott explains elsewhere, "In the experience of the more fortunate baby (and small child and adolescent and adult), the question of separation does not arise, because in the potential space between the baby and the mother there appears the creative playing that arises naturally out of the relaxed state; it is here that there develops a use of symbols that stand at one and the same time for external world phenomena and for phenomena of the individual person who is being looked at" (70).

Using symbols is therefore a way of being in touch with the inner psychic reality—of discovering the self—and is an aspect of what Winnicott calls "creative apperception"—of what first happens when the baby looks into his mother's eyes and, because he discovers himself there, begins also to discover "meaning in the world of seen things" (71). Meaning becomes attached to transitional phenomena, then to playing and to living creatively. For Winnicott the answer to the question "What makes life worth living?" thus includes the idea that life has a quality of reality given by being in touch with the self, which is the same thing as saying that life has meaning. Loss of the play area, which can come about through deprivation, includes "loss of the meaningful symbol" (69).

It is perhaps possible to get the feeling of these ideas by considering the tragedy of Macbeth. The real depth of the tragedy arrives at the point where Macbeth expresses hopelessness in the words "Life . . . is a tale/Told by an idiot, full of sound and fury/Signifying nothing." It comes as a huge relief and indeed as a ray of hope when, confronted by Macduff and the knowledge of doom, he meets his death with fighting words.

The ability to form and use symbols, then, brings meaning to the world of shared reality. But, of course, if enrichment through experience is to take place, it is not enough to say that something in the external world is important to the person only because it corresponds to something within the inner psychic reality. When Winnicott was describing the transitional object, he wrote:

> It is true that the piece of blanket (or whatever it is) is symbolical of some part object, such as the breast. Nevertheless, the point of it is not its symbolical value so much as its actuality. Its not being the breast (or the mother) although real, is as important as the fact that it stands for the breast (or the mother) . . . the transitional object, according to my suggestion, gives room for the process of being able to accept difference and similarity (27).

It is by the *difference* that we grow. This idea is contained in the statements that "a description of the emotional development of the individual cannot be made entirely in terms of the individual, but in certain areas, and this (the potential space) is one of them, perhaps the main one, the behaviour of the environment is part of the individual's own personal development and must therefore be included" (66), and that "when one speaks of a man, one speaks of him *along with* the summation of his cultural experiences. The whole forms a unit" (69).

Winnicott's explanation of the development of his own ideas along these lines is germane here. "It fell to my lot to be a psychoanalyst who, perhaps because of his having been a paediatrician, sensed the importance of this universal [the intermediate area] in the lives of infants and children, and wished to integrate his observation with the theory that we are all the time in the process of developing" (64). Given room at the beginning to develop an area of playing, there is thus no limit or boundary to the development that can take place even into old age, except the limit of our physical capacity to experience and to contain experience.

These considerations, as we have already mentioned, are very much bound up with Winnicott's view of psychotherapy. He believed that where there is space for experiencing in the relationship between the therapist and his patient, or indeed between friend and friend, or parent and child, there is always space for true therapy. The difficulty arises when the play area is lost, or has never developed. In looking at psychotherapy from this point of view Winnicott was able to develop his own therapeutic techniques and to use psychoanalysis in new ways to get back to the place before there was any logic, or form, or use of symbols, so that in the setting provided by his personal reliability, which sometimes meant doing nothing more than being alive and attentive (silently communicating), a point could be reached where a potential space could begin to be (66).

So, in another sense, the concept of the potential space extends the meaning of the word "health." Writing for psychoanalysts about psychoanalysts, Winnicott said, "We seldom reach the point at which we can start to describe what life is like apart from illness or absence of illness." Health in the sense of absence of illness (or worse, in the sense of absence of symptoms) is a negative concept for which Winnicott had no use. "Absence of illness may be health but it is not life," he wrote (69). Life, as we know, included for him the idea of richness of quality—of the capacity to be enriched that comes from an intensity of 'life experience' in relation to a "human mother-figure who is essentially adaptive because of love" (69), and from the ability to carry over something of this intensity of experience to new experiencing in relation to external world phenomena.

It can be seen that these ideas are bound up with his statement that "we are poor indeed if we are only sane" (39). In fact, he found that there were individuals "so firmly anchored in objective reality that they are ill in the direction of being out of touch with the subjective world and with the creative approach to fact." Such people need help because "they feel estranged from dream," because they have lost contact with infantile experience in the merged state (67). "At the theoretical start," Winnicott wrote, "the baby lives in a dream world while awake. What is there when he or she is awake becomes material for dreams" (110). In the creative experience in the potential space, something of this state of affairs reappears. This something is also related to the hallucinations of the schizoid or schizophrenic individual, in the sense that the point of origin of the capacity for enrichment through experiencing is "the exact spot at which a baby is 'schizoid', except that this term is not used because of the baby's immaturity and special state relative to the development of personality and the role of the environment" (67). The same idea is put in another way when Winnicott says that "the phenomena that are life and death to our schizoid or borderline patients appear in our cultural experiences" (69).

This, of course, does not mean that in order to live creatively we need to be on the verge of a mental breakdown, even though it may be true that "breaking down" gives some individuals an opportunity to be creative that has been lost since infancy or childhood. On the contrary, integration needs to be taken for granted in the creative living that involves "a colouring of the whole attitude to external reality" (67) and that is a facet of true health. But it does mean that this true health includes what Winnicott called "the ability to play about with psychosis" (39).

It can also be seen that the more intense the life experiences of the baby at the very beginning, the greater the risk of deprivation of the reliable (predictable) environment that makes involvement safe—of loss of the meaningful object. But the maturational processes include the tendency towards independence and autonomy from both the physical and the psychic point of view (though these are not in fact separate), so where things go well and the reliable environment has time to become internalized, it is *the actual loss* of physical union and of psychic merging that lead to a fulfilling relationship to reality. In the potential space, the loss becomes a gain because "the symbol of union gives wider scope for human experience than union itself" (88).

Speaking of the inevitable loss involved in the transition from the merged to the separate state, Winnicott wrote:

> In some cultures a deliberate effort is made to prevent the mother ever becoming one person so that the child is insured from the beginning against shock associated with loss. In our culture we tend to regard it as normal for the child to experience the full extent of the shock as the mother becomes an external person, but we have to admit that there are casualties. When it works there is a richness of experience which is the main argument in its favour (88).

The casualties, as we have already seen, can produce "have nots," including those in whom the antisocial tendency leads to aggressive acts and all kinds of destructiveness that threaten society. But there are also individuals who can be called partial casualties in this sense, yet who make outstanding contributions to society. Winnicott believed that those creative artists whose "active creation" is compulsive belong to this group; that "anxiety is a drive behind the artist's brand of creativity" (82). For such people there has been a totality of involvement in experience at the very beginning and therefore a richness in imaginative elaboration in the dream world where the personality is in the process of evolving. Subsequently, there has been an unmended failure in the environment. Thus the artist may be antisocial or schizoid "in some localized sense" (53). From this may stem the fact that, together with "the courage to be in touch with primitive processes," the artist has "an astoundingly deep recognition of certain aspects of internal reality which healthy people may miss to their own impoverishment."

But while for the artist there may be self-realization in moments of inspiration when ideas "turn up," the self that is to be found in a relaxed relationship to external reality remains elusive. As Winnicott put it, "A successful artist may be universally acclaimed and yet have failed to find the self that he or she is looking for . . . If the artist (in whatever medium) is searching for the self, then it can be said that in all probability there is already some failure for that artist in the field of general creative living. The finished creation never heals the underlying lack of sense of self" (66). The artist goes on searching; and even though he finds new forms for universal truth, he can never retire: "We cannot conceive of the artist coming to the end of his task" (60).

So we have a paradoxical state of affairs where those who have taken the risk and won are enriched by the creations of those who have taken the risk and in some way lost—lost the enjoyment of life and the "feeling of real" in the outside world because the potential space is invaded by anxiety, or perhaps distorted by self-defence. There is much food for thought (if not for indigestion) in Winnicott's statement that "richness of quality rather than health (absence of illness) is at the top of the ladder of human progress" (53).

Of the essence of the concept of the potential space is the variety and variability that it allows for. Looking at external reality we can see that, as Winnicott put it, this "has its own dimensions and can be studied objectively, and, however much it may seem to vary according to the state of the individual who is observing it, does in fact remain constant" (65). Then, looking at inner psychic reality, we can see that this has at its core the "inherited potential" which allows

for its organization and structure. In the classical Freudian theory—
the theory that was developed especially by Melanie Klein to cover
psychic functioning in early infancy—inner reality is "related to the
psycho-somatic partnership" and in particular to the fantasy that
accompanies orgiastic body functioning (70). In these respects it is
biologically determined and to some extent fixed. It could be said
to give rise to observations about the unchanging quality of human
nature, though of course there are all the variations in the inherited
constitution that are the result of having this particular father and
this particular mother and are peculiar to each individual. But the
area between inner and shared reality is a part of the individual self
that is founded "not on body functioning but on body experiences
. . . that belong to object relating of a non-orgiastic kind" (69). There
is thus here a special kind of variation between person and person
that comes from without, from "the experiences of the individual person (baby, child, adolescent, adult) in the environment that obtains."
The potential space has a capacity to expand: its extent "can be min-
imal or maximal, according to the summation of actual experiences"
(70).

It is this kind of variability, as Winnicott suggested, that can be of
special interest to the social anthropologist, and there is perhaps here
something germane to the "biology and culture" controversy which was
given a new lease of life, particularly in the United States, by the publication of E.O. Wilson's book *Sociobiology: A New Synthesis* in 1975
(152). One aspect of this controversy is the question: How far is culture
biologically determined? At a purely intellectual level Winnicott found
it difficult to escape from the determinism that is implied in theories
about the world and its inhabitants:

> It is true of course that there is no theory of emotional states and of
> personality health and disorder and of behavior vagaries unless there is
> at the basis an assumption that is deterministic . . . The study of the per-
> sonality which is particularly associated with the work of Freud which
> has led to an immense forward stride in man's attempt to understand
> himself is an extension of the theoretical basis of biology . . .

It was his belief that

There is no sharp line anywhere in the theoretical statement of the universe if one starts with the theory of the pulsating star and ends up with the theory of psychiatric disorder and of health in the human being, including creativity or seeing the world creatively which is the most important evidence we have that man is alive and that the thing that is alive is man (92).

This cosmological view of the nature of things was typical of Winnicott's thinking—of his search for form to give meaning to content. Indeed, it could be said that he created a cosmology, using the cultural inheritance that he found ready to be used, whose starting point was not the pulsating star but the beginning and centre of the individual self, from which the whole world took shape and meaning. He did not, however, believe that the determinism of theory was of great practical concern to most people:

The majority of people are not bothered by the understanding, as far as it can be understood, that there is a deterministic basis to life. The subject . . . may become vitally important to anyone for a few moments, but the fact is that the majority of people for most of the time feel free to choose. It is the feeling of being free to choose and of being able to create anew that makes the deterministic theory irrelevant (92).

Yet it does seem that Winnicott's theory of emotional development tells us not only about the *sense* of freedom, but also, through the concept of the potential space, something about an *actual* freedom. In one way the concept of potential space is at the end of a theoretical chain, so that it could be said that nature (or biology) allows for it to come into being. Yet, because it also depends for its existence on the experience of the individual in the (external) environment that obtains, it is *to all intents and purposes* (if not mathematically speaking) capable of infinite variation. It is the place where experience builds upon experience, where the world is continually "woven into the texture of the imagination," so that new patterns of imagining emerge and a man is able to be truly original. This originality can be used in the alteration of the environment itself, and through it local institutions and mores can grow and evolve, influencing the *way* in which man uses his innate morality, so that conditions can obtain in which human beings can live creatively and in turn continue the cultural evolution. The potential space allows to man a certain degree of control over his own destiny.

The late Dr. Neville Gorton, Bishop of Coventry, once expressed the dilemma inherent in the biology and culture controversy in terms of a metaphorical carpet. It was a question of whether mankind simply unrolled the evolutionary carpet or whether he wove it as well. In the potential space we weave.

The reader may with some justification ask: Where is the connection between someone enjoying playing tennis, whether on a tennis court or in a potential space, and man controlling his own destiny? Perhaps there is a clue to this in Winnicott's phrase, "relaxed self-realization" (70). It can be seen that this in the tennis player is what allows him to enjoy his game and to feel alive. He has to acquire the skill and the use of the tennis racquet as an extension of himself, and the weight of the ball and the size of the court have to become a part of him through practice; as he learns something 'clicks' and the self-realization is there, "without too much of the deliberateness of trying" (70). The something that clicks has a place in the history of the individual, in that it owes something to the inherited potential and has been made possible and meaningful because of experiences at the beginning of life—maybe in the handling that has brought about a close-knit psychosomatic collusion. Further, it has a place in the history of the world because we can assume that it was because something clicked with someone using a primitive bat and ball that there developed a game of tennis (or squash, or hockey, etc.), and that there then came to be convenient places for playing these games, and groups of people gathering together to play them, and other groups gathering together to watch the experts and take pleasure in their ability to express themselves in this way, and to put all sorts of their own fantasies and feelings and identifications into the contest.

Winnicott used the same kind of example when describing his own work: "One could compare my position with that of a cellist who first slogs away at technique and then actually becomes able to play *music*, taking the technique for granted" (73). The subject of the evolution of language can be looked at in terms of our use of it to discover and express ourselves and our ideas apart from our immediate needs—to give meaning to things. This applies to science as well as to literature, for language can be used to ask questions;

in science Winnicott saw "the creative impulse appearing as a new question dependent on knowledge of existing knowledge" (81). The evolution of religious groupings, too, can be seen as "a degree of overlapping" of personal potential spaces (27). But this, of course, depends on the individual being free to choose and to create, for at times in the history of the world, and at times in the history of the individual, religion has undoubtedly to be looked at from the point of view of the oppressive boundary and consequent reaction manifested either in submission or rebellion.

In sum, the self-discovery that Winnicott describes as taking place in the potential space is the *same thing* as the realization of individual potential, including the potential to evolve new forms in which potential can be realized. It is crucial to add that he meant realization of the potential apart from where there exists "a state of tension driving towards instinct satisfaction, or else a basking in the leisure of gratification" (70). The distinction, which is at the heart of the matter, is not easy to make: it needs to be understood that it was made by Winnicott because he found the classical concepts of psychoanalysis, even including "the concept of displacement and all the mechanisms of sublimation" (70), not only within himself but also in his clinical practice, insufficient to answer the question: What is life about?

7. Time and Continuity

No statement about form and content can be complete without a mention of the boundary (and therefore the space) provided by time. Winnicott called it "the fourth dimension in integration" (122). It will be remembered that he regarded a sense of continuity in time and of finite time as an achievement; the infant is the merged state lives in infinity, not being aware that there is a past and a future. The "continuity of the line of life," without which it is not possible to describe the infant ego, is in fact supplied by the continuity in maternal care. The sense of continuous time in the infant comes to be added through the completion of *processes*—"processes which from the outside may seem to be purely physiological but which belong to infant psychology and take place in a complex psychological field, determined by the awareness and empathy of the mother" (51).

In particular, Winnicott believed that the benign sequence in the infant of impulsive action, concern, and reparation, acknowledged by a mother who survives, builds up a sense of continuity (54). It is interesting that he found that distortion in the time sense can be a feature not only in the psychotic but also in the deprived individual for whom this benign sequence has been interrupted. The delinquent can have a break in continuity that can affect his ability to connect the past with the present and therefore to imagine the effects of the present upon the future. It can be seen that this idea might tell us enough about the antisocial act to put a question mark over the relevance of the prospect of punishment as a deterrent to certain offenders. It also shows how necessary time and process are in giving form and meaning to life: "In time the end is in sight from the beginning" (122).

It is hardly possible to over-emphasize the importance of continuity in the work of a theorist and practitioner whose whole concept of life was developmental. Development takes place in time, and Winnicott believed that mutative therapy also needs a time span in which to become effective. His idea of cure was very much linked to the idea of care, the word from which it is etymologically derived—care in time that corresponds with the continuity of the holding environment (86).

He believed that for each of us there is a continuity in the handing on of the capacity to *be* as individuals from generation to generation (67). This is dependent upon natural processes facilitated by the environment at the beginning of life and therefore dependent upon us as members of society in providing for such facilitation. Out of the capacity to be arises the capacity to do—to generate as individuals, which means not only replacing the last generation and providing for the next in the biological order but also creating and recreating the cultural environment. It is perhaps the cultural continuity and evolution that principally distinguish the human condition: "Cultural experiences provide the continuity in the human race that transcends personal existence" (69).

Through such experiences each human being as a unique individual can form a bridge leading from the past into the future. But the end of the bridge that is in the past is vital, both in individual history and in the history of mankind, because our culture depends upon experience; therefore "in any cultural field it is not possible to be original except on the basis of tradition" (69). "It is a steadying thing," Winnicott wrote elsewhere, "to find that one's work links with entirely natural phenomena, and with the universals, and with what we expect to find in the best of poetry, philosophy and religion" (86).

It is interesting that Winnicott mentioned the atom bomb in conjunction with the unthinkable anxieties (77, 89). These, it will be remembered, were the different forms that fear of annihilation can take: primitive agonies suffered by the infant in relation to a break in the continuity of being. Winnicott apparently saw in our justifiable fear of the atom bomb an element of the primitive fear of discontinuity (experienced as annihilation)—an implication of the end of all the collected riches of the world built up generation by generation and of all the generations who have not lived. The idea of death is something quite different, because in this sense death is not a discontinuity. Death is a more sophisticated concept than annihilation; it implies that someone has experienced life with a place in continuous time. "There is no death except of a totality," Winnicott wrote. "Put the other way round, the wholeness of personal integration brings with it the *possibility* and indeed the *certainty* of death—and with the acceptance of death there can come a great relief, relief from fear of the alternatives, such as disintegration . . ." (83). The death of the individual does not interrupt the continuity of being in the human race.

Endpiece

There is no doubt that we owe much to thinkers in the round—to those who have had the courage to expose themselves, to risk the I AM of setting out for us a whole way of looking at the world, without tacking or trimming, and in spite of those self-doubts which are inevitable in the integrated person and in the person of integrity. To this achievement Winnicott has added a generosity of spirit not always to be found in the writer on human nature. He has not said to us, "I am telling you how the world is, so you must think as I think." He is rather saying, "On the basis of what we share, and on the basis of how we differ, I may be of use in your own creation of the world." He wanted to be "created into and with," to be "found and used." He hated the idea of being imitated.

In any case he would have been astonished at the idea of himself as philosopher or cosmologist, because it was practice that mattered to him most, and it was out of practice and for practical use that his theory emerged. At the end of a talk given to the Association of Teachers of Mathematics in 1968, he said, "For me, I feel I must get back to my last, which is quite simply the treatment psychiatrically of ill children, and the construction of a better, more accurate, and more serviceable theory of the emotional development of the human being" (83). To these ends he gave "not less than everything."

Our hope is that we may have been able, by introducing Winnicott and his theory to the reader, to allow him or her to enter into whatever has been written by Winnicott, wherever it is found, with ease and enjoyment.

Appendix: The Writing of D. W. Winnicott*

MADELEINE DAVIS

When Donald Winnicott died in 1971 he left, besides clinical material and many letters and drawings, more than 100 papers and lectures that had never been published. Two or three years after his death a committee was set up under the auspices of his widow, Clare, to decide what to do with this material and especially how best to bring his unpublished papers to publication. This project came to include all Winnicott's papers which were scattered about in journals and anthologies and also those which, though in his own books, were permanently out of print in Britain. The idea was to bring together all that he wrote for publication under his own name, so that it would be readily accessible. This was, in fact, in keeping with Winnicott's own wishes, for he had himself planned to have more books published containing a mixture of unpublished papers and papers from journals and anthologies.

Eventually the task of editing and collating the papers fell to the lot of Clare Winnicott, Ray Shepherd (a member of the British Psycho-Analytical Society) and myself. We began in earnest in 1979, meeting on Saturdays at Clare Winnicott's house. Our progress was sometimes slow owing to Clare's illness and need for periods in hospital, but we came increasingly to enjoy the work and to agree over aims, and, when we disagreed about details, to come to what we hope were careful decisions. Clare's knowledge of Donald's life was invaluable to the progress of our work, as was the vitality that she always brought to it.

By the time she died in 1984 most of the papers had been edited. We changed what Winnicott wrote as little as possible, but sometimes

---

*Originally a talk given at a Winnicott Symposium in Zurich, 1985.

we were working with papers in note form, sometimes with two ver-
sions of the same paper, and occasionally with only transcripts of talks.
After Clare Winnicott's death a few more papers were found among
Winnicott's collections of files and letters, and these have now been
added to the proposed publications.

At the outset we had to decide whether we should make a scholarly
"collected works" or whether we should place the papers in categories
according to readership. We decided on the latter course, which
seemed to make sense especially in England, where psychoanalysts are
a relatively small group, and psychoanalysis itself is regarded with a
good deal of suspicion by many people, including "the establishment"
in the medical and psychiatric professions and often in the universities
as well. On the other hand Winnicott himself has a large following in
the other helping professions in Britain, particularly among those
involved in infant and child care. It is a remarkable fact that his book
The Child, the Family and the Outside World still sells more than
10,000 copies a year even though it has existed in its present form since
1964.

We felt, then, that the papers written for people in these other professions, and for parents, should be placed with publishers who cater
for such readers; and we took into account the fact that during
Winnicott's lifetime not only *The Child, the Family and the Outside
World* but also *The Family and Individual Development*—a book
mainly for social workers—had been directed to a readership outside
psychoanalysis.

Clare Winnicott left provision upon her death for a charitable trust
to be set up. This is called The Winnicott Trust, and it exists to ensure
that monies accruing to Winnicott's estate will, in the words of the Trust
Deed, be used to promote "the training and research in the field of psychoanalysis and child health of Paediatricians, Child Psychiatrists and
other professional persons and more particularly to promote the study
of the work of Dr. D. W. Winnicott and to disseminate the results
thereof." To continue the work of publication and to deal with literary
matters she formally provided for three editors, she herself being
replaced by Christopher Bollas, a member of the British Psycho-
Analytical Society.

At this point it might be useful to set out all the titles of Winnicott's
books: first, those published in his lifetime or immediately after his

death which he himself prepared; and second, those which have been prepared since he died.

1. Clinical Notes on Disorders of Childhood 1931
 The Child and the Family 1957
 The Child and the Outside World 1957
 The Child, the Family and the Outside World 1964
 Through Paediatrics to Psycho-Analysis 1958
 The Family and Individual Development 1965
 The Maturational Processes and the Facilitating
  Environment 1965
 Therapeutic Consultations in Child Psychiatry 1971
 Playing and Reality 1971

2. The Piggle 1977
 Deprivation and Delinquency 1984
 Home Is Where We Start From 1985
 Holding and Interpretation 1985
 Selected Letters 1987
 Babies and Their Mothers 1987
 Psycho-Analytic Explorations 1989
 A Study of Human Nature 1987
 Talking to Parents
 Society and the Growing Child

What I should like to do is to relate the content of the new books to the writing already published during Winnicott's life and to relate all of this briefly to the development of his ideas.

Donald Winnicott was born in 1896 in Plymouth in Devon. His father was a merchant who prospered and who was loved and honoured in his lifetime, and Winnicott was proud of him and retained an affectionate relationship with him right until his death in 1948. Near the end of his own life, in 1967, Winnicott was asked to give a talk in Plymouth during what was called "Mental Health Week," and in some brief preliminary notes in his own hand he has written:

 DR D. W. WINNICOTT
 why me here now
 A. **Partly** because born (1896) and bred here till away to school in 1910

Devon name, & proud of it
my father was well-known

(Mayor twice
(Knighted
(& Freedom of City

B. **Partly** because became early interested
in mental health
i.e. became **paediatrician** (early 20's)
(children's doctor)
and from that graduated to **child psychiatry**
i.e. treatment and prevention of
difficulties arising in emotional growth
and development

I think it is of some importance that Sir Frederick Winnicott and his family were religious—they were church-goers belonging to the Wesleyan tradition which of course is nonconformist and which sets great store by the inner religious conviction of the individual. Winnicott tells this story about himself and his father:

My father had a simple (religious) faith and once when I asked him a question that could have involved us in a long argument he just said "Read the Bible and what you find there will be the true answer for you." So I was left, thank God, to get on with it myself (Clare Winnicott, 1978).

The school that the young Donald went to in 1910 was the Leys School in Cambridge, which by all accounts he thoroughly enjoyed. While still at school he read Darwin's *Origin of Species*, and later (in 1945) in a paper entitled "Towards an objective study of human nature" he told of his excitement at finding this book and discovering that "living things could be examined scientifically." This paper, originally published in *The Child and the Outside World* is now out of print in English. It is to be used as an introductory chapter in *Society and the Growing Child*.

No doubt Winnicott's encounter with Darwin was partly responsible for his taking a degree in Biology at Cambridge as a preliminary to his study of Medicine. I believe that it was important also for the theory of emotional development that eventually emerged, and in particular for the ideas behind what he called "the maturational processes," which is half the title of one of his most important books. What seems to be relevant here is that in the Darwinian theory of natural selection *evolution depends upon individuation as well as on reproduction*. Winnicott's emphasis on individuation goes hand in hand with his view that the maturational processes contain much more than the drives behind the adult capacity to reproduce sexually, to work and to have a conscience. He has stated that "there is a biological drive behind progress" and that "progress itself is the evolution of the individual, psyche-soma, personality and mind with (eventually) character formation and socialisation" (1954), to which may be added the capacity to "make a contribution to the world's (cultural) fertility, which is the privilege of even the least of us" (1948).

Of course it is of the essence of Winnicott's theory of development that this evolution of the individual cannot take place without a facilitating environment. But the operative word here *is* "facilitating." Sometimes people talk about infant and child care in terms of "parental *input*"—a thing I believe Winnicott would never have done. It is the baby and child who become able through the facilitating environment to give out what is in each one personally to create and contribute. The experience of the world that itself becomes a part of personal potential is essentially *active*: given "good-enough mothering" at the beginning the baby creates what is there to be found. In a broadcast talk to parents in 1949 Winnicott said:

> In each baby is a vital spark, and this urge towards life and growth and development is a part of the baby, something the child is born with and which is carried forward in a way that we do not have to understand. For instance, if you have just put a bulb in the window-box you know perfectly well that you do not have to make the bulb grow into a daffodil. You supply the right kind of earth or fibre and you keep the bulb watered just the right amount, and the rest comes naturally, because the bulb has life in it.

It is possible that here is to be found one explanation for Winnicott's insistence, which can be puzzling, that the innermost core of the self remains isolated; it remains incommunicado except in terms of life and growth, and, in his own words, "it must never be affected by external reality" (1963a).

Winnicott's medical studies were interrupted by the war, for in 1917 and 1918 he served as Surgeon Probationer with the Royal Navy on a destroyer. At the end of the war he resumed his studies at St Bartholomew's Hospital in London. Around this time he came across the writing of Freud; the account he gave of this event for an article about himself in the *St Mary's Hospital Gazette* is as follows:

> His interest in psychiatry began when, as a student at Bart's, he found that from being a good dreamer, he had ceased to be able to recall his dreams. He called in at Lewis's and asked the Librarian for a book which might enable him to make a recovery. He received a copy of one of Bergson's works, which he found quite irrelevant. He returned the book and was given a work by the Swiss parson, Pfister, on Freud . . . Pfister's book led on to Freud's own works, and reading these led Winnicott to starting his own analysis with James Strachey in 1923.

By 15 November, 1919, he was writing a long letter to his sister Violet explaining what psychoanalysis is, and saying,

> I am putting all this extremely simply. If there is anything which is not completely simple for anyone to understand I want you to tell me because I am now practising so that one day I will be able to introduce the subject to the English people.

A selection of Winnicott's many letters touching on his life and particularly his ideas has been prepared by Robert Rodman, a psychoanalyst and author from California, and has now been published.

Winnicott qualified in medicine in 1920, and in 1923 he obtained two consultant posts as Children's Physician, one at Paddington Green Children's Hospital which he held for forty years, and the other at the Queen's Hospital for Children, where he was in charge of the London County Council Rheumatic and Heart Clinic. Here he was confronted with suspected cases of rheumatic heart disease of epidemic proportion and spent much of his time learning which of his patients were in real danger and trying to see that those who merely came under suspicion were not unnecessarily restricted in their lives. Three trunks full of meticulous notes from this clinic were found in Clare Winnicott's house when she died showing how he listened to his patients and to their mothers. In his more general clinic at Paddington Green, too, he was listening and learning and taking histories, and he was later to say that

> It was as a practising paediatrician that I found the therapeutic value of history-taking . . . Psychoanalysis for me is a vast extension of history-taking, with therapeutics as a by-product (1963b).

He also wrote specifically of the value of history-taking to the mother:

> I very quickly discovered as long as forty years ago that the taking of case-histories from mothers is in itself a psychotherapy if it be well done. Time must be allowed and a non-moralistic attitude naturally adopted, and when the mother has come to the end of saying what is in her mind, she may add: Now I understand how the present symptoms fit into the whole pattern of the child's life in the family, and I can manage now, simply because you let me get at the whole story in my own way and in my own time.

This is from a paper given to a non-analytic audience in 1961 called "Varieties of psychotherapy," and it is included in *Home Is Where We Start From.*

Winnicott's training analysis with James Strachey, begun in 1923, lasted for ten years. Through this analysis, in a very special way, Winnicott became a kind of grandson to Freud himself, for it is apparent that Strachey's deep knowledge of Freud's writing and first-hand experience of the classical technique were passed on to his patient. It is possible to find throughout Winnicott's writing nuances and implications which derive from a close familiarity with Freud which he always assumed that his psychoanalytic colleagues shared.

Winnicott's clinical experiences during this period resulted in the writing of his first book, *Clinical Notes on Disorders of Childhood* (1931), in which the day to day practice of a paediatrician is looked at, taking into account the anxieties and conflicts belonging to the inner life of the child. It was a courageous book to publish at the time, marking him off from his paediatric colleagues. It is hoped that this book, which has never been translated into another language and which is long out of print, will be annotated by two paediatricians who knew him and possibly republished in the not-too-distant future. Two of its chapters are reproduced at the beginning of *Through Paediatrics to Psycho-Analysis*, and I would like to quote a passage from one of these which seems to me to be entirely characteristic of Winnicott's philosophy and of the respect which he always had for the personal process in his patients whether in the practice of medicine, psychoanalysis or child psychiatry. Winnicott is talking about a child of 2½ referred to him for loss of appetite after the birth of a baby brother.

A doctor who does not understand the processes underlying such unwellness and will think out a diagnosis and treat the illness as determined by physical causes. A doctor who understands a little about psychology will guess the underlying cause of the illness and take active measures to help the patient; for instance, he will instruct the parents not to make a difference in their treatment of the child after the baby's arrival, or will send the child away to stay with an aunt, or advise the parents to allow the child animal pets. As a prophylactic measure he will advise parents to answer fearlessly their children's questions about where babies come from, and generally to act without anxiety.

It is possible to go further and to say that a doctor who knows still more about psychology will be content to hold a watching brief, and do nothing at all, except be a friend. For he realizes that the experiencing of frustrations, disappointments, loss of what is loved, with the realization of personal unimportance and weakness, forms a significant part of the child's upbringing, and, surely, a most important aim of education should be to enable the child to manage life unaided. Moreover, the forces at work in determining the behaviour both of the parents and of the child are so hidden, with foundations so deep in the unconscious, that intellectual attempts to modify events resemble the scratching of initials on the pillars of a cathedral—they do little more than reflect the conceit of the artist.

From this period sprang Winnicott's life-long aim that there should be more people like himself versed in both paediatrics and psychoanalysis, and that child psychiatry and physical paediatrics should be brought under one umbrella and become two sides of a single subject. Unfortunately by the end of his life he became disillusioned about this aim. In an addendum to a paper written for the Association of Child Psychology and Psychiatry in 1970 he said:

There was a splendid open field for exploration in the mid-twenties. I thought that child psychiatry should be the other half of paediatrics. Those physically orientated should be glad to work with those psychiatrically orientated. I think I have proved that in this country paediatrics will never allow this. The opportunity was already lost in the late thirties and again in the mid-forties after the war, when physical paediatrics failed to relish the idea of a twin brother. We have now settled down into a state of affairs in which paediatrics has lost its psychological half to academic psychology and to adult psychiatry, nurtured in mental hospitals and the physical treatment of mental disorders, built on the assumption that mental disorders are diseases like physical diseases, which they are not.

Nevertheless his ideas had influence on a generation of paediatricians, especially those who knew at first hand the value of his clinical work. Several of these became and remained his friends.

Winnicott's unpublished writings on the different kinds of professional work involving children and on the interrelationship of the professions are included in the book *Society and the Growing Child*. Also in this book is a paper about the organization of the clinic at Paddington Green. This is interesting because Winnicott's clinic there was unique. It started off as an ordinary paediatric out-patients clinic and changed into a psychiatric clinic as he himself changed over the years, until it became so famous that it had visitors from all over the world. The change, however, was never *officially* noted: it just came gradually to be accepted.

In 1926 Melanie Klein came to England, and not long after this Winnicott was sent by James Strachey to see her. She became his supervisor in child analysis, and eventually he went to Joan Riviere, a follower of Klein's, to continue his own analysis. Winnicott has described (1962) how he found the classical theory insufficient for explaining emotional difficulties that he recognized in very small children and in babies, and how he had begun to formulate his own theories about these. Klein produced just what was needed at the time. He found her development of the classical concept of fantasy and her insistence on its primacy particularly useful. Through her work his own definition of fantasy as the "imaginative elaboration of somatic parts, feelings and functions" emerged. Especially important was the *localization* of fantasy by the

child: as he later said, in an informal talk about the origins of his ideas
given in 1967,

> From my point of view people knew about inner psychic reality
> through Freud and they knew about fantasy and dream, but it was she
> who pointed out the importance of the localization of all that goes on
> between eating and defaecation, and that it had to do with the inside
> of the body. I feel that she taught me all this without which I couldn't
> do the psycho-analysis of children at all.

And indeed, the Kleinian influence is, I think, clearly visible in the
child analysis described under the title of *The Piggle*, though of course
one has to say that if Klein herself had been doing this analysis it would
have sounded completely different.

Winnicott in fact never considered himself a "Kleinian" in spite of
his acceptance of many of her ideas. During the Second World War,
when the split occurred in the British Society as a result of the dif-
fering views of Klein and of Anna Freud and her associates, Winnicott was quietly doing his work as Physician in Charge of the
Child Analysis Department—a post which he held for twenty-five
years. After the war Winnicott's differences with Klein became manifest and to some extent explicit, the most pervasive of these being
that he believed she did not pay enough attention to the *actual*
environment that obtains in early infancy. He was convinced that it
was impossible even in theory to talk about early psychic functioning in terms of the baby alone, for without maternal care "there is
no such thing as a baby." It is interesting that his own account of
the Kleinian concept of the "depressive position," which became an
integral part of his theory of development, differs from the original
formulation at exactly this point. In the Kleinian account the conflict
leading to guilt in the infant (and eventually to social activity) is initially brought about through the antithesis *in fantasy* of the mother
as the object of instinctual love on the one hand and instinctual
aggression on the other; whereas in Winnicott's account (1963c) the
mother of instinctual aim and fantasy is simply called the "object-
mother," and the contrast is made between this object-mother and
the "environment-mother" who actually holds and handles the baby
and adapts to his needs. Winnicott wrote several papers about

Klein's ideas, most of which are reproduced in *Psycho-Analytic Explorations* along with much that he wrote about the work of other analysts as well.

It was, in fact, Winnicott's unfolding need to think and write about the early environment that led to his parting in the 1940's with Riviere, who apparently strongly disapproved of his preoccupation with the subject. A further difficulty had also presented itself, and this had to do with the attitude of workers involved with children outside of psychoanalysis. As he himself has described it (in the informal talk quoted above, which is part of *Psycho-Analytic Explorations*),

> The psychoanalysts were the only people for about ten or fifteen years in this country who knew there was anything *but* environment. Everybody was screaming out that everything was due to somebody's father being drunk. So the thing was, how to get back to the environment without losing all that was gained by studying the inner factors.

It was Winnicott's experience in the Second World War, when he was appointed Consultant Psychiatrist to the Government Evacuation Scheme in Oxfordshire, that really enabled him to put the two things, the environment and inner reality, together in his theory.

It is relevant here, I think, to mention two men versed in psychoanalysis who were pioneers in linking behaviour disorders to deprivation. One is August Aichhorn who in 1925 in his remarkable book *Wayward Youth* wrote about his experience as residential warden in an institution for delinquent adolescents, and the other is John Bowlby who in 1940 published, inter alia, a formal study of 150 children seen by him in a Child Guidance Clinic in London, in which he showed a direct link between stealing and separation from the mother during infancy. Winnicott's own findings in the war confirmed what these two had found. Children were sent from the big cities to foster-parents in the country, but a number of these children were too difficult for the foster-parents to cope with or they ran away. Hostels were set up to take these difficult children, and it was found that these were the ones who had originally come from unsettled homes, or homes where the environment was obviously deficient. Winnicott was brought face to face with the urgent problems presented by these children. Years later, in one of the last lectures he gave (1970), he told of these experiences in a description of the work done by David Wills, the warden of a hostel housed in a former Poor Law Institute at Bicester. Here is a passage from the lecture:

It was exciting to be involved in the life of this wartime hostel for evacuation failures. Naturally it collected the most unmanageable boys in the area, and a familiar sound was like this: a car would drive up at some speed, the bell-pull would start up a clatter of bells, someone would open the front door; the door would bang to the accompaniment of a car whose engine had been left running making off as if chased by a fiend. It would be found that a boy had been slipped into the front door, often with no warning phone call, and a new problem had been put on the David Wills plate . . .

At first in my weekly visits I would see a boy or two, give each a personal interview in which the most astonishing and revealing things would happen. I would sometimes get David and some of his staff to listen while I told the story of the interview, in which I made smashing interpretations based on deep insight, relative to material breathlessly presented by boys who were longing to get personal help. But I could feel my little bits of sowing falling on stony ground.

Rather quickly I learned that the therapy was being done in the institution, by the walls and the roof; by the glass conservatory which provided a target for bricks, by the absurdly large baths for which an enormous amount of wartime coal had to be used up if the water was to reach up to the navel of the swimmers.

The therapy was being done by the cook, by the regularity of the arrival of food on the table, by the warm enough and perhaps warmly coloured bedspread, by the efforts of David to maintain order in spite of shortage of staff and a constant sense of the futility of it all, because the word success belonged somewhere else, and not to the task asked of Bicester Poor Law Institution . . .

When I came to look further into what was going on I found that David was doing important things based on certain principles that we are still trying to state and to relate to a theoretical structure . . . We have to examine the things that come naturally in the home setting in order that we may do these things deliberately and adapt what we do economically to the special needs of individual children or meet special situations as they arise . . .

For me watching this work was one of the early educational knocks which made me understand that there is something about psychotherapy

which is not to be described in terms of making the right interpretation
at the right moment.

Out of such experiences arose Winnicott's particular theory of the
antisocial tendency in which he distinguished two sorts of deprivation: loss of the "good object" and loss of the reliable framework
within which the impulsive and spontaneous life of the child is safe.
He was also able to make a distinction between deprivation on the
one hand—a state of having had something and lost it, and privation
on the other—a state of never having had, with mental hospital illness, or domination by psychosis, as a consequence; and he was able
to show how in practice the antisocial tendency can overlap at one
point with the psychoses and at another with the psychoneuroses.
Especially he linked deprivation with failure to achieve the depressive position and a sense of social responsibility within the individual. At the same time he came to see the antisocial acts of the
recidivist and the psychopath, which so patently display a compulsion to repeat, and which have become hardened into a way of life,
as acts which in their first manifestations in the individual (usually
in childhood) are "signs of hope." The hope is that what has been
lost will be found again, or given back, and that the maturational
processes which have been dammed up will once more be freed. In
this way he was able to explain at least some of man's actual inhu-
manity to man without recourse to the concept of an inherited
death instinct.

We have gathered together most of what Winnicott wrote specifically
about the antisocial tendency in the book called *Deprivation and Delinquency*, which has now been published in several languages. It includes
his wartime broadcasts about evacuation and also a description of the
setting up and management of the wartime hostels, written with Clare
Britton, the Psychiatric Social Worker who worked with him at the time
and who later became his wife.

The quarter century from 1945 until Winnicott's death saw an almost
incredible surge of activity. In this period he became a master of psy-
chotherapeutic technique as well as of a theory of emotional development that was truly his own. When one considers the activities quite
apart from clinical work and routine lecturing that he was engaged in,
his achievements seem nothing short of astonishing.

He continued for many years to be Physician in Charge of the Child Department of the Institute of Psychoanalysis, responsible for training in child analysis. He held the post of Scientific Secretary to the British Psycho-Analytical Society, then Training Secretary. He was President of the Society from 1956 to 1959 and again from 1965 to 1968. He served terms of office as Chairman of the Medical Section of the British Psychological Society, President of the Paediatric Section of the Royal Society of Medicine and President of the Association for Child Psychology and Psychiatry. He took part in UNESCO and WHO study groups, and was Chairman of the committee responsible for setting up the Finnish Psychoanalytical Society, with whom he spent some time lecturing and giving seminars. He was invited to lecture throughout the U.S. in 1962–63 and in many other parts of the world at various times.

In addition to all this, at the end of the war and for about ten years thereafter, Winnicott waged a fierce battle with his colleagues in adult psychiatry over the use of leucotomy and convulsion therapy in the treatment of the mentally ill. In 1944 he organized a symposium on shock therapy at the British Psycho-Analytical Society, and he conducted a long correspondence on the subject in the columns of the *British Medical Journal* in an attempt to get medical practitioners to consider the psychological effects of ECT. To leucotomy he was passionately and at times bitterly opposed, and, particularly in the early 1950's, he spent a great deal of time and energy trying to find ways of drawing public attention to the ethical issues involved in its use. About it he wrote such things as

I realize that the correct procedure is for us to speed up research into the psychology of insanity and so to provide a scientific basis for mental hospital work, but in the meantime are we to see our countryside littered with "cured" mental hospital patients with permanently deformed brains? And what happens if these physical therapy methods spread to the treatment of criminals? What guarantee have we that a Bunyan in prison will be allowed to keep his brain intact and his imagination free, or, to take a more ordinary case, that a political prisoner should be allowed to maintain his political convictions and his brain? (1945)

The fundamental principle for which I think we must fight is that the human being has the right to suffer, and even to commit suicide, with the brain, the somatic basis for the psyche, inviolate (1951).

Several of his articles and papers on these subjects have been grouped together and placed at the end of *Psycho-Analytic Explorations*.

Perhaps the most significant professional event of the immediate post war period was Winnicott's reading of his paper "Primitive emotional development" to the British Psycho-Analytical Society in 1945. Here his thesis of early psychic functioning involving ego-integration, psychosomatic collusion and the role of illusion in the infant's adaptation to shared reality are set forth, inextricably intertwined with the maternal provision that meets the infant's needs. It was a revolutionary paper.

At the same time he was giving the series of broadcast talks to parents and others connected with children that appeared in his two books *The Child and the Family* and *The Child and the Outside World*. In these talks his new ideas were embedded in common and familiar English, without a trace of technical language or a jargon word. The "average expectable environment" being talked about by Heinz Hartmann in America had turned up in England as "the ordinary devoted mother," undergoing a sea change in the process; for I doubt if anyone has spoken with such immediacy about how ordinary parents and their babies and children actually behave and feel towards each other. Most of these original broadcast talks, as is well known, were reproduced in the new book which appeared in 1964 entitled *The Child, the Family and the Outside World*. Before Winnicott's death this book had been reprinted four times, and he was able in 1967 to attend the party given to celebrate the 50,000th copy being sold.

Around 1960 Winnicott broadcast some more talks to parents, mostly about young children. These have not been published, and they form the content of the book *Talking to Parents*, now in process of publication. This contains, among other things, talks about jealousy, about saying "no" and about what in the young child's behaviour particularly irks or annoys the mother. The book has an added interest in that during these talks Winnicott was commenting on recorded conversations between mothers themselves about these subjects, and we have been able to obtain transcripts of these conversations from the B.B.C. so that they may be included.

It was during the hugely productive time of the late 1940's and early 50's that Winnicott began to have a few patients in analysis who showed a need for prolonged regression. In 1953 he wrote in a letter to Clifford Scott, a psychoanalytic colleague and friend,

> I am now very much strengthened by my experience of having allowed
> a psycho-analytic patient to regress as far as was necessary. It did really
> happen that there was a bottom to the regression and no indication of
> a need to return following the experience of having reached the bottom
> . . . The experience of having a few regressing cases enables me to see
> more clearly what to interpret. As an example I would say that since
> experiencing regressions I more often interpret to the patient in terms
> of need and less often in terms of wish.

Several things were consolidated and emerged from these analyses,
many of them involving a fresh look at the Freudian concepts of
impingement and trauma and their implications for very early development. Not least of these, I believe, was the concept of the "false self."
While it is possible to see origins of this idea in other writers—most
noticeably, perhaps, in Ferenczi (1930, 1931)—its development and use
were very characteristic of Winnicott. Especially so was his emphasis
on the compliant aspect of the false self organization, for he had always
hated compliance, seeing it as inimical to growth and the realization
of potential. The concept of the false self could be used to explain how
schizoid elements and even schizophrenia can remain latent and unob-
served until something precipitates a breakdown in adulthood. Moreover, it was found by Winnicott to be invaluable in the diagnosis of cases
for analysis. Other ideas were also helped along by the experiences with
regressed patients: the idea, for instance, of the intellect of the infant
being exploited in order to make up for a deficient environment, which
he saw as a possible factor in the aetiology of obsessional neurosis; and
then, too, his well known elucidation of the concept of annihilation of
the ego in terms of the psychotic or "unthinkable" anxieties. All of these
ideas appear in *Through Paediatrics to Psycho-Analysis*, mostly in
papers first read at Scientific Meetings of the British Psycho-Analytical
Society. In his paper "Metapsychological and clinical aspects of regression" (1954) he wrote about the implications of this work with regard
to classical psychoanalysis, giving his own views of how the method that
Freud evolved could be used to supply some of the positive elements
that had been missing in the patient's early environment. From around
this time also dates the fullest account that Winnicott wrote of a period
in an actual analysis, using the notes that he took during the sessions.
Previously published in an anthology, this has now appeared as a sep-

arate book under the title of *Holding and Interpretation*. It has the bonus of an introduction by Masud Khan, a friend and colleague of Winnicott's who worked closely with him over the editing of his books and papers during his lifetime.

In the meantime, in 1951, there emerged the concept that had been brewing for a long time: namely that of transitional objects and transitional phenomena. This was of course based on direct observation, using Winnicott's own observations in his clinics and in the wartime hostels, and also taking into account, I believe, Willi Hoffer's observations of the hand-to-mouth activities of tiny babies in the Hampstead War Nurseries where Hoffer worked under the auspices of Anna Freud.

From all of this it was not a long step for Winnicott to gather together his ideas about the facilitating environment that had found expression especially in his broadcast talks and to present them in a more formalized way. This he did in such papers as "Primary maternal preoccupation" (1956) and the vastly important "Theory of the parent-infant relationship" (1960) where "holding" came into its own as a concept that could be developed and used both in psychotherapy and in broader areas of social work. This paper appeared in *The Maturational Processes and the Facilitating Environment*, where, as is well known, details of the early environment are developed in other talks, many of which were given to psychoanalytic audiences in the U.S.A. A further collection of papers on the subject of the environment as it affects the newborn, given to groups outside psychoanalysis, has been put together under the title of *Babies and Their Mothers*; and it is hoped that this book, published in 1987, may reach those who are professionally concerned with this area of life.

A Study of Human Nature was written by Winnicott in 1954. Its prehistory goes back a long way—to 1936, in fact, when he was asked by Susan Isaacs to lecture to post-graduate teachers at the Institute of Education in London on the subject of child development. He continued to give these lectures for twenty years, and one or two of them have survived in the form of transcripts and will be included in *Society and the Growing Child*. Through the giving of these lectures Winnicott was asked to lecture also on a regular basis to post-graduate social work students at the London School of Economics, which he did for fifteen years. In 1954 Clare Winnicott suggested to him that he should put the contents of these lectures together, and the result was this book, *A*

Study of Human Nature. It was written explicitly for post-graduate students with some knowledge of dynamic psychology, and in an introduction to it Clare wrote,

> The opportunities for regular lecturing which continued until Winnicott's death in 1971 were much valued by him because they provided him with a constant incentive to clarify his own understanding and to modify his ideas in the light of his interaction with students, and of his own experience. Winnicott evolved his own special way of communicating the material of his lectures, and year after year the students gave up trying to take notes and became involved with him in the actual process of growth and development. The original purpose of this book was to supply the notes that the students could not take, and to make them available to all students of human nature.

The book was annotated by Winnicott from time to time, especially in the last years of his life. It is unique in that is is the only place that Winnicott talks at length about the Freudian theory of the psychosexual origins of the psychoneuroses. From here the book goes backwards through the depressive position of Klein to early psychic development in the infant.

During the 1950's Winnicott also perfected the Squiggle Game which he used in the therapeutic consultations with children, mostly of latency age, for which he became famous in his lifetime. Many of these cases are of course gathered together in his book *Therapeutic Consultations in Child Psychiatry* which was published just after his death. A description of the Squiggle Game and a description of the usefulness of the single therapeutic consultation are included in *Psychoanalytic Explorations.* Winnicott himself has said that he only really became proficient at squiggles at around the age of 60, and it seems likely that this new proficiency corresponded with the immense capacity he had during the last twenty or so years of his life to do the thing that he called playing. Throughout these years he made many hundreds of squiggles and drawings of his own as a way of relaxing, and even his signature on letters became a source of this kind of pleasure, like those in *Figure 1.*

His obvious enjoyment of life during these years, along with the extraordinary surge of freedom and originality in the area of his work, I am sure owed much to his second marriage, to Clare Britton, whose essay about him and about their life together has been included in *Psycho-Analytic Explorations.* In addition to this, Clare's involvement in social work and her position as Director of Child Care Studies at the Home Office reinforced Winnicott's concern that those doing professional work with children should have a firm basis for what they did. Many of his lectures to social workers are to be found in *The Family and Individual Development,* a book that he dedicated to Clare, and others will be published in *Society and the Growing Child.*

In the 1960's when Winnicott was elaborating his ideas about the "good-enough environment" he elaborated also the other side of the picture—the psychoses as "environmental deficiency disease." Three

Figure 1

papers from this era have been included in *Psycho-Analytic Explora-tions*; one of them is his account of "Fear of breakdown" as the fear of a breakdown that has already happened in infancy through environmen-tal failure. Besides this, he continued to develop his ideas about playing and about symbolism, linking the playing of the child backward to the use of transitional phenomena and forward to the mature individual's capacity to discover the self in all aspects of the environment, and in so doing to make a contribution to the world. In his book *Playing and Reality* (1971) he acknowledges his debt in this area to Marion Milner and to an exchange of ideas with her that began in the early 1940's. Another name that should be mentioned in this connexion is that of Margaret Lowenfeld, whose association with Winnicott dated from the 1920's, and whose vast experience and detailed descriptions of the play of children undoubtedly helped in the shaping of his ideas.

Although most of the papers that Winnicott wrote in the later 1960's about playing were included by him in *Playing and Reality,* a few that are peripheral to the subject were found after his death, marked at the top with the words "Belonging to Book." Some of these have been put into *Psycho-Analytic Explorations*, and two have found their way into *Home Is Where We Start From.* This last book contains a selection of papers that we considered of interest to a very wide readership: besides dealing with individual development they embrace such topics as war, democracy, freedom and feminism. It has now been published in sev-eral languages.

In 1968 Winnicott gave a lecture to the New York Psychoanalytic Society about his newest concept, the "use of an object," which describes how infants and also patients in treatment can emerge from the realm of the magic effects of fantasy, including the magical behav-iour of an object (person), and can live in a world of real relationships. This comes about through the destruction in fantasy of the object, which is then seen to survive in actuality without change to retaliation. The lecture did not meet with a very favourable reception at the time, but there is no doubt that Winnicott considered the expression of his idea, which had a long pre-history in experience gleaned from the prac-tice of psychoanalysis, as extremely important to his scheme of emo-tional development. It was a bit of the foundation of his edifice that had hitherto remained unlaid. In his book *A Study of Human Nature* he left a footnote concerning his view of the primary nature of destructiveness in the individual, and to this he added, in 1970, that the reason he had not been able to publish the book was that he had only lately arrived at the "use of an object" concept.

As was his wont, Winnicott tied his concept down to infant development—not only to the purely psychic but also to cognitive development, because for him these were inseparable. In this way he added a new dimension to what is known to developmental psychology of the achievement of object permanence. But it is perhaps especially to psychoanalysts and psychotherapists that this concept speaks, finding as it does in the destructiveness of the patient a drive towards a wholeness that can become actual because of the survival of the therapist, of his professionalism and of his technique.

The original lecture on "the use of an object" is in *Playing and Reality,* but some preliminary work for it and his answers to the criticisms it evoked are included in *Psycho-Analytic Explorations.* So too is an unfinished paper dating from 1969 called "The use of an object in the context of Moses and Monotheism" which links the concept to the writing of Freud and involves a discussion of the place of the father in the infant's life—something rare in Winnicott's theoretical work.

Psycho-Analytic Explorations also contains material relating to another of Winnicott's last ideas, which was to take a look at very early psychic functioning in terms of the pure male and female elements that are to be found mingled in each individual. He linked the female element to "being" (identity) and the male element to "doing." In this way he arrived at the phrase "the doing that arises out of being" as a definition of creativity, or living creatively, or playing, which he believed to be "the most important evidence we have that man is alive and that the thing that is alive is man."

APPENDIX REFERENCES

AICHHORN, A. (1925). *Wayward Youth.* London: Imago.

BOWLBY, J. (1940). The influence of early environment in the development of neurosis and neurotic character. *Int. J. Psychoanal.,* 21: 154–178.

FERENCZI, S. (1930, 1931). Notes and fragments. In *Final Contributions to Psycho-Analysis.* London: Hogarth Press, 1955.

WINNICOTT, C. (1978). D. W. W.: A reflection. In *Between Reality and Fantasy,* ed. S. Grolnick & L. Barkin. New York: Jason Aronson.

WINNICOTT, D. W. (1945). Physical therapy in mental disorder. *Brit. Med. J.,* 22 December 1945.

————(1948). Paediatrics and psychiatry. In *Through Paediatrics to Psycho-Analysis.* London: Hogarth Press, 1975.

————(1949). The baby as a going concern. In *The Child, the Family and the Outside World.* London: Penguin Books, 1964.

————(1951). Ethics of prefrontal leucotomy. Letter to the Editor. *Brit. Med. J.,* 25th August 1951.

————(1954). Metapsychological and clinical aspects of regression. In *Through Paediatrics to Psycho-Analysis.* London: Hogarth Press, 1975.

————(1962). A personal view of the Kleinian contribution. In *The Maturational Processes and the Facilitating Environment.* London: Hogarth Press, 1965.

————(1963a). Classification. In *The Maturational Processes and the Facilitating Environment.* London: Hogarth Press, 1965.

————(1963b). Training for child psychiatry. In *The Maturational Processes and the Facilitating Environment.* London: Hogarth Press, 1965.

————(1963c). The development of the capacity for concern. In *The Maturational Processes and the Facilitating Environment.* London: Hogarth Press, 1965.

————(1970). Residential care as therapy. In *Deprivation and Delinquency.* London: Tavistock Publications, 1984.

Bibliography

Part A of this list includes all the papers by D.W. Winnicott from which we have quoted in the text. It is not a complete bibliography. The papers are given in the order in which they appear in Winnicott's own books, but we have also placed in parentheses before the title the date on which a paper first appeared, either in a previous publication, as a lecture, or as a broadcast talk. Part B includes other authors to whom we have referred. In all cases the arabic numeral corresponds to the same numeral in the text.

PART A

(a) *The Child, the Family and the Outside World* (London: Penguin Books, 1964 etc.; U.S.: Addison-Wesley, 1987)

   1. (1957) Introduction
   2. (1949) A Man Looks at Motherhood
   3. (1944) Getting to Know Your Baby
   4. (1949) The Baby as a Going Concern
   5. (1944) Infant Feeding
   6. (1949) Close-up of Mother Feeding Baby
   7. (1949) The World in Small Doses
   8. (1949) The Baby as a Person
   9. (1949) Weaning
  10. (1947) Further Thoughts on Babies as Persons
  11. (1949) The Innate Morality of the Baby
  12. (1944) What About Father?
  13. (1946) What Do We Mean by a Normal Child?
  14. (1945) The Only Child
  15. (1942) Why Children Play
  16. (1944) Support for Normal Parents
  17. (1946) Educational Diagnosis

18. (1946) Aspects of Juvenile Delinquency

(b) *Collected Papers: Through Paediatrics to Psycho-Analysis* (London: Hogarth, 1975; N.Y.: Basic Books, 1958)

19. (1931) A Note on Normality and Anxiety

20. (1941) The Observation of Infants in a Set Situation

21. (1945) Primitive Emotional Development

22. (1948) Paediatrics and Psychiatry

23. (1949) Birth Memories, Birth Trauma, and Anxiety

24. (1947) Hate in the Countertransference

25. (1950) Aggression in Relation to Emotional Development

26. (1952) Psychoses and Child Care

27. (1951) Transitional Objects and Transitional Phenomena

28. (1949) Mind and Its Relation to the Psyche-Soma

29. (1954) The Depressive Position in Relation to Normal Emotional Development

30. (1954) Metapsychological and Clinical Aspects of Regression

31. (1956) Primary Maternal Preoccupation

32. (1956) The Antisocial Tendency

(c) *The Family and Individual Development* (London: Tavistock; N.Y.: Basic Books, 1965)

33. (1958) The First Year of Life: Modern Views on Emotional Development

34. (1960) The Relationship of a Mother to Her Baby at the Beginning

35. (1950) Growth and Development in Immaturity

36. (1960) On Security

37. (1957) Integrative and Disruptive Factors in Family Life

38. (1958) The Family Affected by Depressive Illness in One or Both Parents

39. (1960) The Effect of Psychosis on Family Life

40. (1959) The Effect of Psychotic Parents on the Emotional Development of the Child

41. (1961) Adolescence: Struggling Through the Doldrums

42. (1960) The Family and Emotional Maturity

43. (1958) Theoretical Statement of the Field of Child Psychiatry

44. (1957) The Contribution of Psycho-Analysis to Midwifery

45. (1950) The Deprived Child and How He Can Be Compensated for Loss of Family Life

46. (1955) Group Influences and the Maladjusted Child: The School Aspect

47. (1950) Some Thoughts on the Meaning of the Word Democracy

(d) *The Maturational Processes and the Facilitating Environment* (London: Hogarth; N.Y.: I.U.P., 1965)

48. (1965) Introduction

49. (1958) Psycho-Analysis and the Sense of Guilt

50. (1958) The Capacity to Be Alone

51. (1960) The Theory of the Parent-Infant Relationship

52. (1962) Ego Integration in Child Development

53. (1962) Providing for the Child in Health and Crisis

54. (1963) The Development of the Capacity for Concern

55. (1963) From Dependence towards Independence in the Development of the Individual

56. (1963) Morals and Education

57. (1957) On the Contribution of Direct Child Observation to Psycho-Analysis

58. (1960) Ego Distortion in Terms of the True and False Self

59. (1962) A Personal View of the Kleinian Contribution

60. (1963) Communicating and Not Communicating Leading to a Study of Certain Opposites

61. (1963) Training for Child Psychiatry

62. (1963) Psychotherapy of Character Disorders

63. (1963) The Mentally Ill in Your Caseload

(e) *Playing and Reality* (London: Penguin Books, 1974; N.Y.: Basic Books, 1971)

64. (1971) Introduction

65. (1968) Playing: A Theoretical Statement

66. (1968) Playing: Creative Activity and the Search for the Self

67. (1970) Creativity and its Origins

68. (1968) The Use of an Object and Relating Through Identifications

69. (1967) The Location of Cultural Experience

70. (1970) The Place Where We Live

71. (1967) Mirror-role of Mother and Family in Child Development

72. (1968) Contemporary Concepts of Adolescent Development

(f) *Therapeutic Consultations in Child Psychiatry* (London: Hogarth; N.Y.: Basic Books, 1971)

73. (1970) Introduction

74. Case 1 'Iiro' aet 9 years 9 months

(g) *Deprivation and Delinquency* (London and N.Y.: Tavistock, 1984)

75. (1947) (with Clare Britton) Residential Management as Treatment for Difficult Children

76. (1939) Aggression

77. (1966) The Absence of a Sense of Guilt

78. (1946) Some Psychological Aspects of Juvenile Delinquency

79. (1965) Do Progressive Schools Give too much Freedom to the Child?

80. (1961) Varieties of Psychotherapy

(h) *Home Is Where We Start From* (London: Penguin Books; N.Y.: W.W.Norton, 1986)

81. (1961) Psycho-Analysis and Science: Friends or Relations?

82. (1970) Living Creatively

83. (1968) Sum, I AM

84. (1964) The Concept of the False Self

85. (1967) Delinquency as a Sign of Hope

86. (1970) Cure

87. (1957) The Mother's Contribution to Society

88. (1966) The Child in the Family Group

89. (1965) The Price of Disregarding Psychoanalytic Research

90. (1964) This Feminism

91. (1940) Discussion of War Aims

92. (1969) Freedom

93. (1970) The Place of the Monarchy

(i) *Babies and Their Mothers* (London: Free Association Books; U.S.: Addison-Wesley, 1987)

94. (1966) The Ordinary Devoted Mother

95. (1968) Breast-Feeding as Communication

96. (1966) The Beginning of the Individual

97. (1967) Environmental Health in Infancy

98. (1968) Communication Between Infant and Mother, and Mother and Infant, Compared and Contrasted

99. (1967) Preliminary notes for the above (see appendix)

(j) *Psycho-Analytic Explorations* (London: Karnac Books; Boston: Harvard, 1989)

100. (1957) Excitement in the Aetiology of Coronary Thrombosis

101. (1963) Fear of Breakdown

102. (1965) The Concept of Trauma

103. (1965) The Psychology of Madness

104. (1965) New Light on Children's Thinking

105. (1966) A Note on the Mother-Foetus Relationship

106. (1967) The Concept of Clinical Regression Compared with that of Defence Organisation

107. (1969) The Use of an Object in the Context of Moses and Monotheism

108. (1969) The Mother-Infant Experience of Mutuality

109. (1970) Basis for Self in Body

110. (1970) Individuation

111. (1968) The Squiggle Game

112. (1962) The Beginnings of a Formulation of an Appreciation and Criticism of Klein's Envy Statement

113. (1947) Physical Therapy of Mental Disorder

114. (1969) Physiotherapy and Human Relations

(k) *Talking to Parents* (in process of publication)

115. (1957) Health Education Through Broadcasting

116. (1969) The Building Up of Trust

117. (1956) How Much Do We Know about Babies as Cloth Suckers?

118. (1960) On Saying No

119. (1960) What Irks

(l) *Society and the Growing Child* (in process of publication)

120. (1945) Towards an Objective Study of Human Nature

121. (1948) Primary Introduction to External Reality

122. (1961) The Time Factor in Treatment

123. (1954) Pitfalls in Adoption

124. (1966) Autism

125. (1968) Sleep Refusal in Children

126. (1967) The Association for Child Psychology and Psychiatry Observed as a Group Phenomenon

127. (1970) A Personal Statement about Dynamic Psychology

128. (1970) The Practice of Child Psychiatry

129. (1968) A Link Between Paediatrics and Child Psychiatry

(m) *The Spontaneous Gesture* (Boston: Harvard, 1987)

130. (1969) Letter to Robert Tod

PART B

131. Bower, Tom "How Much Can Babies Take In?" in *The Perceptual World of the Child* (Glasgow: Fontana, 1977)

132. Bower, Tom "Perception and Development" in *The Perceptual World of the Child* (Glasgow: Fontana, 1977)

133. Brazelton, T.B. Discussion following "Human Maternal Behaviour after Delivery" in *Parent-Infant Interaction:* Ciba Foundation Symposium 33 (new series) (Amsterdam: Elsevier, Excerpta Medica, 1975)

134. Brody, Sylvia "Transitional Objects: Idealisation of a Phenomenon" in *The Psychoanalytic Quarterly,* XLIX, October, 1980

135. Dare, C. "Psychoanalytic Theories" in *Child Psychiatry: Modern Approaches* ed. Rutter and Hersov (Oxford: Blackwell, 1976)

136. Fairbairn, W.R.D. *Psychoanalytic Studies of the Personality* (London & Boston: R.K.P., 1952 etc.)

137. Ferenczi, Sandor "Stages in the Development of the Sense of Reality" in *First Contributions to Psycho-Analysis* (London: Hogarth, 1952; N.Y.: Basic Books, 1955)

138. Freud, Sigmund *Formulations Regarding the Two Principles of Mental Functioning* Standard Edition XII

139. Freud, Sigmund *The Ego and the Id* Standard Edition XIX

140. Isaacs, Susanna "Donald Woods Winnicott 1896–1971" in *Scientific Bulletin No.57* (The British Psycho-Analytical Society)

141. Khan, M. Masud R. "Text for the Winnicott Memorial Meeting, 19th. January, 1972" in *Scientific Bulletin No. 57* (The British Psycho-Analytical Society)

142. Klaus, Marshall H. and Kennell, John H. "Human Maternal and Paternal Behaviour" in *Maternal-Infant Bonding* (St. Louis: C.V. Mosby Co., 1976)

143. Liedloff, Jean *The Continuum Concept* (London: Futura; U.S.: Addison-Wesley, 1976)

144. MacFarlane, Aidan "Life Before Birth" in *The Psychology of Childbirth* (Glasgow: Fontana, 1977)

145. Piaget, Jean "Explanation of Play" in *Play, Dreams and Imitation in Childhood* (London: R.K.P., 1967)

146. Piaget, J. and Inhelder, B. "The Semiotic or Symbolic Function" in *The Psychology of the Child* (London: R.K.P., 1969)

147. Rose, Steven "Where Brains Fail: Madness and Mysticism" in *The Conscious Brain* (Penguin Books, 1976)

148. Schaffer, Rudolph "The Organisation of Infant Behaviour" in *Mothering* (Glasgow: Fontana, 1977)

149. Schaffer, Rudolph "Do Babies Need Mothers?" in *Mothering* (Glasgow: Fontana, 1977)

150. Tizard, J.P.M. "Obituary: Donald Winnicott" in *International Journal of Psycho-Analysis* 52, (1971)

151. Winnicott, Clare *D.W.W.: A Reflection in Psycho-Analytic Explorations* (London: Karnac; Boston: Harvard, 1989)

152. Wilson, E.O. *Sociobiology: A New Synthesis* (Boston: Harvard, 1975)

Index

Adolescence, 9, 81–5, 149,
Adoption of children, 92, 108, 156
Aggression, 20, 58, 69, 72, 76, 78–79,
  84, 118, 146, 149, 164,
  and adolescence, 84
  and antisocial tendency, 80
  and capacity for concern, 74–6
  and death instinct, 3, 69
  and depressive position, 182
  Kleinian view of, 13, 69
  as life force, 69
  and separation of me/not me, 70
  and object permanence, 70–71
Aichhorn, August, 183
Alone, the capacity to be, 34–36, 61
Ambivalence, 75
Anencephalic infants, 50
Annihilation, 44, 171, 188
Antisocial tendency, 15, 78–81, 84, 145,
  148, 164, 170, 185
  and adolescence, 84, 149
  and democracy, 145–6
  and deprivation, 78, 164, 185
  and destructiveness, 78, 80, 164
  and family management, 78–80
  and hope, 79–80, 185
  and psychopathy, 80, 185
  and stealing, 78, 80
  and time sense, 170
Anxiety, 3, 9, 14, 19, 44, 46, 58, 75,
  76, 80, 148, 152, 157, 165, 171,
  in Spatula Game, 19
  unthinkable, 44, 46, 80, 171, 188

Apperception, 65
Artists:
  and creativity, 165
  and form 139, 140
  and integrity, 49
Association for Child Psychology and
  Psychiatry, 180, 186
Association of Social Workers, 100
Association of Teachers of
  Mathematics, 172
Asthma, 18–19
Autism, 46, 47, 115
Autonomy and self-control, 142

Babies. See Infants
Babies and Their Mothers (Winnicott),
  175, 189
Baby, no such thing as a, 30–31, 182
Benzie, Isa, 122
Being:
  vs. annihilation, 44, 106, 171
  continuity of, 33, 40, 45, 89, 97–8,
    115, 169–71
  and female element, 89, 103
  and doing, 89, 103, 170, 193,
Bergson, H.L., 178
Bicester Poor Law Institution, 184
Biology, 9, 11, 27, 166–7, 176
  and adolescence, 9
  and culture, 166
  and inner psychic reality, 166
  and mothers, 87–90
  and psychoanalysis, 11

Birth:
  experience/memory of, 90, 92–3,
    153–4
  trauma from, 45
Bisexuality, 89
Body. *See also* Personalization;
    Psychosomatic collusion
  and coordination, 37–8, 101–2
  as dwelling place of the self, 37–8,
    100, 103
  experience, 19, 166
  functioning, 19, 28, 29, 37–8, 89,
    100, 103, 166
  involvement, 39, 62, 92–3, 154–5,
  reaction, 44, 105–6
Bollas, Christopher, 174
Bonding, parent-infant, 105
Borstal Governors, 78
Bower, Tom, 38, 67,
Bowlby, John, 16, 183
Brazelton, T. Berry, 94–5,
Breakdown, fear of, 47, 192
Breast-feeding, 40–41, 103–5, 155. *see
    also* Infants; Mothers
British Medical Journal, 186
British Psycho-Analytical Society, 173,
    174, 182, 186, 187
British Psychological Society, 186
Britton, Clare, 185, 190–1. *See also*
    Winnecott, Clare
Broadcast talks to parents, 187
Brody, Sylvia, 59

Cambridge University, 176
Cathexis, 69, 71
Child and the Family, The (Winnicott),
    175, 187
*Child, the Family and the Outside
World, The* (Winnicott), 174, 175, 187
Child and the Outside World, The
    (Winnicott), 175, 176, 187
Child Guidance Clinic, 183
Child Psychiatry, and physical
    pediatrics, 180–1

Children, *xii*, 6–8. *See also* Infants;
    Mothers; Playing
  antisocial tendency in, 15, 78–81, 84,
    164
  and authority, 153
  and family, 131–36
  handicapped, 101
  handling of, 100–2
  holding of, 97–100
  imagination in, 108–9
  irksomeness in, 123–4, 187
  and object presenting, 103–10
  observation of, 16
  playing of, 61–3, 91, 121, 133,
    156–60, 161
  and schooling, 148–9
  and Second World War, 15
  self-control of, 144
  sexuality of, 14
*Clinical Notes on Disorders of
    Childhood* (Winnicott), 10, 139,
    175, 179–80
"Close-up of Mother Feeding Baby"
    (Winnicott), 103
Cognitive development, 67, 71, 193
Convulsion Therapy, 186
Communication:
  arising out of need, 115
  direct/indirect, 114–15, 121
  and ego-relatedness, 113–21
  having no means of, 44
  and playing/potential space, 65, 121
  of reliability, 112–13, 115
  in psychoanalysis, 12, 114, 163
  and Squiggle Game, 21–22
Completion:
  of experiences, 21, 76
  of processes, 95–7, 98, 169–70
Compliance, 4, 48, 49, 51, 56, 65,
    73–4, 79, 143–4, 147, 156, 188.
    See also False self
Compromise:
  in adolescence, 83
  in inner reality, 142

social, 49, 74
Concern:
  the capacity for, 73–8, 109
  and constructive work, 75–6
  and responsibility in infants, 75
  and responsibility in parents, 91–2
Continuity, 43, 169–71. *See also* Being;
  Time
  of Culture, 66, 170–71
Continuum Concept, The (Liedloff), 102
Creativity, 3–4, 64, 88, 115, 161–5,
  167, 169, 193
  and compulsion, 60, 165
  creative apperception, 64, 118, 119,
  161
Culture:
  and biology, 166
  and continuity, 66, 170–71
  and opportunity for, 109, 152, 177
  and playing/potential space, 61, 66,
  159–69
  and transitional objects, 59

Darwin, Charles, 8, 88, 176, 177
Davis, Madeleine, 173–93
De-adaptation/failure, 51, 52, 73,
  110–13, 127
Death, 171
Death instinct, 3, 69, 185
Defiance, 83
Delinquency. *See* Antisocial tendency
Delusions, 64
Democracy, 144–7, 151, 192. *See also*
  Freedom
Dependence, 30–31, 46, 48, 50, 53, 66,
  69, 86, 106
  absolute, 31, 39, 46, 99, 107, 110,
  120, 123, 126, 153–6
  in adolescence, 83
  and fear of domination, 127–8
  of infants, 30–31, 53, 127, 153–6
  and intellectual development, 49–52
  and mothers, 126–8, 153
  relative, 31, 53, 78, 110

stages of, 31
Depersonalization, 101. *See also*
  Personalization
Depression, 76, 96, 150–51
Depressive position, 182, 185, 190
Deprivation:
  and antisocial tendency, 78–81, 148,
  164, 183
  and environmental failure, 78–81,
  113, 164
  vs. privation 78, 185
  value of, 81
Deprivation and Delinquency
  (Winnicott) 175, 185
Destructiveness:
  and aggression, 69, 72, 192
  and antisocial tendency, 78, 79–80,
  164, 193
  by chance, 69, 73
  and concern, 74–5
  and object permanence, 70, 75
Devotion, maternal, 121–6. *See also*
  Mothers
Diagnosis, 12, 16, 18, 46, 140
Displacement, 169
Doing, 40, 89, 103, 193
Donne, John, 66
Dream (ing):
  of creating children, 91
  estrangement from, 163
  of flying, 108
  and playing, 61
  vs. waking life, 71
  world of infant, 163

Ego, 29, 50, 113, 188. *See also* Self
  boundary of, 120
  and communication, 113–21
  competence of, 89
  defences in 46–8, 158
  dissociation/splitting of, 46, 77
  and holding, 101–102
  of infants, 28–29, 65, 113–21

integration of, 33–5, 75, 101–102,
    187
and maturation, 81
needs of, 115
and object relating, 40
psychology of, 28, 30–1
relatedness of, 35, 56, 65, 69,
    113–21
support of, 43, 46, 54, 73, 78, 79,
    98–100, 105
Ego and the Id, The (Freud), 37
Electroconvulsive therapy (E.C.T.), 23,
    186
Empathy, 72, 98, 112, 117, 121, 124
Environment: *see also* Merging; Setting
    182–3
deficiency in, 46–7, 188
facilitating, 177
indestructible, 79, 130, 148
vs. internal processes, 31, 86
facilitating, 177, 189
failure of, 43–4, 79, 192. *See also*
    Impingement
good-enough, 31, 34, 47, 51, 78, 191.
    See also Mothers
growth of, 7, 110
holding-, 44, 99, 159
-mother, 74, 114, 182
Winnicott's observation of, 7
Esther, history of, 96–7
Evolutionary approach, 88, 177
Experience, Experiencing:
area of, 56, 64–5
body, 19, 169
completion of, 19, 76
cultural, 62, 66, 162, 164, 170
and fantasy, 19
vs. inherited tendencies, 160, 166
life-, of infant and child, 160, 162,
    164
in mothers, 90–2, 106
of mutuality, 65, 92, 116–7
of omnipotence, 39–43, 50, 56, 63–4,
    106, 111, 116

in parents, 90–2
and playing/potential space, 63–4,
    65, 159–66

Fairbairn, W.R.D., 114
False self, 48–9, 188. *See also*
    Compliance
and intellect, 49–52
and morality, 74
Family, 131–36, 142–3. *See also*
    Parents
break-up of, 79, 132
interference with, 152, 157–9
and management, 80, 147–8
and playing/transitional
    phenomena, 134–5
and security, 134, 143–4, 148
and society, 132–3, 134, 143, 151–2
and symbolism, 135, 160–1
and therapy, 80–1, 135, 152–3
and unconscious fantasy, 136
Winnicott's family, 3–4
Family and Individual Development,
    The (Winnicott), 13, 174, 175, 191
Fantasy, 29, 34, 68, 70, 71, 82, 89, 91,
    101, 181–2, 192
of infants, 19–20, 40, 44, 89, 182
of mothers, 92–3, 101–2
and Kleinian contribution, 181–82
and mutuality, 117
definition of, 181
unconscious and adolescence, 82
unconscious and destruction of
    object, 70–71
unconscious and family, 136
unconscious and object-mother, 74–5
unconscious and sex, 91–2, 132
unconscious and Spatula Game,
    19–20
Fathers, 92, 128–30, 193. *See also*
    Mothers
strength of and family circle, 148
Winnicott's father, 4, 176
"Fear of breakdown," (Winnicott), 192

Female element, 89, 103, 193
Feminism, 128, 192
Ferenczi, Sandor, 42, 188
Fetus. *See also* Infants
    and familiarity with mother, 106–7
    and healing, 100–101
    mobility/motility of, 69
Finnish Psychoanalyitcal Society, 186
Form and content, 143–5. *See also*
    Setting
*Formulations Regarding the Two
    Principles of Mental Functioning*
    (Freud), 41
Freedom, 192. *See also* Democracy
    vs. anxiety, 158
    vs. determinism, 167
    of instincts, 76, 89, 143, 160
    and personality, 146
    strain of, 146
    support for, 158–9
    the threat to, 157
    and vigilance, 157
Freud, Anna, 15, 16, 182, 189
Freud, Sigmund, 3, 11, 13–14, 16,
    28–29, 33, 37, 40, 41, 42, 43, 54,
    69, 88, 89, 113, 120, 166, 178,
    179, 188, 190, 193

Gorton, Neville, 168
Government Evacuation Scheme, 183
Guilt, 76, 79, 80, 91–2, 182
Guy's Hospital, 25

Hallucination, 41, 58, 163
Hampstead War Nurseries, 189
Handling of infants 38–9, 100–3
Hartmann, Heinz, 187
Hate:
    and aggression, 69
    in infants, 69, 130
    in mothers, 123–4
    and sentimentality, 123, 149–50
    Winnicott's, of delinquent boy, 6–7
Health:

and absence of illness, 163
    and normality, 20
    and richness, 165
Health education, 156
Heraclitus, 141
Heredity, 46, 89, 160, 165–6
History-taking, 24, 179
Hoffer, Willi, 189
Holding, 89, 97–100, 189
    concept of, 21, 35
Holding and Interpretation (Winnicott),
    175, 189
Home Is Where We Start From
    (Winnicott), 175, 179, 192
Horder, Lord, 24
Hughes, Ted 127
Human Nature (Winnicott), 175,
    189–90, 192
Human nature, 9, 13–14, 88, 166, 172
Hypnotism, 11

'I am', 33, 34, 52, 74, 82, 143, 172
Id, 36, 40, 50, 75, 76, 115. *See also*
    Instincts
    and adolescence, 82
    demands of, 28
    needs of, 115
Identification
    with authority, 145
    with children, 133
    maternal-infant, 89–90, 92–3, 97,
        106, 122–3. *See also* Merging;
        Primary maternal preoccupation
    with others, 71, 115, 120–1, 127–8
    with society, 145
Illusion, 55–6, 60, 64, 66, 67, 108, 187.
    See also Omnipotence
Impingement, 40, 43–5, 48, 66, 143,
    151, 188. *See also* Stimulus
Incorporation/elimination fantasies, 20
Individuation, 177
Infant(s). *See also* Children; Fetus;
    Mothers; Omnipotence; Playing
    aggression in, 69–70

and de-adaptation/failure, 110–13
and dependence, 30–31, 53, 127,
    153–4
ego of, 29–30, 66, 113–21
and environment, 86–7
and false self, 48–9
and family, 131–6
fantasy of, 19–20, 41, 44, 89,
and father, 193
handicapped, 101, 111
handling of, 100–102
holding of, 97–100
and illusion, 56–7
and impingement/trauma, 43–5
integration of, 32–7, 68
and morality, 73–8, 142
and object relations/omnipotence,
    39–43, 103–10
observation of, 17
separation of, 68, 142, 161
sexuality of, 14
and Spatula Game, 17–24, 111
subjective state of, 39, 164
theory of emotional development in,
    15, 27–28
and time, 68, 76, 169–70
and transitional objects/phenomena,
    57–61
Inherited potential, 31, 33, 44, 169,
In Memoriam (Tennyson), 25, 72
Innate Morality of the Baby, The
    (Winnicott), 139
Insanity, psychology of, 186
Instincts, 3, 14, 28, 39, 69 76, 88, 89,
    98, 113. *See also* id
Institute of Education, 189
Institute of Psychoanalysis, 186
Integration, 32–34, 37, 52, 68, 74, 77,
    78, 99–100, 142, 171
Intellect. *See also* Thinking
and awareness of maternal care 51,
    52
and adaptation to reality, 51
and the false self, 49–52, 188

and thinking, 50–51
Internalized good environment, 36, 93,
    101, 142, 164. *See also* Introjection
Introjection, 48, 120
and projection, 120
I.Q., 12
Isaacs, Susan, 16, 189
Isolation of the self, 177

Jealousy, 187
Jesus College, Cambridge, 9

Kennell, John, 114, 119–20
Keynes, John Maynard, 157
Khan, Masud, 189
Klaus, Marshall, 114, 119–20
Klein, Melanie, 13, 15, 16, 19, 29, 54,
    69, 74, 120, 166, 181–2, 190

Lacan, Jacques, 118
Language, 116, 168
Leucotomy, 23, 186
Leys School, 176
Liedloff, Jean, 102
Little's disease, 46
London County Council Rheumatic
    and Heart Clinic, 178
London School of Economics, 189
Love:
    affectionate, 66, 75, 114, 116
    and aggression, 70
    and destruction, 70, 75
    and ego-relatedness, 113-4
    the infant's, 70, 76, 130, 182
    the mother's, 98, 101, 113–4, 123,
        163
Lowenfeld, Margaret, 192

Macbeth, 161
Male elements, 193
Management:
    in adolescence, 81, 83, 149
    and the antisocial tendency, 81, 145
    in the family, 80, 148–9

in infancy, 104–5, 180
and permissiveness, 149–50
in society, 143, 148, 151
vs. theory, 8, 83
Man Who Came to Dinner, The, 122
Marriage, 92, 132
Maternal-Infant Bonding (Klaus and Kennell), 119–20
Maturational Processes and the Facilitating Environment (Winnicott), 175, 189
Maturity, 3–4, 55, 176–7
and emotional development, 21, 35
and morality, 73–4
Me/not me, 33, 39, 53–4, 57, 68, 70, 103, 111, 142, 160
Memory, 50
Mended failures, 113, 115–6
Merging, 52, 64, 68, 95–6, 99, 103, 111, 112, 115, 127, 129, 134–5
"Meta psychological and clinical aspects of regression," 188
Metapsychology, 93
Milner, Marion, 192
Mind, 50–1
Mirror-role of mother, 118
Monarchy, 147
Morality:
  of infants, 69–73, 142
  innate, 20, 69–73, 167
  and maturity, 73–4
  and mothers, 73–4, 77
Morley, Robert 122
Mothering (Schaffer), 87
Mother(s), 56, 58, 87–136. *See also* Primary maternal preoccupation
and adaptation, 40, 44, 50–1, 105, 111, 163–4
and aggression, 69–73
and biology, 87–90
and communication, 113–21
and dependence, 126–8, 153–4
education of, 124, 156
and ego-relatedness, 35, 74, 113–21

environment/object-mother, 75, 114, 182–3
and experience accumulation, 90–3
and false self, 48–9
good-enough, 31, 34, 48, 91, 177
and handicapped infants, 101
and handling, 100–102
and hate, 123–4
and holding, 35, 89, 97–100
and identification, 93, 106, 127
illness in, 96, 107, 147
instinct in, 90
interference with, 154, 158
mirror-role of, 118
and morality, 73–4, 77
naturalness of, 124–5
and object relating, 40–3, 103–5
ordinary devoted, 123–6, 187
and personality, 87
predictability of, 41–2, 43, 106–7, 118, 164
and separation, 143
strictness of, 77, 130
as witch, 112, 127
Motility, primitive, 69–70
Mutuality, 65, 93, 116–21
and fantasy, 117

Natural selection, 177
Narcissism, primary, 33
National Childbirth Trust, 155
Neuropharmacology, 11
Neurophysiological development, 110
Neurosis, 14–15, 21, 188
New Statesman, 157
New York Psychoanalytic Society, 192
Normality and health, 20
Nursery School Association, 122

Object(s):
  -mother, 74, 182
  permanence of, 67–71, 193
  placing of outside the self, 67–73
  presenting, 42, 48, 103–10

relating, 32, 39, 43, 48, 53, 70, 74,
    134
seeking, 114
subjective, 39–40, 114
transitional, 57–61, 70, 161
use of, 67–73, 192
use of the term, 39
Observation, direct/indirect, 16, 19–20,
    86, 189
*Observation of Infants in a Set
    Situation* (Winnicott), 17
Obsessional neurosis, 188
Occupational therapy, 102
Oedipus complex, 14–15
Omnipotence, 39–43 48, 50, 56, 59, 63,
    106, 111, 116. *See also* Experience
Origin of Species (Darwin), 8, 176

Paddington Green Children's Hospital,
    5, 14, 17, 178, 179, 181
Paediatrics, 10, 24
    and child psychiatry, 180–81
Panic, 38
Parents:
    as centre of family, 132, 135–6
    education of, 156–7
    and experience accumulation, 90–3
    and fantasy, 90–3, 135–6
    interference with, 151–2
    and responsibility, 92–3, 132, 133–4,
        153
    and security, 142–3
Parliamentary government, 147
Part-object, 74. *See also* Object
Penicillin, 10
Persecution, expectation of, 52, 84, 143
Personalization, 32, 37–9, 100. *See also*
    Body; Psychosomatic collusion
Personality, 11, 20, 38, 135, 177
    and biology, 166
    core of, 29–30
    evolution of, 165
    and freedom, 145–6
    and integration, 33

and mothering, 87
richness of, 163, 165
schizoid, 46–7, 96, 163, 165
Physics, 9, 11
Physiology, 9–10, 11, 13, 29
Physiotherapy, 102
Piaget, Jean, 33, 62
Piggle, The (Winnicott), 175, 182
*Play, Dreams and Imitation in
    Childhood* (Piaget), 63
Playing, 61–3, 91, 121, 134, 160, 161,
    192, 193. *See also* Potential space
Playing and Reality (Winnicott), 159,
    192, 193
Pleasure principle, 55
Potential space, 57–61, 63–5, 121,
    159–69. *See also* Playing
Primary maternal preoccupation, 89,
    93–7, 111, 114, 189. *See also*
    Mothers
"Primary Maternal Preoccupation"
    (Winnicott), 189
Primitive agonies, 44, 106, 171, 185
"Primitive Emotional Development"
    (Winnicott), 187
Privation and deprivation, 78
Progress, drive behind, 177
Projection, 120
Propaganda, 66, 154, 156, 157
Psyche, 23, 37, 190. *See also* Ego Self;
    absence of, 38
    and intellect, 49–50
    as term, 54
Psychiatry, 46
    and physical treatment, 23
Psychoanalysis, 11, 12–17, 18–24,
    75–6, 81, 86, 94, 120, 163, 174,
    179
    on aggression, 69–70
    classical theory of, 13–14, 69–70,
        114, 169, 181, 188
    and communication, 114
    and freedom, 158
    and individual dignity, 23,

objects in, 39
and observation, 11, 16, 19–20, 86,
    178
setting in, 11, 140–1, 163
unconscious in, 12, 14
Psycho-Analytic Explorations
    (Winnicott), 175, 183, 187, 190,
    191, 192, 193
Psychology and science, 11–14
Psychoneuroses, 185, 190
Psychosis, 46–8, 94, 106, 164, 185, 191
Psychosomatic collusion, 37–8, 49, 101,
    166, 168, 187. *See also* Body;
    Personalization
Psychotherapy, 179, 184–5
Puberty, 81

Queen Elizabeth's Hospital, 14
Queen's Hospital for Children, 178
Questionnaires, standardized, 12

Reaction. *See also* Impingement;
    Stimulus
to antisocial individuals, 149
to impingement, 36, 40, 44–5,
    105–6, 146–7, 155–56, 169
Reality:
external or shared, 28, 53, 67, 71,
    108–9, 117, 142, 160, 163, 165,
    177
inner psychic, 28–29, 40, 53, 54–5,
    89, 142, 165, 187
Reality principle, 53–4, 55, 73, 108,
    111
Reality testing, 56, 71, 106
Reflecting back, 117–20
Reflex, grasp, 17
    rooting and sucking, 105
Regression, 47, 68, 112, 187–8
Religion, 4, 56, 155, 157, 169, 176,
Revenge Fable (Hughes), 127
Revenge, public, 150
Risk taking, 76, 154. *See also*
    Security/risk

Riviere, Joan, 181, 183
Rodman, Robert, 178
Romulus and Remus, 126
Rose, Stephen, 23
Royal Society of Medicine, 186

St. Bartholomew's Hospital, 24, 178
St. Mary's Hospital Gazette, 178
Schaffer, Rudolf, 87, 90
Schizoid personality, 46–7, 96, 163,
    165, 188
Schizophrenia, 46–7, 163, 188
Schools, 148–9
Scientific method, 13
    and psychology, 14–16
Scott, Clifford, 187
Second World War, 151, 183; and
    children, 15
Security/risk, 141–4, 148, 154
Selected Letters (Winnicott), 175
Self. *See also* Ego
and communication, 114–5
concept of, 27–28
consciousness of, 28
defence of, 46–48
defence of and freedom, 157–8
discovery of, 65, 101, 121, 124, 145,
    161, 165, 168
isolation of core of, 177
in mature individual, 192
Self-control, 77, 144
and autonomy, 142
Sensuous coexistence, 75, 155
Sentimentality, 123, 149–50
Serenity, 157
Setting, 11, 103–4, 140–1, 163
Sex and unconscious fantasy, 91, 132
Sexuality, child/infant, 14
Shepard, Ray, 173
Socialization, 49, 74, 142, 177, 185
Society and the Growing Child
    (Winnicott), 175, 176, 181, 189,
    191
Sociobiology (Wilson), 166

Spatula Game, 17–24, 111
Spontaneity, 3, 21, 22, 28, 40, 55, 60, 77, 88, 118, 140, 141, 143, 145, 160, 185
Squiggle Game, 22, 137, 190
Squiggles, 190
Stages in the Development of the Sense of Reality, (Ferenczi), 42
Stealing, and separation from mother, 183
Stimulus and reaction, 36, 105
Strachey, James, 178, 179, 181
Study of Human Nature, A (Winnicott), 175, 189, 190
Subjectivity in science, 11–12
Sublimation, 169
Symbolic play, 62–63
Symbols and transitional phenomena, 160–3, 192

Taking to Parents (Winnicott), 175, 187
Tennis, 160
Tennyson, Alfred Lord, 25, 72
Theory, 8–17
   determinism in, 166–7
"Theory of the parent-infant relationship," 189
Therapeutic Consultations in Child Psychiatry (Winnicott), 21, 24, 175, 190
Therapists, 12, 14
   and hierarchy, 22
   training of, 12–13
Thinking, 50
Through Paediatrics to Psycho-Analysis (Winnicott), 175, 180, 188
Thumbsucking, 57–60
Time:
   and continuity, 169–71
   and integration, 34
   and sense of, in delinquents, 170
   and sense of, in infants, 68, 76
Tod, Robert J.N., *ix*

"Towards an Objective Study of Human Nature" (Winnicott), 176
"Transitional Objects: Idealization of a Phenomenon" (Brody), 59
Transitional objects/phenomena, 57–61, 159–69, 189
   and culture, 58–9
   and first 'not me' possession, 57–61
   and paradox, 59
   and playing, 61–2, 161, 192
   relationship of infant to, 58–9
   survival of, 58, 70–1
   and symbolism, 161–3
"Transitional Objects and Transitional Phenomena" (Winnicott), 59
Trauma, 44–45, 80, 107, 188
Truancy, 6

Unconscious, 12, 14, 70, 71, 97
   fantasy, 19, 70–71, 75, 81, 90–3, 132, 135
   and psychoanalysis, 12, 14
   and revenge, 150
UNESCO, 180
Unintegration, 32–37
Unthinkable anxieties, 44, 46, 47, 80, 171, 188
"Use of an object in the context of Moses and Monotheism, The," 193

"Varieties of Psychotherapy," 179
Vertue, St. John, 25
Vigilance and freedom, 157

Wallbridge, David, *ix*
Wayward Youth (Aichorn), 183
Weaning, 75, 76–7, 150
WHO, 186
Wilson, E.O., 166
Wills, David, 184
Winnicott, Donald W.,
   achievements of, 185
   and biology, 9, 11
   books of, 174–5

his childhood, 3
and children, 5
and compliance, 4
his cosmology, 167
and delinquent boy, 6–7
his education, 9–10, 14, 15, 24
as "enfant terrible," 4, 5
his faith in human nature, 3
his family, 3, 4
his father, 4, 175, 176
and First World War, 9, 183–84
and Freud, 11, 13–14,
and history-taking, 24
his house, 141
and importence of environment, 7,
    84–5
his integrity, 12, 22–24, 172
and jargon, xi–xii
and Klein, 13, 15, 16, 182
and observation, 7–8, 16, 19, 57, 86
and paediatrics, 10, 16, 24

philosophy of, 180
and physical treatment of mental
    illness, 22–23
his practicality, 7, 172
and psychoanalysis, 11–14, 15–16
and religion, 4, 176
and Second World War, 15
and Spatula Game, 17–24
and Squiggle Game, 22
his style, xi–xii
his theory, 8–9, 14–15, 19–20
writing of, 173–93
Winnicott, Sir Frederick (father), 176
Winnicott, Violet (sister), 178
Winnicott Publications Committee, ix
Winnicott Trust, 174
Woman, fear of, 126–8
Work, constructive, 76, 181

Yequena Indians, 102